Higher Education Assessments

Other Titles in the Series

Leading the Campaign: Advancing Colleges and Universities
  by Michael J. Worth

Leaders in the Labyrinth: College Presidents and the Battlegrounds of Creeds and Convictions
  by Stephen J. Nelson

Academic Turnarounds: Restoring Vitality to Challenged American Colleges/ Universities
  edited by Terrence MacTaggart

Managing Diversity Flashpoints in Higher Education
  by Joseph E. Garcia and Karen J. Hoelscher

The Art and Politics of Academic Governance: Relations among Boards, Presidents, and Faculty
  by Kenneth P. Mortimer and Colleen O'Brien Sathre

Strategic Leadership: Integrating Strategy and Leadership in Colleges and Universities
  by Richard L. Morrill

Leadership Legacy Moments: Visions and Values for Stewards of Collegiate Mission
  by E. Grady Bogue

The Indispensable University: Higher Education, Economic Development, and the Knowledge Economy
  by Eugene P. Trani and Robert D. Holsworth

Peak Performance for Deans and Chairs: Reframing Higher Education's Middle
  by Susan Stavert Roper and Terrence E. Deal

Presidential Transitions: It's Not Just the Position, It's the Transition
  by Patrick H. Sanaghan, Larry Goldstein, and Kathleen D. Gaval

Changing Course: Making the Hard Decisions to Eliminate Academic Programs, Second Edition
  by Peter D. Eckel

Searching for Higher Education Leadership: Advice for Candidates and Search Committees
  by Jean A. Dowdall

Other Duties as Assigned: Presidential Assistants in Higher Education
  edited by Mark P. Curchack

The "How To" Grants Manual: Successful Grantseeking Techniques for Obtaining Public and Private Grants, Sixth Edition
  by David G. Bauer

Leaders in the Crossroads: Success and Failure in the College Presidency
  by Stephen James Nelson

International Students: Strengthening a Critical Resource
  edited by Maureen S. Andrade and Norman W. Evans

Faculty Success through Mentoring: A Guide for Mentors, Mentees, and Leaders
  by Carole J. Bland, Anne L. Taylor, S. Lynn Shollen, Anne Marie Weber-Main, and Patricia A. Mulcahy

Higher Education Assessments

Leadership Matters

Edited by
Gary L. Kramer
and
Randy L. Swing

Published in partnership with the

ACE AMERICAN COUNCIL ON EDUCATION
® The Unifying Voice for Higher Education

ROWMAN & LITTLEFIELD PUBLISHERS, INC.
Lanham • Boulder • New York • Toronto • Plymouth, UK

Published in partnership with the American Council on Education

Published by Rowman & Littlefield Publishers, Inc.
A wholly owned subsidary of The Rowman & Littlefield Publishing Group, Inc.
4501 Forbes Boulevard, Suite 200, Lanham, Maryland 20706
http://www.rowmanlittlefield.com

Estover Road, Plymouth PL6 7PY, United Kingdom

British Library Cataloguing in Publication Information Available

Library of Congress Cataloging-in-Publication Data
Higher education assessments : leadership matters / edited by Gary L. Kramer and Randy L. Swing.
    p. cm. — (The American Council on Education series on higher education)
"Published in partnership with the American Council on Education."
Includes index.
ISBN 978-1-4422-0620-5 (cloth : alk. paper) — ISBN 978-1-4422-0622-9 (electronic)
    1. Universities and colleges—United States—Evaluation. 2. Education, Higher—United States—Evaluation. 3. Universities and colleges—United States—Administration. 4. College administrators—United States. 5. Leadership—United States. I. Kramer, Gary L., 1945– II. Swing, Randy L., 1954–
    LB2331.63.H54 2010
    378.1'07—dc22

                                                                            2010020803

Printed in the United States of America

Contents

List of Figures and Table   vii

Foreword   ix
  Peter T. Ewell

Acknowledgments   xiii

Introduction   xv
  Gary L. Kramer and Randy L. Swing

PART I: LEADING ASSESSMENTS ON THE CAMPUS

1   Championing the Assessment of Learning: The Role of
    Top Leaders   3
    Trudy Bers and Randy L. Swing

2   Assessment Frameworks That Can Make a Difference in
    Achieving Institutional Outcomes   27
    Gary L. Kramer, Coral Hanson, and Danny Olsen

**PART II: BRIDGING LEARNER OUTCOMES:
FINDING COMMON GROUND**

3   Assessment and Student Diversity   59
    Vasti Torres

4   Assessments in Student Services That Foster Student and
    Program Success   73
    John H. Schuh

5 Documenting Student Learning: Valuing the Process   95
      Kay H. Smith and Raymond D. Barclay

6 Learning Outcomes, Assessment, and Program Improvement   119
      Russell T. Osguthorpe, Bryan D. Bradley, and Trav D. Johnson

**PART III: ASSESSMENTS THAT TRANSFORM THE
LEARNING CULTURE**

7 Student Engagement and a Culture of Assessment   135
      Jillian Kinzie

8 Assessment in the Disciplines   161
      John Muffo

9 Assessment That Transforms an Institution   179
      Peter J. Gray

10 Putting Students First as Partners in the Learning Enterprise   213
      Gary L. Kramer and Thomas E. Miller

Epilogue   237
      Gary L. Kramer and Randy L. Swing

Subject Index   241

Name Index   247

About the Contributors   253

Figures and Table

FIGURES

2.1 Factors with Institution-Level, Program-Level, and Course-Level Assessment Plans   30

2.2 Stakeholder Benefits of a Systems Approach   31

2.3 Model for Culture Change: Moving toward a "Culture of Evidence"   46

2.4 Establishing a Culture of Evidence: A Systems Approach   47

2.5 Hypothetical Institutional Strategic Plan: History of Activity   48

2.6 Hypothetical Unit Review Data Flow: Degree-Level Assessment   49

2.7 Hypothetical Department Path to Graduation: Timing of Direct and Indirect Assessments   50

5.1 Assessment for Learning   99

9.1 Assessment Process   180

9.2 Teaching, Learning, and Evaluation Matrix   197

10.1 Partnerships That Lead to Student Success, Development, and Learning   233

TABLE

6.1 A Framework for Linking Student Learning with Program Improvement   122

Foreword

The second decade of the twenty-first century promises tough times for higher education. Money is short, infrastructure continues to crumble, and there are far too many students for an increasingly contingent and discontented faculty to teach. For a president or academic leader to put aside these urgent problems and consider assessment seems the height of indulgence. Why pay any attention to this topic at all?

The answer is that the assessment of student learning and development is at the heart of all these other problems and one of the key management tools available to colleges and universities to work their way out of them. At the most visible level, the aftermath of the Spellings Commission has signaled accountability for results as a major immediate challenge for American higher education. And unlike previous accountability surges in our history, this one is unlikely to go away. Policy and corporate leaders are aware that the performance of higher education in turning out capable and thoughtful citizens and workers is critical to our future. They also know that our performance in doing this as a nation in a global context is no longer unmatched. These accountability demands are real, they are justified, and they are likely to be permanent. Evidence about the academic achievements of our students is at the heart of them. These developments mean that assessment now constitutes a noticeable slice of every academic administrator's mental pie chart. As I have written elsewhere, an institution today can no more do without assessment than it can do without a development office.

All academic leaders at some level already know this. This is why the level of attention devoted to assessment has become so generally pervasive, as results of the recent survey—*More Than You Think, Less Than We Need*—released by the National Institute for Learning Outcomes Assessment (NILOA) reveals.

But as the chapters in this volume argue, it is the *way* we do assessment, not just doing it, that matters. The temptation is strong to simply deal with the matter and move on. Join the Voluntary System of Accountability (VSA) or one of its cousins, administer the Collegiate Learning Assessment (CLA) or another of the alphabet soup–like panoply of standardized tests to a handful of students, administer an alumni survey, post the results somewhere on the institution's website, and be done with it.

Granted, these are all steps that need to be done, and institutions should go about doing them. But the challenge is deeper than that. The White House has called upon postsecondary education to generate an unprecedented number of college-educated individuals, at a time when doing so will require far more cost-effective approaches to teaching and learning because of the sheer numbers of students to be accommodated on lower base budgets. On top of this, the changing demographics of our future students—increasingly underprepared and older—will make the job harder. Increased numbers of postsecondary credentials will mean nothing if they are not degrees with integrity—representing mastery of the full panoply of knowledge and skill that the decades ahead demand. On the home front at every institution, meanwhile, the challenge is to systematically use assessment to find areas where teaching and learning can be improved, to deliberate as a community about what changes are necessary, and to set aside the means and the will to make them happen. In doing this, moreover, it is important to remember that assessment is not just about finding fault. Sometimes the process uncovers things that are working spectacularly, providing both the opportunity to tell this to the rest of the world and to examine things more closely so we can apply what we learn elsewhere in the institution. In either case, the challenge of the next decade will be to not just take stock of student learning but also *get better* at generating it, intentionally, systematically, and continuously.

The chapters in this volume are designed to help you do this. They remind you, first of all, that the management of assessment is much like the management of anything else. You need an explicit plan, consistent with your institution's mission and values, that documents in sufficient detail what needs to be done and who is to do it. You need to pay regular attention to how these activities are implemented, motivating the right people at the right times, establishing and enforcing appropriate lines of accountability, and monitoring progress and celebrating success. And you need to assess the whole process every few years to identify things that are not working and get rid of them. But there are also important ways in which assessment is special. It requires unusual attention to unpacking and discussing your institution's core values and aspirations. And it is singularly collective—especially with respect to the active involvement of large slices of the faculty and student affairs professionals. Spaces to talk about these things are in very short supply on today's campuses, and you need to make room for them—perhaps at the expense of necessary, but more quotidian, tasks.

It is also easy to misperceive assessment as a process that you can simply put in place and keep running. What you will discover through this volume is that it is part of a *system* that includes virtually everything that your institution is about with respect to teaching and learning including curriculum, pedagogy, faculty recruitment and development, student activities in and out of the classroom, equipment purchase and maintenance, physical planning, and a good deal more. Just as it is tempting when flying to sit back and think about the airplane you are traveling in as a thing unto itself—forgetting the vast infrastructure of industry, runways, people movers, security, and traffic control that keeps the thing up there—you will need to consider the many ways assessment is connected to how your institution does all of its business.

In so doing, two big lessons in particular stand out. First, as the recent NILOA survey underscores, a couple of decades of practice means that we are a whole lot better at doing assessment than we used to be, but we have made far less progress in using its results. Consequently, much of the accumulated experience that this volume contains is about how to make assessment results accessible to people on the ground who have to actually do the work, and how to help them appropriately convert the hidden messages these results contain into concrete action. Second, successfully implementing assessment demands unusual attention to the arts of servant leadership and motivating people. Faculty members are frequently reluctant partners in assessment, at least at first. In many disciplines—especially those in the arts and sciences unaffected by specialized or programmatic accreditation—they are predisposed to see the assessment process as an imposed management charade that threatens the ineffability of their craft. They are also incredibly busy. Convincing them that they have something to gain through the process and that the essence of assessment is really just turning the arts of scholarship and inquiry, in which they have all been trained, onto the core enterprise of teaching and learning, is one key to successful implementation. You also need to realize that you don't need to convince everybody to move forward. Good leaders do not just discover consensus, they *create* it.

Finally, the construction of this volume itself models good practice in assessment. Each chapter begins with a clear statement of what the authors want you to learn. Each contains multiple opportunities for you to practice and apply what you have read, usually through a well-framed set of questions that you can tailor to your circumstances. Links to assessment resources are ample, but assessment "technique" does not get in the way of the things you really need to know about the topic as a president or academic leader. We hope that you will learn much from these pages and will do even more. Both the country and the academy need this to happen.

Peter T. Ewell
Vice President, National Center for Higher
Education Management Systems (NCHEMS)
Senior Scholar, National Institute for
Learning Outcomes Assessment (NILOA)

Acknowledgments

Gary and Randy would like to thank their author-colleagues who have shared their experiences and scholarship on what really matters in higher education assessments. Clearly, without them and their demonstrated good works over the years, there would be no book! Our colleagues have challenged us with ideas and strategies to align institutional claims with achieving outcomes in all performance areas of the campus—to rally assessments around improving student success, learning, and development. They have taught us that it is the way we do assessment, not just doing it, that matters.

Special thanks go to Sharon Black of Brigham Young University for her marvelous and professional assistance in editing the manuscript and organizing all the details associated with the final manuscript. As well, thank you Susan Slesinger and Paula Moore of ACE and Patti Belcher of Rowman & Littlefield for your wonderful support and guidance throughout this book project.

Thank you also to our senior leader reviewers: Earl Potter, president, St. Cloud State University; Catherine Anderson, associate provost, Gallaudet University; Elizabeth Paul, provost, Stetson University; William Sederberg, commissioner, Utah State Higher Education System; Joe Crowley, president emeritus, University of Nevada, Reno; Andrew Phillips, provost, U.S. Naval Academy; and Cecilia Lopez, vice president of academic affairs, Harold Washington College, City Colleges of Chicago. This book is better because of their insightful comments. They helped focus this volume on what is most useful to know about assessments in higher education from a leader's perspective, especially in leading assessments on the campus.

And finally, Gary expresses appreciation to colleagues in the McKay School of Education at Brigham Young University, especially department chair Steven Baugh. His support and patience made this work possible. And Randy acknowledges Missy Wiggins for the long hours in manuscript preparation. We would be amiss if we didn't also acknowledge our wives and families for their willingness to adjust their needs and expectations to allow us the time and energy to complete this work. Thank you.

Introduction

Gary L. Kramer and Randy L. Swing

Another book on assessment? Who needs it? Two assumptions underlie these questions. First, the questions assume that we have already perfected the assessment wheel. And second, there is an underlying assumption that this book is primarily about *how to do* assessments, suggesting that it is intended only for assessment directors and providers. This group and others are included in the readership because they are very much involved with student learner outcomes, development, and success; however, it is the senior campus leaders to whom this volume is directed. The book focuses on essential imperatives and key principles, or *what leaders need to know and do to lead assessment successfully* on the campus. Chapter contributors have focused their scholarship and research on what senior administration leaders need to know as they set the tone and facilitate institutional assessments—assessments that really matter in aligning the institution with its claims and in achieving institutional outcomes.

THE PURPOSE OF THE BOOK

This book reflects the work of a multitude of researchers, scholars, and practitioners in higher education assessments. The scholar-researcher-authors of this book have brought to the forefront key issues, concepts, and principles relevant to both leading and advancing assessments in higher education culminating in improvement of student learning and development. The extraordinary scholarship of our author-colleagues is brought together in the epilogue. Here we summarize essential imperatives for senior leaders to apply their political wisdom and leadership talents before, during, and after assessments have taken place. In doing so, we recognize that forming a vision for campus assessment operations is both a challenging and necessary leadership task.

The book's core theme is to measure what is of value and to inform decision making from what is measured; this notion is integrated throughout the entire book, unifying its principles, examples, and recommendations. Intentional, purposeful assessments must reflect valuing of those items measured and capacity to apply the measurements to institutional decisions and changes. Clearly, data alone cannot drive decisions. People make decisions, but data ought to inform the decisions made. As this book and its chapters show, intentional assessments should be guided by senior administration to connect with an institutional assessment plan and strategy that engage stakeholders to improve student learning and development. Such assessments can have a powerful influence when campus leaders use purposeful assessments and derived data for decision making in all key performance areas of the campus.

Finally, this volume seeks to identify and present assessment strategies to assist senior leaders to address the following: (1) How will the institution be dramatically better in five years as a result of current senior leadership? (2) What is or will be the campus narrative? (3) What are the areas of assessment that matter most? In short, what will be measured five years from now to *empirically demonstrate progress in aligning institutional claims with student learning and development, and overall in achieving institutional outcomes?*

To assist in addressing these questions and aims, the chapters in this volume address assessments that matter most as senior administrators focus on assessment and diversity, assessment in student affairs, documentation of student learning, student engagement related to a culture of assessment, ways to bridge learner outcomes, assessment in the disciplines, how assessments can transform a culture, and putting students first as partners in the learning enterprise. The premise of this book is to connect and explore these foundational pillars of assessment reform by

1. adopting rigorous standards to create a campus-wide assessment infrastructure, one that measures what is of value and sustains an evidence-based culture that grounds the improvement process; and
2. using a data systems approach including intentional assessments that are aligned with institutional claims and enable a demonstrable culture of evidence that supports student development and learning, indeed, tracking and celebrating the student achievement and the institutional outcomes story.

HIGHER EDUCATION ASSESSMENT
AND THE RESEARCH LITERATURE

Several significant studies and researchers have set the context for the chapters in this book. Researchers, scholars, administrators, and practitioners have long sought to understand and address what matters most in higher education assessments and what makes a difference in driving change to improve student learning and development. The principles, standards, and frameworks are well developed and established in the research literature (Angelo, 2007; Banta, 2005; Banta, Jones, and Black, 2009; Banta and Associates, 1993, 2002; Baxter Magolda and King, 2004; Boyer, 1990; Chickering and Gamson, 1987; Council for the Advancement of Standards in Higher Education, 2009; Ewell, 2004, 2007; Keeling, 2006; Keeling, Wall, Underhile, and Dungy, 2008; Kuh, 2009; Kuh, Kinzie, Schuh, and Whitt, 2005a, 2005b; Pascarella and Terenzini, 2005; Schuh and Associates, 2009; Schulman, 2007; Tinto 1987, 1993; Tinto and Pusser, 2006).

Noteworthy are the following research milestones, educational movements, and scholarly works on accountability in higher education, which this book acknowledges and on which it is built.

- *The Student Personnel Point of View* (American Council on Education, 1949 [1937]) called for better services and improved intentional assessments.
- *Education and Identity* (Chickering, 1969; Chickering and Reisser, 1993) is still cited today as a useful resource for understanding college students' psychosocial development process along with theories on student mattering. "Clear and consistent objectives," observed Arthur Chickering and Linda Reisser (1993) in a second edition, "stated in terms of desired outcomes for learning and personal development, are critically important in creating an educationally powerful institution" (p. 287).
- Vincent Tinto (1987, 1993) and Alexander Astin (1977, 1985) provided the context and foundation for student success theories of integration and involvement.
- *A Nation at Risk* (National Commission on Excellence in Education, 1983) focused on the condition and needed reform of K–12 education, which in turn directly called for change on college campuses.
- "Seven Principles of Good Practice in Undergraduate Education" (Chickering and Gamson, 1987) promoted more effective teaching and learning approaches in higher education undergraduate studies.
- Ernest Boyer (1990) elevated the scholarship of teaching to the scholarship of discovery, thus leading to the scholarship of teaching and learning;

both of these movements require assessment to demonstrate the changes in student learning.

- *How College Affects Students* (Pascarella and Terenzini, 1991, 2005) provided a comprehensive resource on understanding the concept of a long-term, value-added approach to studying student learning.
- Sandia National Laboratories (1993), charged by U.S. secretary of energy James Watkins, called for "upgrading the quality of educational data" and making major improvements in the data used to analyze U.S. education.
- The Wingspread Group on Higher Education (1993), released *An American Imperative: Higher Expectations for Higher Education*, which charged higher education with failing to meet society's needs for a better educated, more skilled, and more adaptable citizenry—calling for higher standards and greater accountability.
- *The Student Learning Imperative* (American College Personnel Association, 1994) outlined conditions that enhance student learning.
- *Learning Reconsidered: A Campus-Wide Focus on the Student Experience* (Keeling, 2004) was followed by *Learning Reconsidered Part 2: A Practical Guide to Implementing a Campus-Wide Focus on the Student Experience* (Keeling, 2006), culminating in *Assessment Reconsidered: Institutional Effectiveness for Student Success* (Keeling et al., 2008). All three emphasized the role of student affairs as a partner in the broader campus curriculum, that is, linking mission to practice.
- George Kuh (2009) and others (Kuh et al., 2005a, 2005b) identified through the Documenting Effective Educational Practices (DEEP) project many colleges and universities that were effective in promoting student success and, most important, described the relationships between student engagement, persistence, satisfaction, learning, and personal development.

In conclusion, these landmarks in accountability research laid the foundations for ongoing improvements in higher education, not only setting the context for this book but also framing its basic premises. Past and current research efforts affirm that higher education continues to examine the current and past progress of assessment use on campuses to improve student development and learning. In this respect, there is still work to be done to create a qualitative institutional assessment infrastructure, one that permeates the campus. While in part this book seeks to inform its readers about what really matters in assessment and how it can be done more effectively, its primary emphasis is on what campus leaders need to know to be successful in leading a coherent, consistent, and campus-engaged assessment plan.

Atul Gawande (2007), a medical doctor who wrote *Better: A Surgeon's Notes on Performance*, advised his audience to look for opportunities to make a difference. While medicine and other professions (including education) have imperfections, he argues, we should not embrace every new trend that comes along but rather recognize the inadequacies in what we do and seek out solutions (p. 257). Like medicine, higher education is replete with uncertainties and failures, but it is in the end likewise worthwhile. So our challenge to our readership—like Gawande's to his—is to explore change, especially in assessments that, as emphasized in the chapters in this volume, have the potential to drive change that matters most—to achieve institutional outcomes—and inform decisions in higher education that improve student learning and development and in all key performance areas of the institution.

INTENDED AUDIENCES

This book is specifically addressed to higher education leaders on campuses: presidents and vice presidents, provosts, and deans. Its intended audience also includes all those on the president's team, including department chairs, faculty members, and assessment administrators who are concerned with addressing the following:

1. assessing learner outcomes by establishing a meaningful and consistent assessment culture within the campus community, one that fulfills institutional priorities as well as accreditation standards—determining what really matters in assessments and aligning assessments with institutional claims;
2. supporting and improving student learning, performance, development, and achievement based on educational claims by measuring what is valued and informing decisions from what is measured; and
3. establishing an assessment plan to monitor student progress toward and achievement of learning outcomes through an evidence-based culture that enables the use of data to contribute to improving program and student development on the campus.

Notably, each chapter focuses on benefits and processes relevant to leading assessments on the campus, specifically what senior administrators need to know and do. While this book is addressed to senior campus leaders, it is also intended to help academic and student life administrators, faculty members, and other campus leaders use evidence gained from assessment processes to inform discussions, design assessments that align with institutional policies and practices, shape policy, inform change, and essentially—via an established culture of evidence—improve student learning and development on the campus.

ORGANIZATION OF THE BOOK

This book is organized into three broad constructs or parts, and the specific chapters, as indicated, address each.

Part I: Leading Assessments on the Campus

Chapter 1: "Championing the Assessment of Learning: The Role of Top Leaders"

Trudy Bers and Randy L. Swing explore the senior leader's role in institutional assessments. This chapter is designed specifically for senior leaders who are charged with oversight of a higher education institution or unit to provide leadership and inspiration and to ensure compliance with internal and external demands for assessment and improvement. This chapter is not a guide for the person who spends every day designing and implementing assessment; there is a rich and growing literature in the "how to do assessment" genre. Rather, this chapter is intended to assist a senior leader who must confirm recommendations from an assessment staff member, discuss assessment matters with regional accrediting bodies, and set the tone and vision for assessment on his or her own campus. The chapter begins with the belief that senior campus leaders would not reach their positions without a deep commitment to creating the best student learning opportunities possible. Leading assessment is just one more tool for accomplishing high levels of student learning and thus institutional success. Additionally, the engagement of senior leaders—whether from academic affairs, student affairs, the president's office, or a system office—is mandatory for institutional success in assessment efforts.

Chapter 2: "Assessment Frameworks That Can Make a Difference in Achieving Institutional Outcomes"

Gary L. Kramer, Coral Hanson, and Danny Olsen begin this chapter by acknowledging that assessments that contribute to decision making in all key performance areas of the institution are extensive and involve a variety of challenges and constraints. Assessment becomes especially challenging when consideration must be given to the place of assessments and reporting in the larger context of aligning institutional claims with outcomes projected for all performance areas of the campus. Senior leaders must assert, they claim, their political wisdom and leadership talents in directing use of purposeful assessments to guide strategic planning within existing budget constraints in meaningful and credible ways, which include managing and supporting behavior change based on broad engagement of the campus community. While the authors offer no panacea for creating and managing an integrated database to support campus-wide decision making, the chapter does offer essential, established principles and conditions concerning assessment frameworks that can influence achievement of institutional outcomes. To accomplish this, the chapter is divided into two main sections: (1) creating and managing an integrated database that supports informed, decision making in key performance areas of the institution and (2) using assessment planning principles and developing conditions to establish a sustainable culture of evidence from which the institutional data story can be told, one that aligns evidential data with the aims and claims of the institution.

Part II: Bridging Learner Outcomes: Finding Common Ground

Chapter 3: "Assessment and Student Diversity"

Vasti Torres explains in this chapter that as the number of students attending college increases so does their diversity. As a result, colleges and universities are challenged to manage environments that include students of diverse races and ethnicities, genders, social classes, and levels of academic preparation. When a diversity issue rises to the level of senior administrators, it typically appears in the form of a letter or memorandum from concerned faculty members, students, or staff members asking for some type of action to address previous incidents or past inaction. This chapter focuses on the historical issues institutions confront regarding diversity, as well as the struggle to define what diversity is within any given campus community. Diversity influences student learning, and challenges arise when institutions embrace diverse students; institutional data can contribute to decisions that help settle issues for concerned faculty members, students, or staff members. In considering the issues involved with assessment and student diversity, this chapter explains the theoretical foundation of the concept of diversity as a positive influence in higher education. Following this explanation is a discussion of the contextual dimensions of defining diversity, the types of diversity assessment institutions should consider, and the issues institutions should reflect on when embracing diversity with a desire to create change.

Chapter 4: "Assessments in Student Services That Foster Student and Program Success"

John H. Schuh examines selected issues related to assessment in student services that contribute to student success and, by extension, to program success.

This chapter focuses on foundational aspects as well as identifies selected contextual issues that frame assessment in student affairs; the chapter also discusses several theoretical and conceptual foundations of assessment in student affairs. Then it presents an assessment model and some tools that can be used by those interested in conducting assessments in student affairs. It concludes with some examples from institutions that are engaged in successful assessments in student affairs. This chapter identifies selected issues related not only to the assessment of student affairs programs and services but also to the experiences that lead to student and institutional success. Contextual issues discussed lend a theoretical and conceptual foundation for assessment in student affairs. Promising assessment programs at several institutions are described briefly. The chapter asserts that assessment has become a central activity in student affairs. Those student affairs divisions that embrace assessment and conduct assessments on a routine basis will thrive; those that do not may not.

Chapter 5: "Documenting Student Learning: Valuing the Process"

Kay H. Smith and Raymond Barclay caution in this chapter that, in higher education assessment, campus leaders may easily get lost or bogged down in approaches, vocabularies, scales of operation, disciplinary needs, accreditation pressures, and accountability reports. Such topics represent substantive issues that must be understood and managed in order to create a coherent approach to assessment at the institutional level. Yet, in response to the ever-increasing demands for institutional effectiveness and evidence of student learning, leadership tends to address these external pressures by providing evidence in the form of simple inputs and outputs aimed primarily at satisfying external accreditation and accountability processes. But approaching assessment focused only toward external audiences can cause administrators to neglect authentic assessment and documentation of student learning: what students learn, how they learn, what they can do with their learning, and how this recursively informs instructional design and support services aimed at increasing learning.

Chapter 6: "Leaner Outcomes, Assessment, and Program Improvement"

Russell T. Osguthorpe, Bryan D. Bradley, and Trav D. Johnson raise a question and then address it in this chapter: "Why learning outcomes?" University administrators must be concerned with the quality of their academic programs so that their institutions can meet requirements for accreditation. They must also find ways to convince the faculty that meeting such requirements will actually improve teaching and lead to increased student learning. Some faculty members wonder if writing learning outcomes is a meaningless exercise to meet an imposed requirement, since some have taught successfully for years without articulating such outcomes. The key to helping these faculty members see the value of learning outcomes is to focus on the assessment of student performance—helping the faculty see that careful course and program design can improve what students learn in their courses. This chapter describes the process and potential benefits of aligning learning outcomes with course, program, and institutional goals. From an institutional perspective, learning outcomes provide articulated and measurable sets of skills that instructors are accountable for teaching, modeling, and facilitating for their students. Assessment of student learning within the aligned framework and context of learning outcomes is critical in order to verify and evaluate the degree to which students have learned and mastered the intended skills and knowledge.

Part III: Assessments That Transform the Learning Culture

Chapter 7: "Student Engagement and a Culture of Assessment"

Jillian Kinzie asserts that many campuses have made significant advances in assessment practices that drive improvements in student learning and success. This chapter introduces a framework for assessment based on student engagement and success, then highlights nine characteristics of campus assessment activities associated with improvements to student learning. For convenience, characteristics are grouped according to their focus on (1) strong leadership, (2) inclusive involvement, or (3) outcome-based program function. Most institutions still find it hard to use evidence for systematic improvement, and few report having well-developed assessment plans to sustain a culture of assessment. Fortunately, effective and inspirational models have been developed by many institutions that have adopted an effective student engagement framework for assessing and improving the conditions for students' success leading to improvements in their learning. In this chapter, the lessons learned from twenty educationally effective institutions are reexamined in light of information from additional institutions that have advanced a framework for student engagement and success.

Chapter 8: "Assessment in the Disciplines"

John Muffo argues the importance of senior system and campus leaders understanding the major principles of assessment for the purpose of leading a system or institution. He provides a conceptual shift of sorts by moving in a slightly different direction without contradicting anything in prior chapters. Muffo contends that assessment in the disciplines usually presupposes simultaneous assessment by the institution. Disciplinary assessment just takes the focus a level or two closer to where the learning actually takes place—at the college, school, department, or unit level. An understanding of disciplinary assessment is important to a senior leader, particularly one with major academic or academic support responsibilities, because the leader may spend a great deal of time and energy dealing with such matters in the course of his or her career, especially if the assessment program is mandated externally: for example, by the state or federal government or by professional or specialized accreditation. (Additionally, most academic assessment matters involved in institutional accreditation take place at the unit level first and are then aggregated upward.) Thus, comprehending the assumptions behind the processes and methods employed in disciplinary assessment and the related area of disciplinary accreditation can only enhance one's effectiveness as a senior leader in higher education. The fact that many decisions resulting from these processes have major budgetary implications, some of which may differentially impact academic and administrative units, only heightens the importance of comprehension.

Chapter 9: "Assessment That Transforms an Institution"

Peter J. Gray defines assessment not in terms of *tests and measurement* but rather as a generic process that provides *a means of systematic inquiry in support of continuous improvement and accountability*. This process is grounded in the mission and goals of an institution, department, or program; focuses on academic and nonacademic practices and procedures; uses qualitative and quantitative methods to answer important evaluation questions; and, based on the results, provides feedback for improvement and accountability. The process of assessment is a means for guiding systematic, incremental positive changes that over time add up to the transformation of institutions or departments in order to better achieve their goals and objectives and meet the demands of accountability. And when assessment is an integral part of the change process, it too becomes embedded in the institutional culture and in this sense is also transformative. Thus, the purpose of this chapter is to describe a way of conceiving and implementing assessment so that it becomes embedded in the culture as a systematic and continuous process of improvement and as a way to provide valid and reliable information for accountability. This involves designing meaningful, manageable, and sustainable assessment practices that help institutions and departments fulfill institutional priorities, especially related to their educational purposes, as well as meeting accreditation and other standards regarding institutional effectiveness.

Chapter 10: "Putting Students First as Partners in the Learning Enterprise"

Gary L. Kramer and Thomas E. Miller conclude part III with a discussion on engaging students as partners in the learning enterprise, particularly in the assessment processes. Doing this, they assert, is both challenging and essential as higher education seeks to improve student learning and development. But students need to be involved in discussing and planning assessment rather than just giving feedback about learning and program outcomes. While assessments are most effective when they intentionally involve students as partners, this ideal is difficult to achieve. Many students cannot see the benefits or connections involved in bringing curricular and cocurricular program and unit interventions together with associated learner outcome assessments. Recognizing that student success is a result of partnerships and collaboration within the campus community, this concluding chapter addresses this question: *In five years, what will the campus narrative be for putting students first as partners in the learning process?* This chapter is intended to guide senior administration in establishing a culture of evidence that supports student success in the learning enterprise—not only to engage students as partners in assessments but also to clearly identify their expectations and experiences in relation to the institution's aims and claims.

Epilogue

In this concluding section on what leaders need to know, Gary L. Kramer and Randy L. Swing summarize essential imperatives to assist senior leaders to apply their political wisdom and leadership talents before, during, and after assessments have taken place. What can senior leaders do to rally assessments around improving student success, learning, and development? It would be easy to reply that every campus is unique and each leadership team must find its own way into and through assessment processes. There is no one-size-fits-all approach to assessment. Institutions *do* have unique and varied missions that must be addressed, but as the epilogue points out, a close look at the chapters in this volume reveal that the authors seldom needed to qualify their advice by stipulating that it only applies to one type of institution or another. The book is not segmented into sections for community colleges, liberal arts colleges, research universities, and so forth. The unspoken, but shared, belief is that there are common leadership imperatives that influence the ultimate success of assessment efforts no matter what sector, type, or size of institution is involved.

REFERENCES

American College Personnel Association. (1994). *The student learning imperative: Implications for Student Affairs*. Alexandria, Va.: Author.

American Council on Education. (1949 [1937]). *The student personnel point of view*. Washington, D.C.: Author.

Angelo, T. A. (2007, November 6). Can we fatten a hog *just* by weighing it? Using program review to improve course design, teaching effectiveness, and learning outcomes. Materials for a concurrent workshop in the 2007 Assessment Institute, Indianapolis.

Astin, A. W. (1977). *Four critical years: Effects of college on beliefs, attitudes and knowledge*. San Francisco: Jossey-Bass.

Astin, A. W. (1985). *Achieving educational excellence: A critical assessment of priorities and practices in higher education*. San Francisco: Jossey-Bass.

Banta, T. W. (2005). What draws campus leaders to embrace outcomes assessment? *Assessment Update, 17*(3), 14–15.

Banta, T. W., & Associates. (1993). *Making a difference: Outcomes of a decade of assessment in higher education*. San Francisco: Jossey-Bass.

Banta, T. W., & Associates. (2002). *Building a scholarship of assessment*. San Francisco: Jossey-Bass.

Banta, T. W., Jones, E. A., & Black, K. E. (2009). *Designing effective assessment: Principles and profiles of good practice*. San Francisco: Jossey-Bass.

Baxter Magolda, M. B., & King, P. M. (Eds.). (2004). *Learning partnerships: Theory and models of practice to educate for self-authorship*. Sterling, Va.: Stylus.

Boyer, E. L. (1990). *Scholarship reconsidered: Priorities of the professoriate*. Princeton, N.J.: Carnegie Foundation for the Advancement of Teaching.

Chickering, A. W. (1969). *Education and identity*. San Francisco: Jossey-Bass.

Chickering, A. W., & Gamson, Z. F. (1987, June). Seven principles of good practice in undergraduate education. *AAHE Bulletin, 39*(7), 3–7.

Chickering, A. W., & Reisser, L. (1993). *Education and identity* (2nd ed.). San Francisco: Jossey-Bass.

Council for the Advancement of Standards in Higher Education. (2009). *CAC professional standards for higher education* (7th ed.). Washington, D.C.: Author.

Ewell, P. T. (2004, November). The changing nature of accountability in higher education. Paper prepared for the Western Association of Schools and Colleges (WASC) Senior Commission.

Ewell, P. T. (2007, November). Assessing assessment: Successes, failures, and the future. Presentation given at the Assessment Institute of Indiana University–Purdue University Indianapolis.

Gawande, A. (2007). *Better: A surgeon's notes on performance*. New York: Picador.

Keeling, R. P. (Ed.). (2004). *Learning reconsidered: A campus-wide focus on the student experience.* Washington, D.C.: National Association of Student Personnel Administrators and the American College Personnel Association.

Keeling, R. P. (Ed.). (2006). *Learning reconsidered part 2: A practical guide to implementing a campus-wide focus on the student experience.* Washington, D.C.: American College Personnel Association, and others.

Keeling, R. P., Wall, A. F., Underhile, R., & Dungy, G. J. (2008). *Assessment reconsidered: Institutional effectiveness for student success.* Washington, D.C.: International Center for Student Success and Institutional Accountability.

Kuh, G. D. (2009). Understanding campus environments. In G. S. McClellan & Associates (Eds.), *The handbook of student affairs administration* (pp. 59–80). San Francisco: Jossey-Bass.

Kuh, G. D., Kinzie, J., Schuh, J. H., & Whitt, E. J. (2005a). *Assessing conditions that enhance educational effectiveness.* San Francisco: Jossey-Bass.

Kuh, G. D., Kinzie, J., Schuh, J. H., Whitt, E. J., & Associates. (2005b). *Student success in college: Creating conditions that matter.* San Francisco: Jossey-Bass.

National Commission on Excellence in Education. (1983). *A nation at risk: The imperative for educational reform.* Washington, D.C.: U.S. Government Printing Office.

Pascarella , E. T., & Terenzini, P. T. (1991). *How college affects students: Findings and insights from twenty years of research.* San Francisco: Jossey-Bass.

Pascarella, E. T., & Terenzini, P. T. (2005). *How college affects students: A third decade of research.* San Francisco: Jossey-Bass.

Sandia National Laboratories. (1993). Summary of issues. *Journal of Educational Research, 86*(5), 309–310.

Schuh, J. H., & Associates (Eds.). (2009). *Assessment methods for student affairs.* San Francisco: Jossey-Bass.

Schulman, L. S. (2007). Counting and recounting: Assessment and the quest for quality improvement. *Change: The Magazine of Higher Learning, 39*(1), 20–25.

Tinto, V. (1987). *Leaving college: Rethinking the causes and cures of student attrition.* Chicago: University of Chicago Press.

Tinto, V. (1993). *Leaving college: Rethinking the causes and cures of student attrition* (2nd ed.). Chicago: University of Chicago Press.

Tinto, V., & Pusser, B. (2006, November). Moving from theory to action: Building a model of institutional action for student success. Paper presented at the National Symposium on Postsecondary Student Success, Washington, D.C.

Wingspread Group on Higher Education. (1993). *An American imperative: Higher expectations for higher education.* Racine, Wisc.: Johnson Foundation.

Part One

LEADING ASSESSMENTS ON THE CAMPUS

Chapter One

Championing the Assessment of Learning: The Role of Top Leaders

Trudy Bers and Randy L. Swing

This chapter is intended for senior leaders who oversee a higher education unit or institution. These campus leaders wear many hats: managing the staff, controlling budgets, establishing a vision to guide future actions, scanning the environment for threats and opportunities, and more. Most campus leaders have a role that includes leadership for institutional assessment—a role that may have come as a surprise and may include functions for which the individual has had little if any formal training. Because assessment may be new to some leaders, we have included information about its operational aspects as well as its purposes and goals.

The organizational level that has most direct authority and responsibility for assessment varies by institution, but the basic premises and expectations regarding assessment should be common. At some institutions this information may be of greater practical utility for chief academic officers (CAOs) and other administrators and faculty members whose responsibilities focus on implementing assessment programs. At smaller institutions the CAO is likely to be most directly responsible. However, we assert that chancellors and presidents of larger institutions, who are unlikely to have direct responsibility for assessment, should still be informed in order to offer leadership and guidance.

Over the past two decades, expectations have increased rapidly for presidents, CAOs student affairs officers, deans, and directors to provide leadership and inspiration to ensure compliance with internal and external demands to demonstrate institutional effectiveness. Institutional leaders are now in the center of a large and growing national conversation about quality assurance, transparency, and the value of higher education. Many college leaders are rather uncomfortable in what may seem to be the uncharted waters of leadership for measuring and using student learning outcomes to inform campus decisions. Some hesitation is understandable.

The purpose of this chapter is to help leaders move beyond that hesitation by articulating important ways in which leaders both provide a context in which assessment is valued and ensure adequate support for a sustainable, cyclical, organized assessment program. We acknowledge that there are no one-size-fits-all solutions for successful learning outcomes assessments. Just as learning is complex and often messy, so are efforts to measure and evaluate it.

As authors, we begin with the belief that senior campus leaders would not reach their positions without a deep commitment to creating the best student learning opportunities possible. We hold that leading assessment is just one tool for fostering high levels of student learning and thus institutional success. Additionally, we hold that the engagement of senior leaders—whether they represent academic affairs, student affairs, the president's office, or a system office—is mandatory for institutional success in assessment efforts. Regardless of the individual's leadership style, assessment can contribute to presenting the institution or unit vision by recounting stories and providing evidence needed to support a case for continuing practices that are effective or for changing those that are not. We hope that, after reading this chapter and those that follow, each leader will find his or her own voice for fostering a campus vision for assessment.

We begin the chapter by addressing definitions and perspectives of assessment, neither of which are consistently defined or agreed upon across higher education or even within single institutions. We then move to a discussion of the contemporary context within which assessment takes place, a context characterized by growing expectations that colleges and universities will demonstrate that students are learning. Next we move to a more microscopic discussion, identifying purposes of learning outcomes assessment and approaches to assessment. Finally, we identify leadership challenges and suggest ways in which leaders can affirm the importance of assessment and foster an institutional climate in which learning outcomes assessment is valued by all stakeholders, implemented on a regular basis, and used to improve learning.

DEFINITIONS AND PERSPECTIVES

Over the past three decades a number of constructs have fallen, accurately or inaccurately, into the category of assessment. Specialists in the field carefully segment measurement, evaluation, institutional effectiveness, and assessment into separate arenas, but many in higher education use *assessment* as an umbrella term for a variety of quality enhancement and accountability efforts.

The vocabulary of assessment is not standardized across higher education. Because of the inconsistent use of language, we feel it wise to begin any discussion with a brief definition of *assessment* as it will be used in our chapter. It is likely that institutional leaders and faculty members use the term differently with various stakeholders and even with one another. It is especially important for senior leaders to understand the terminology used at their institutions and also to be sure that others understand how they define terms such as assessment. Absent a common vocabulary, the already messy world of assessment will be even more confusing.

In brief, we view assessment as a process, the purpose of which is to discern student learning, performance, and achievement in the aggregate. Assessment focuses on students and their learning at the course, program, and institutional levels. It is about students and their acquisition of knowledge, skills, and sometimes even attitudes.

Assessment is not the same as evaluation, accountability, or performance standards. Evaluation involves making judgments about efficacy, utility, efficiency, quality, or satisfaction with people, programs, policies, practices, and procedures. Professionals also agree that assessment is not the same as *accountability* or *standards of quality*. Accountability is a process of using assessment results to demonstrate and document achievement of quality standards (Suskie, 2009). Assessment and accountability are both rooted in the institutional mission and goals; thus, institutions should focus their assessments on learning outcomes consistent with mission and goals and demonstrate accountability for outcomes consistent with their missions. A community college with a mission that includes preparing students for careers should assess whether students have learned the technical and general knowledge and skills for successful performance on the job. And for accountability the institution might also examine whether alumni obtain and succeed in jobs in those careers. A university with a mission that includes original research should examine the extent to which it obtains research grants and the frequency with which faculty members publish research articles and books or present at professional research meetings. Both university examples speak to accountability; they are not assessments of student learning.

Confusion occurs when assessment of learning outcomes is not differentiated from appraisals gauging effectiveness in other dimensions, such as research, faculty productivity in teaching, student satisfaction with support services, or financial health of the institution. Such dimensions and outcomes are important but are not indicators of learning.

While generally defining assessment may splinter into esoteric discussions, parameters must be set for a particular discussion of assessment that is intended to sharpen understanding and shape action. Because various stakeholders will carry individual ideas and associations for the term, a campus leader must seek common ground in order to communicate clearly and to set a common vision for assessment initiatives.

Uses and Misuses of Assessments

An important component of a vision for assessment is the degree to which results will be used to improve programs (based on aggregated data) versus the degree to which results will be used to evaluate individuals (faculty members or students). Most assessment instruments used by colleges and universities do not rise to the level of precision necessary to evaluate individual students in terms of their own learning. Licensure and graduate entrance exams are examples of highly precise academic assessments, but these rarely have pretests that allow for a measure of value gained. Tests of general education competencies and disciplinary exams that test learning in the student's major are precise enough, when aggregated, to measure program outcomes, but they should not be used to assign students to remediation or other academic services.

Similarly, assessments that are good enough to measure program-level outcomes should not be used to evaluate faculty members. Students are not randomly assigned to faculty members or courses, so there are potentially multiple reasons that one class might perform on a higher or lower level than another. Yet, the fear that assessments will be used as a form of faculty evaluation is often a concern that must be considered and addressed by senior leaders.

A clear vision for assessment places the work as an exploration of how well the institution is doing, rather than how individual students or faculty members are performing. Certainly, higher education is not a solo sport for students, faculty members, or administrators. Acknowledging that it takes all players to create an excellent learning environment and outstanding learning outcomes is at the core of a vision for assessment efforts that matter.

CONTEMPORARY CONTEXT OF ASSESSMENT

The need to evaluate individual student learning is well integrated into the American system of higher education. Tests, capstone projects, exit examinations, and an elaborate system of grading individual students are ingrained in the American college experience. In fact, a common argument is that there is no reason for assessment since colleges already issue grades, which should be adequate quality assurance.

Grades as Assessments

We recognize that grades do provide valuable information. They also have shortcomings. Most college teachers can recite examples of final grades that were not an accurate expression of a student's learning. Bright students sometimes choose to skip a test or assignment and settle for grades below their actual achievement level. And some overachievers may earn high grades by collecting bonus points and maintaining perfect attendance, thereby receiving grades above their actual level of learning. As all academics are aware, different faculty members teaching the same course may show little consistency in the ways they evaluate students; standardized rubrics are rarely adopted on the department or university level. Since grading standards are not consistent across institutions, transfer students are often overrated or underrated as they shift their schooling to a new context. Grades are an important omnibus measure of student achievement and performance, which includes learning, but even at best they are seldom limited to learning or adequately calibrated for comparability.

Moreover, many educators assert that learning is cumulative across courses so that learning outcomes cannot be adequately assessed until the student has completed a program or sequence of courses. The allocation of considerable resources to assessments of core curricula, general education, and overall programs is premised on the assumption that measuring learning outcomes requires more than simply aggregating course grades.

Assessments across Institutions

Obviously higher education is a messy business. Few bottom-line measurements exist that can prove an institution's worth, particularly as institutions enroll vastly different students and work to achieve widely varying missions. Yet, as access to higher education has expanded and the cost of a college degree has increased, the demands from consumers (student, parents, Congress, and state legislatures) to be able to compare institutions of higher education have increased. The Spellings Commission (Secretary of Education's Commission on the Future of Higher Education, 2006) brought national attention to the need for consumer information about higher education by calling for increased efforts to assess student learning and to tie learning to accreditation. Higher education leaders were painfully aware of the difficulties of achieving some of the ideals expressed in the debates of the Spellings Commission. Yet the commission's report spurred action by both private and public colleges to provide better consumer information.

The Voluntary System of Accountability (VSA) is one example of this response. The VSA is a voluntary initiative developed by the higher education community to meet the following objectives:

• provide a useful tool for students during the college search process;
• assemble information that is transparent, comparable, and understandable;
• demonstrate stewardship and accountability to the public; and
• measure educational outcomes to identify and enhance effective educational practices.

Sponsored by the Association of Public and Land-Grant Universities (APLU), formerly the National Association of State Universities and Land-Grant Colleges (NASULGC), and the American Association of State Colleges and Universities (AASCU), the VSA requires participating institutions to administer and publish results from one of three standardized assessments of learning outcomes: the Collegiate Assessment of Academic Proficiency (CAAP) from the ACT; the ETS® Proficiency Profile (formerly the Measure of Academic Proficiency and Progress [MAPP]); or the Collegiate Learning Assessment (CLA). Institutions publish VSA data using a standard format on www.collegeportraits.org/.

More recently, the American Association of Community Colleges, the Association of Community College Trustees, and the College Board have collaborated and, with support from the Lumina Foundation, begun developing a Voluntary Framework for Accountability (VFA). The VFA is intended to be analogous to the VSA but with measures appropriate to community colleges. At present (December 2009), the VFA is forming work groups to research current state and system data collection efforts, conceptualize and test potential measures, consider how data may be used by and benefit colleges, and develop a plan to encourage participation. A particular challenge for the VFA will be to incorporate information about student learning without mandating participants to administer standardized tests or presuming that learning outcomes assessments are comparable across institutions.

Another national assessment initiative is the VALUE (Valid Assessment of Learning in Undergraduate Education) project of the Association of American Colleges and Universities (AAC&U). The project entails developing rubrics to assess a wide range of skills in three broad areas: intellectual and practical skills, personal and social responsibility, and integrated learning. Fifteen rubrics have been developed (see www.aacu.org/Rising_Challenge/index.cfm).

Questions and Challenges

The national debate continues, playing out specifically in the regional accrediting bodies. Campus leaders will not be able to ignore national and regional contexts for assessment. The Council of Regional Accrediting Commissions' (C-RAC; 2003) principles for good practice related to student learning are among several declarations that drive accreditation policies at the regional accrediting agencies.

At the core of these new approaches are a number of questions: for example, "What are students learning?" "Is it the right kind of learning?" "What difference is the institution making in students' lives?" "What evidence does an institution have that ensures what a student learns is worth his or her investment?" These are questions that an institution must be prepared to discuss with regional and disciplinary accrediting bodies. Depending on the team visiting the institution, these questions might be posed to senior leaders, most likely the CAO, or to deans, faculty members, and assessment directors.

A particularly useful source of information on assessment is the National Institute for Learning Outcomes Assessment (NILOA; www.learningout comeassessment.org). Established in 2008, this new organization has chosen as its primary objective "to discover and disseminate ways that academic programs and institutions can productively use assessment data internally to inform and strengthen undergraduate education, and externally to communicate with policy makers, families and other stakeholders." Campus leaders need to think about external forces such as accrediting agencies and state governing or coordinating board mandates, but they must also be aware of the local campus history with assessment. Many institutions now have twenty or more years of experience with some form of assessment practices. On some campuses the process has left scars and deep divisions, while on others assessment is among the standard operating procedures. Most campuses are in between, with many faculty members still skeptical about the value of assessment and with perceptions of the importance of assessment varying over time. Campus leaders should expect these questions to be explored:

• What is understood as the local culture of assessment? Do faculty and staff unions agree about assessment activities? Is assessment driven from a central office or decentralized to campus units and individuals?

- What resources are allotted to assessment activities, and what are the sources of assessment funding?
- Is assessment viewed as an initiative for accountability or for improvement? Can it be both?
- To what degree has the campus reached consensus on issues of academic freedom and faculty autonomy in terms of assessment across courses and programs?
- To what degree is the campus willing to acknowledge weaknesses and areas needing improvement in publicly available reports and documents? Do local sunshine laws apply to assessment findings and materials?
- Has the institution experienced significant turnover among assessment leaders or made multiple "fresh starts" in assessment that send the faculty and staff back up the learning curve or imply that assessment doesn't really matter?
- Has the institution been cited by accrediting agencies for weak or inadequate learning outcomes assessments? If so, what responses have been required from the institution?

It is likely that the area of least agreement will center on whether assessment is primarily for accountability or for improvement. It is easy to suggest that the two can occur simultaneously, yet in reality tensions surround these purposes. Assessment for accountability includes inherent pressures to find positive results and must focus on what external stakeholders consider to be of most value. Assessment for improvement may provide greater incentives for candor but may also include inherent pressures to find minor flaws that can be resolved with increased resources.

Having discussed the distinctions between assessment broadly conceived and the assessment of learning outcomes, and having noted a number of contextual factors that shape the environment within which learning outcomes assessment occurs, we turn now to a more focused discussion of the assessment of student learning outcomes. Again we acknowledge that top-level leaders are unlikely to be engaged at this level of assessment, but we offer the information as a brief overview for senior leaders who feel uncertain about their knowledge of assessment or who want to pass along the information to those with more day-to-day involvement.

PURPOSES OF LEARNING OUTCOMES ASSESSMENT

Learning outcomes assessment is driven by multiple purposes, both internal and external to the institution. Many of them are discussed individually in the sections that follow.

Establish and Refine Learning Objectives

To Articulate and Clarify What Students Should Know and Be Able to Do as a Result of Taking Courses and Programs

A first step in developing an assessment plan and process is for departments to clearly articulate the learning objectives for their programs and courses. Unfortunately, they do not always do so. In many institutions curricula were in place long before the assessment movement began, and only brief descriptions of program and course contents were submitted to explain the curricula. Learning objectives are different: they typically begin with a verb indicating an active, observable result (*describe, explain, compare, analyze,* etc.), then specify knowledge, skills, and attitudes as objects of that verb (e.g., "describe the process" or "analyze the causes"); they focus on what students, rather than instructors, will do. Consider the difference between a course description and a set of learning objectives for an American government course.

Course Description

This course presents philosophical principles, governmental machinery, and political processes of the federal government. Content includes political culture, the Constitution, civil liberties and rights, government institutions, political parties and interest groups, public opinion, and public policy decision making.

Learning Objectives

• Explain the primary roles of the three branches of the federal government.
• Describe the historical and philosophical underpinnings of the U.S. Constitution.
• Explain the influence of interest groups, political parties, and political action committees (PACs) on campaigns and elections for the U.S. Congress and presidency.
• Analyze the voting behavior of American subgroups characterized by racial, ethnic, religious, socioeconomic, gender, geographic, and political party distinctions.
• Evaluate contemporary political issues and potential solutions from different theoretical perspectives.

Learning objectives should be measurable so that another faculty member assessing students' work would come to the same basic conclusion about the extent of learning as the instructor teaching the course.

Learning outcomes reflect whether students have acquired the knowledge, skills, and even attitudes specified as objectives. In reality, the terms *learning objectives* and *learning outcomes* are often used interchangeably or are used differently from one institution to another. As noted earlier in this chapter, to minimize confusion we urge institutions to adopt a consistent and common vocabulary and definitions for assessment-related terms.

The faculty is central to the development of learning objectives. Across institutions in all higher education segments, the process of articulating learning objectives forces faculty members to wrestle with different conceptions of the same course, the fundamental content they believe should be included, and the learning that should take place.

To Foster Common Learning Objectives across Multiple Sections of the Same Course

When faculty members agree on the core learning to take place in a course, there is an assumption that all sections will deal with the same core content, although it may be presented in a variety of formats, supporting materials, and pedagogical approaches. Flexibility may be provided for faculty members to add or emphasize topics within the basic course framework, add learning objectives, assign different readings (unless a standard text or course packet is required), and use a variety of assignments to evaluate students' knowledge and skills. From the institutional perspective, what is important is that regardless of who teaches the course or how it is taught, all students successfully completing that course will achieve the same core learning objectives, giving the course credibility beyond the individual instructor and even beyond the institution. This form of credibility allows an institution to assume that students who successfully complete a course will be prepared for the next level course in a sequence and enables transfer institutions to accept credits without examining the specific class syllabus or credentials of the instructor delivering the class.

Measure Achievement and Generate Action

To Identify Areas in Which Learning Objectives Are Not Being Met and to Change Course or Program Contents and Teaching to Achieve Greater Learning

When learning outcomes assessments demonstrate that students are not achieving the desired level of learning (i.e., they are not able to demonstrate the knowledge or skills faculty members expect in the course), assessment results can trigger a variety of responses. Faculty members may revise pedagogy and materials, perhaps giving students more frequent feedback, using computer-based exercises to augment lectures and class discussions, preparing new instructional materials to supplement or replace ineffective resources, incorporating more active or problem-based learning into a lecture course, or devoting more class time to particularly difficult topics. In some cases the faculty members and administrators may find that they need to change the method of assessment or the standard of performance expected of students. While such responses are sometimes appropriate, they must not be used to explain away poor results or shift attention from the learning and teaching of course subject matter.

To Meet Accountability, Accreditation, and Public Expectations That Students Are Learning What the Institution Asserts They Are Learning

All colleges make claims about what their students learn, though the statements are often framed as assertions of broad institutional purposes for students: what graduates will be prepared to do in their careers, in their personal lives, and as citizens. But as the climate of higher education has changed, public and private agencies are seeking evidence to substantiate claims of student learning and achievement. While the lay public may focus primarily on traditional indicators such as number of degrees and graduates' success in being admitting to graduate school or obtaining jobs, the academy itself recognizes differences between these measures and direct evidence that students have acquired the knowledge and skills implied by the traditional indicators. Learning assessments can be part of that evidence.

To Identify and Address Gaps in Meeting Learning Objectives among Student Subgroups (Gender, Age, Race and Ethnicity, Remedial and College Ready, and Major)

When assessment results are disaggregated by student subgroups, gaps in performance among subgroups are often revealed. Through additional research, institutions can identify students' attributes, patterns of enrollment, participation in support services, and perceptions of barriers and supports associated with successfully attaining learning objectives. For example, the institution might find that part-time students in one department regularly meet learning objectives but part-time students in another department do not. Using research results, institutions or departments can design and implement interventions to improve student learning as well as identify and share good practices that might account for a department's success. It should be noted that research of this nature often requires compiling data at the student level, whereas most learning assessments are reported at subgroup, department, or institutional levels. This, in turn, requires skillful researchers who have access to data, know how to use them, and respect the need for confidentiality in sharing results.

Recognize and Value Achievement

To Measure Value Added

Some proponents of learning outcomes assessments, particularly those using standardized tests, argue that assessment results measure the value added by an institution to a student's knowledge and skills. For example, the CLA aggregates students' scores to the institutional level to indicate how students as a whole are performing. After the CLA is administered to samples of freshmen and seniors, results for the two groups are compared. The CLA Institutional Report states, "The CLA is designed to measure an institution's contribution, or value-added, to the development of . . . competencies, including the effect of changes to curriculum and pedagogy" (Council for Aid to Education, 2009).

Others dispute the claim that assessments measure value added. For example, Trudy Banta (2007) summarized conclusions she and her colleagues reached in their studies of standardized tests as measures of value added. According to Banta, standardized tests fall short of measuring value added because they

- "test primarily entering ability,
- are not content neutral,
- contain questions and problems that do not match the learning experiences of all students at any given institution,
- measure at best 30% of the knowledge and skills faculty want students to develop in the course of their general education experiences,
- cannot be given to samples of volunteers if scores are to be generalized to all students,
- cannot be required of some students at an institution and not of others."

Most attempts to measure value added rely on comparing cross-sectional data: data from two groups taking the assessment at the same time, with one group assumed to represent students at the beginning of a learning experience and the other assumed to represent students at the end. While quantitative data can be used to compare groups' similarities on a variety of characteristics (e.g., age, gender, program, ACT or SAT, high school GPA), it is far more problematic, if not impossible, to parse out the collegiate and noncollegiate experiences that contributed to learning demonstrated by the second group on their assessments. Particularly at this time—when students swirl among institutions, discontinue for a term or more, work while going to school, and take more than two years to complete an associate degree and four years to complete a baccalaureate degree—assuming that the institution assessing the end-of-experience learning is responsible for that learning is shaky at best.

To gauge the value added to learning by an institution, longitudinal studies are required in which work of the same students is assessed over time, with student attributes and other variables that might account for learning outside the institution controlled. Such research is difficult to conduct. Some assessment approaches, especially portfolios, permit institutions to examine students' changes over time, but assuming the institution is responsible for the changes is risky. Using assessments to demonstrate value added is the most controversial of assessment purposes.

To Understand and Value Out-of-Class Learning through Articulating Learning Objectives for Co- and Extracurricular Activities and for Support Services

Many institutions have strengthened service-learning, study-abroad, and internship programs but may not have identified, let alone measured, the learning objectives students are expected to achieve as a result of participating in them. Even less effort has been expended in examining the learning that can occur when students are involved with support offices: for example, writing scholarship applications for financial aid or completing a Free Application for Federal Student Aid (FAFSA). Documenting student learning from such activities may illustrate the importance of out-of-class experiences, build a case for continuing to fund offices and programs sometimes viewed as marginal to the institution, and demonstrate that teaching and learning occur across the campus and involve all employees, not just the faculty.

APPROACHES TO ASSESSMENT

There are many approaches to assessment. In this section we touch briefly on the most common, although we recognize that some institutions have developed remarkably innovative and unusual methods that are less known but equally if not more substantive and meaningful for that institution.

Measurement Dimensions

Before identifying approaches, we note two important measurement dimensions that characterize assessments: one categorizes measures as direct or indirect, and the other categorizes data as quantitative or qualitative.

Direct measures rely on students demonstrating that they have gained the knowledge and skills being assessed. Demonstrations take many forms, including answers to test questions covering the content, performances, presentations, papers, lab solutions, accounting ledgers, and so on. The accuracy of direct measures depends on the explicit correspondence between the work evaluated and the learning outcome the work is designed to display. *Indirect measures* rely on perceptions that the knowledge or skill has been attained, using proxies from which these inferences can be made. Examples of indirect measures include self-reports of students, satisfaction of graduates' employers, and analyses of course syllabi.

Quantitative data are numeric—amenable to statistical analyses. For example, the percentage of correct answers on a test or the number of minutes required to correctly solve a problem are quantitative measures. *Qualitative data* include almost any information that is not numeric; these data approximate a characteristic, property, or attribute and are used primarily to describe the qualities of a phenomenon. For example, students' journals describing what they learned in a class are qualitative measures.

Most national attention today is focused on direct, quantitative measures of student learning outcomes. However, institutional leaders should be aware that rich and informative assessments also occur with qualitative and indirect approaches.

Common Assessments

To simplify and to emphasize that no approach is necessarily better than another, we present the most popular approaches in alphabetical order. Some approaches may include both quantitative and qualitative data.

Capstone Courses (Direct and Qualitative or Quantitative)

At the end of a program, students may be required to take a class that integrates material covered in earlier courses and allows them to demonstrate their learning through various combinations of tests, papers, portfolios, simulations, team assignments, presentations, and other methods that demonstrate learning. Such a course is designed to approximate the totality of key learning expected of students completing the program. Therefore, course learning outcomes are interpretable as program learning outcomes as well.

Course-Embedded Assessment (Direct and Qualitative or Quantitative)

Assessment practices may be embedded in academic courses, most commonly by gathering student data based on questions selected by the department. Questions intended to assess student outcomes are incorporated or embedded into final exams, research reports, and term papers or projects. This work is evaluated by two or more faculty members to determine whether or not the students are achieving the prescribed educational goals and objectives of the department. This assessment is a *separate process* from that used by the course instructor to grade the exam, report, or term paper.

Course Progression and Success (Indirect and Quantitative)

Assessment may be designed to track the performance of students through each course in a defined sequence. Assuming the curriculum is well aligned so that the competencies of the first class are prerequisites for the second, this method can provide relevant information about how much students are really learning.

Culminating Project (Direct and Qualitative or Quantitative)

A culminating project may be linked with a capstone course or internship experience or may stand alone as a requirement for program completion. The project needs to be broadly defined, but it must reflect students' learning and ability to integrate information from across the curriculum. Grading may be by faculty, by outside experts, or by a combination of internal and external evaluators. Such a project differs from a portfolio in that a portfolio is a collection of student work gathered throughout the student's time at the institution, whereas the project is a more focused work that addresses a particular situation or simulation. For example, students in fashion merchandising might be required to put together a marketing campaign—including sample ads, budgets, media schedules, and displays—to promote a new line of sportswear targeted to young teens, and then to present the campaign to an audience of faculty members, peers, and industry representatives. In the performing arts, a "juried performance" is evaluated by outside experts.

Curriculum and Syllabus Analyses (Indirect and Qualitative or Quantitative)

By analyzing the curriculum in terms of course syllabi, assessors can chart which courses will cover which of the objectives that have been defined for general education, the discipline area, or the program. Use of the chart assures the department that students enrolled in a specific program or advancing through general education coursework will have had the opportunity to achieve those objectives if they have followed the prescribed sequence. Syllabus analysis is especially useful when multiple sections of a course are offered with a variety of instructors. Assessors can easily discern whether each section will cover essential points without having to prescribe the specific teaching methods to be used.

Employer Surveys (Indirect and Qualitative or Quantitative)

Surveys can be taken of alumni employers to learn their perspectives on the competency, knowledge, skills, workplace behaviors, and other relevant attributes graduates bring to their workplace performance. Implementing employer surveys can be challenging for several reasons, which include identifying employers or supervisors who have direct knowledge of the individual's performance, overcoming reluctance on the part of employers to provide student-specific information or feedback that could prompt litigation or other negative consequences, obtaining alumni permission to contact employers or supervisors, and determining what knowledge and skills the alumni learned at the institution or at other institutions and worksites.

Employment and Job Placement Rates (Indirect and Quantitative)

Employment and job placement rates are often examined, as these data can indicate the relevance of program curriculum as well as student attainment of expected learning outcomes. Some states link student data with unemployment data to identify students who have been reported by employers to be employed within a given quarter. Other databases may be accessible to track employment by the U.S. Postal Service, federal government, or military units. The student's Social Security number is used to match files across these data sets. In some states, such as Illinois, the state agency does the matching but provides the college with aggregate information, not student-specific data.

Focus Groups and Exit Interviews (Indirect and Qualitative)

Focus groups and exit interviews with current and former students can be important sources of information about students' learning, their academic skills, and their perceptions about their experiences at the college and within the programs. Information from these sources should not be generalized and should always be used in conjunction with results from other research approaches.

Institutional or Departmental Tests (Direct and Quantitative)

These tests are developed by the faculty to cover all or most essential elements of a course or program. They may be administered to all students or to an appropriate sample of students at the completion of the course or program. Because students take the test regardless of instructor and at or near the end of the learning experience, results may be interpreted as indicating acquisition of knowledge or skills across the department for that course or program. Where departments create their own assessments, evaluating test reliability and validity may be a daunting project; frequently, faculty members rely on face validity and assume that their professional judgment is sufficient to give the test credibility.

Licensure Exams (Indirect and Quantitative)

In some fields, especially in health careers and some business programs (e.g., accounting and real estate), individuals must pass a state or national licensure or board exam before being able to practice their profession. Results on such exams are considered indicators of student learning, because it is assumed that students who pass the exams have acquired the necessary knowledge and skills. Unfortunately, not all agencies report exam results to the student's institution, so colleges must rely on students' self-reports.

Portfolio Assessment (Direct and Quantitative or Qualitative)

A portfolio is a collection of a student's work that demonstrates learning and development. Work is carefully assessed by the faculty or other content-area experts and typically evaluated holistically. Portfolios can consist of hard or electronic copies of students' work, including such artifacts as student-written papers, projects, videotapes of presentations, resumes, sample letters of application for jobs, and other materials that give evidence of achievements. For program-level assessment, portfolios must contain documentation of learning and development across the spectrum of program objectives.

Rubrics (Direct and Quantitative or Qualitative)

A rubric functions as a scoring guide: a list, chart, or set of descriptive phrases that indicate the criteria that will be used to score or grade an assignment. Rubrics are not independent assessments, but they provide information to students and evaluators about what attributes, behaviors, information, or skills need to be apparent in a student's work to warrant a particular evaluation. Rubrics foster uniformity in evaluations of student learning across multiple sections of the same course among multiple instructors and among multiple evaluators.

Satisfaction and Self-reported Learning Surveys (Indirect and Quantitative)

Student and alumni satisfaction surveys may be designed to include self-reported estimates of learning. Results provide indirect evidence of student learning outcomes. Though most powerful when results are triangulated with more direct assessments of learning, satisfaction surveys can be especially helpful when respondents are currently working in the field and are providing feedback about whether what they believe they learned in the program has adequately prepared them for the workplace. Satisfaction surveys are available through a number of commercial providers or may be developed by the institution.

Standardized Tests (Direct and Quantitative)

Standardized tests are administered and scored in a consistent manner, with items selected after trials for appropriateness, clarity, and difficulty. Norm-referenced tests are used to compare individual or group scores to the score of a larger group. Criterion-referenced tests are used to determine how well an individual or group has learned a particular body of knowledge or skills. Testing agencies that produce standardized tests can provide information about validity, reliability, and norm-referenced or criterion-referenced results for prior test takers.

Transfer To and Success In Another Institution (Indirect and Quantitative)

A record of the numbers of students who move to other institutions, including degrees earned if available, can be a useful tool for program, discipline, or institution assessment. The primary purpose of community college transfer programs is to provide students with the first two years of undergraduate work, helping them gain the necessary knowledge and skills to succeed in upper division courses. Thus, acceptance at and transfer to a four-year college or university is an indirect indicator of student learning. Community colleges can find out if and where many of their students transfer through the National Student Clearinghouse Student Tracker program. Four-year colleges can also track progress of students who have left their institution and entered programs at other colleges or universities. The Clearinghouse claims to have data for 92 percent of U.S. college students (www.studentclearinghouse.org/about/default.htm).

Vendor or Industry Certification Examination (Indirect and Quantitative)

Certification examinations administered by vendors or professional and industry organizations provide external validation that the student has the knowledge and skills identified by the vendor or industry as essential for a particular job or credential. The examining body may not care where test takers obtained their knowledge or whether this was achieved through formal coursework or self-study.

ISSUES OF LEADERSHIP

Failing to establish an effective assessment program would be cited as a significant shortcoming by most accrediting agencies. But building an assessment program that consumes resources without returning useful information is arguably worse. Doing assessment as an end in itself is unjustifiable, but meaningful assessment is useful. A test of quality assessment is that it either produces actions for improvement or confirms existing practices in ways that protect and preserve them (Swing, 2004). Senior leadership must make continual efforts to guide assessment in these directions.

Assessment of Assessment

The process of using assessment results to inform decisions and actions is frequently referred to as "closing the loop." The intention, of course, is to make changes that lead to future assessments showing higher levels or more widespread learning—a verifiable hypothesis. Thus, assessment is a cycle of testing, interpreting results, implementing changes, and retesting to measure the impact of change.

Campus leaders should ask the following questions:

- How do we know that our selected assessment measurements are measuring what we think they measure (measurement validity)?
- How do we know that our measurements of the concepts of interest are consistent (measurement reliability)?
- What adjustments have been made based on findings from past assessment efforts?
- How were those changes tested through additional assessment efforts?
- Did learning improve as a result of campus adjustments?
- Did learning improve for all students or only for certain subpopulations?

A common mistake is to repeat assessments too quickly. Time is required for new procedures to be fully implemented and to begin working as intended. Campus leaders must consider and advocate for assessment timelines that do not shortchange the process. This means campuses need assessment programs that stretch into the future, with identified projects, timetables, reporting processes, responsible parties, and budgets. It also means assessment documents should include data and information about past assessments, including results, ways the results were used to change courses and programs, and subsequent measures to determine the impact of those changes.

Administrators should remember that small changes usually create small results. Though small improvements in what students know and can do may be pragmatically important, they may not be adequately detected by assessment instruments. Large changes may produce highly visible results, but they usually take significant amounts of time and resources to fully implement. Outcomes of measurable magnitude may require more than a year to achieve.

Leadership Imperatives

As we consider the role of institutional leaders in assessment, six specific imperatives emerge. For an institution to build and sustain a strong assessment program that serves the institution as well as external constituencies, we urge leaders to emphasize these areas.

Set expectations that assessment will be implemented and results used for decision making, including planning and budgeting. To translate expectations into reality, ask for the evidence to support recommendations for course and curriculum changes and for new or reallocated resources; schedule presentations about student learning to leadership colleagues and other key stakeholders; ensure that information about assessment and student learning is prominent on the website and in other publications; and acknowledge and applaud good assessment practices and results. Yet another strategy is to include knowledge of or even demonstrated experience with assessment in ads for senior academic leaders, if not as a requirement, at least as a preferred attribute. This strategy signals both internally and externally that assessment is important to the institution.

Build and sustain an infrastructure to support assessment. Institutions may use a variety of approaches for building and sustaining an assessment infrastructure. While we do not advocate a particular structure, we do suggest that an office or offices be designated with authority and responsibility to coordinate and cultivate learning outcomes assessment. We note the possibility of there being more than one office because in large, complex universities assessment may be better handled at the college or even department level than at the university level, while at small institutions a single office will probably be both sufficient and appropriate. The offices may have a variety of roles, but it is most important that assessment professionals not supplant faculty members and do assessment for them. Rather, assessment professionals serve as mentors, coaches, and consultants, helping with logistical tasks that must be expedited for assessment to occur. The infrastructure is related to the next imperative: providing resources.

Provide resources to support assessment, including money, staff, space, computer support, and professional development. It is naive to assume assessment can be done as an add-on to existing responsibilities and without additional dollars. For example, most faculty members require professional development to learn to plan, implement, interpret, and use results of assessment. Attending and presenting at assessment conferences is not only an opportunity for professional development but also an affirmation of the value of assessment to the institution and recognition of faculty members' contributions to assessment. Assessment requires time, and often alternate time is a powerful incentive that both permits and encourages the faculty to be involved. Professional support from institutional research and assessment offices provides the faculty and others with the help they need to both manage assessment projects and compile and interpret results. We say "others" because learning outcomes assessment may take place in academic support and student affairs units as well as in academic departments and programs. Standardized tests cost money as well. These are some of the more obvious and real costs associated with assessment.

Pay attention to assessment by asking questions, visiting the assessment office, championing assessment outside the institution, and having the courage to protect the institution from inappropriate expectations and unfunded assessment mandates.

Use results by explicitly linking assessment to decisions and *telling people you are doing so*. A common mistake is to make positive changes but fail to clearly articulate how the changes were informed by assessment results, even if other considerations were also included in the decision-making process.

Celebrate successes in assessment. Success is more than just positive results that affirm student learning. Success includes innovative and effective assessment processes and tools that return meaningful results and engage the faculty and staff, even if the results do not depict the level or extent of learning desired.

Major Leadership Challenges

No matter how well designed and carefully implemented, assessment efforts will be challenging for campus leaders on a variety of fronts. Senior leaders need to apply political wisdom and leadership talents before, during, and after assessments have taken place. Balancing positive and negative findings is not always an easy process.

Positive Results

There is nothing wrong with focusing early assessment efforts on documenting what a campus is doing well. Senior leaders will find joy in having clear evidence of successful programs and gains in student learning. Citing the results and widely disseminating them are useful and important. Yet, there will be myriad decision points even when results are positive. For example, should successful programs be rewarded with additional resources? (Program leaders may feel penalized if resources are frozen because they are already doing well.) Although a program is successful, are there areas where improvement is needed or where resources could be reduced without harming the overall result? The best assessment efforts should provide evidence about specific aspects that are working well, so that the core elements of success can be protected as changes are made in future years or programs are scaled up. Identifying successful practices can also help other departments adopt or adapt them.

Disappointing Results

Of course some assessments will show that students have not learned as desired or that programs are not resulting in the desired level of success. Though senior leaders may be tempted to hide such findings, they must bring their best leadership skills to the task of using disappointing findings to improve future performance. As they deliver such findings to various stakeholders, senior leaders must craft their messages appropriately. Some faculty and staff members who have given their best efforts to a program may be sensitive and frustrated if the results have been ultimately disappointing. Leaders would do well to explain to stakeholders the lessons learned by the institution and staff members involved, along with ways those experiences will inform future efforts. Disappointing results should be met with action. Should a program receive increased resources in hopes of improving performance? Are there other organizations that could serve as models because of their higher levels of success?

Continued Resistance

Most assessment professionals report that resistance to assessment tends to decline after the initial assessment cycle. But some resistance is likely to continue. Even as assessment becomes institutional, some individuals will continue to hope that assessment is a passing fad that will fade over time. Senior leaders can defuse resistance by using assessment data constructively and widely reporting how they do so. Senior leaders should continue to emphasize the need for data to ensure quality and confirm their willingness to support such efforts.

Management Challenges

Assessment efforts need to be renewed and adjusted over time. Senior leaders should question assessments that do not focus on what matters most. Many assessment efforts lose meaning over time; it is important to know when to stop conducting certain assessments or when to reduce frequency of a specific procedure.

   Perhaps the most challenging issue for senior leaders is to avoid micromanaging assessment but still lead the effort to ensure that assessment does not become an end unto itself. Successful assessment efforts can change incrementally over time to focus more on the number of assessments rather than their level of service to the campus. Similarly, assessment efforts can drift away from the institutional aims and mission as they are used to measure satisfaction, document levels of participation, measure change in knowledge, and track multiple student behaviors. Maintaining focus on what the institution controls and which assessments most impact desired outcomes requires decisive leadership.

CONCLUSION

This chapter sets the stage for the remainder of this volume. Toward this objective, we have provided a general discussion of assessment broadly defined and narrowed to a focus on student learning outcomes; we have considered the external and internal environments shaping learning outcomes assessment, described purposes and approaches that contribute to successful assessment, and concluded with the role of senior leaders in supporting and overseeing assessment, along with challenges these leaders face in building, institutionalizing, and sustaining assessment programs. Particularly in the current context of academia, with demands for understandable data and information about student performance rising while resources fall, the need for campus leaders to develop and convey clear, consistent messages about assessment and to use assessment results in making decisions is critical.

Senior leaders will quickly discover that assessment is not optional for an accredited institution of higher education. It is also not likely to just bubble up as an excellent campus effort without the encouragement of senior campus leaders. Forming a vision for campus assessment operations is a challenging and necessary leadership task.

REFERENCES

Banta, T. W. (2007, January 26). A warning on measuring learning outcomes. *Inside Higher Education*. Retrieved from www.insidehighered.com/views/2007/01/26/banta.

Council for Aid to Education. (2009). 2007–2008 Collegiate Learning Assessment (CLA) institutional report, University College. Retrieved from www.cae.org/content/pdf/CLA_0708_R_University_College.pdf.

Council of Regional Accrediting Commissions. (2003). Regional accreditation and student learning: Principles for good practice. Retrieved from www.ncahlc.org/download/0412AssessmentAccredLearningPrinciples.PDF.

Secretary of Education's Commission on the Future of Higher Education. (2006). A test of leadership: Charting the future of U.S. higher education. A report of the commission appointed by Secretary of Education Margaret Spellings, U.S. Department of Education. Retrieved from www2.ed.gov/about/bdscomm/list/hiedfuture/reports/final-report.pdf.

Suskie, L. A. (2009). *Assessing student learning: A common sense guide* (2nd ed.). San Francisco: Jossey-Bass.

Swing, R. L. (Ed.). (2004). *Proving and improving. Volume II: Tools and techniques for assessing the first college year* (Monograph No. 37). Columbia: National Resource Center for the First-Year Experience and Students in Transition, University of South Carolina.

WEBSITES

Association of American Colleges and Universities (AAC&U)
www.aacu.org/Rising_Challenge/index.cfm

College Portrait of Undergraduate Education
www.collegeportraits.org

Council for Aid to Education's Collegiate Learning Assessment
www.cae.org/content/pdf/CLA_0708_R_University_College.pdf

National Student Clearinghouse
www.studentclearinghouse.org/about/default.htm

Chapter Two

Assessment Frameworks That Can Make a Difference in Achieving Institutional Outcomes

Gary L. Kramer, Coral Hanson, and Danny Olsen

In chapter 1, Randy Swing and Trudy Bers make a very good case for the importance of assessment for a campus. However, we begin this chapter by acknowledging that assessments that contribute to decision making in all key performance areas of the institution are extensive and involve a variety of challenges and constraints. Assessment becomes especially challenging when consideration must be given to the place of assessments and reporting in the larger context of aligning institutional claims with outcomes projected for all performance areas of the campus. Senior leaders must assert their political wisdom and leadership talents in directing use of purposeful assessments to guide strategic planning within existing budget constraints in meaningful and credible ways, which include managing and supporting behavior change based on broad engagement of the campus community.

Such challenges and constraints provide impetus for this chapter. While the authors can offer no panacea for creating and managing an integrated database to support campus-wide decision making, the chapter does offer essential, established principles and conditions concerning assessment frameworks that can influence achievement of institutional outcomes. To accomplish this, the chapter is divided into two main sections: (1) creating and managing an integrated database that supports informed, data-driven decision making in key performance areas of the institution and (2) using assessment planning principles and developing conditions to establish a sustainable culture of evidence from which the institutional data story can be told, that is, one that aligns evidential data with the aims and claims of the institution. Moreover, in this context, data become most helpful in constructing and understanding the underlying paradigms governing assessment in institutions.

A careful reading of this chapter should inform the reader on what and how to change in leading toward stronger, more congruent assessments on the campus: ensuring that every measurement used is of value, even *intentional*, and that decisions driven by these data positively promote and improve *student learning and development*—the core purpose of assessments in higher education. Given institutional financial constraints and the all-important return on investments, senior leaders will want to give particular attention as they read this chapter to the following: (1) deciding what matters most and what should be done differently as they lead assessments on the campus, (2) identifying factors of a campus assessment system, and (3) creating a culture of evidence that supports and aligns the institutional claims and mission.

Regular application of the principles and concepts discussed in this chapter should assist campus leadership and other stakeholders to accomplish the following:

- Access and query essential information (data) on student progress, development, and learning in a timely way.
- Determine whether the program and student learner outcomes have been achieved—what is working and where improvements need to be made.
- Ensure that assessment tools are intentional (purposeful) and aligned with and able to qualitatively measure institutional and departmental claims.
- Consistently address and update through the assessment process what is of value (intentional assessment) and, most important, inform decisions from what is measured—while keeping student learning and development at the core of most campus assessments.
- Limit the number of assessments and be selective in measuring what is most important.
- Use an established culture of evidence to tell the data story to various constituencies in and outside the institution, that is, address various accountabilities through readily available data.

What can be done to improve the campus assessment process? Without a clearly defined purpose, collecting data can consume a great deal of time and yield mounds of information that have no direct connection to the assessment inquiry. It is important to avoid measuring just to be measuring; the stakes are too high in costs and human resources given the instrument validity and reliability factors also involved. If the primary driver for assessments on the campus is the attempt to measure student learning, success, and development, then assessments should be organized around measuring what is of value and informing decisions for improvement in terms of what is measured.

FACTORS OR CONDITIONS OF AN
ASSESSMENT SYSTEM OR PLAN

Clearly, to lead assessment consistently and qualitatively year in and year out is not easy. Yet, while leading assessments has its ups and downs, doing so is most effective, as we explore in this section, when assessments are intentional (purposeful)—especially when what we measure is of value and the data derived are used to inform decisions for program improvement or change. No simple task or easy answers are involved. But based on a premise of this chapter, key factors or conditions of a systems plan, which are applicable across institutional types, can influence a systematic and continuous process of purposeful assessment. Thus, the following factors of an assessment plan or system built around student learning, engagement, development, and success can more directly assist campus leaders in telling the data story and improving student learning and development (see figures 2.1 and 2.2):

- *intentional (purposeful) assessments* from which the data align with and support campus claims—measuring consistently and persistently what is of most value to the campus;
- *engaged stakeholders* who are directly connected to the assessment system, with the president's office providing leadership and vision for building assessment partnerships with faculty members, students, and staff members;
- *an integrated and relational database* that provides stakeholders with comprehensive and user-friendly data access, query, and reports;
- *a master calendar* that emphasizes accountabilities of various units of the campus community in the assessment system, including timelines for data collection, assessment, data analysis, reporting, and follow-up or feedback essential to improving student learning initiatives;
- *timely reports* that tell the data story; and
- *data to inform decisions* based on what is measured, comprising the culture of evidence.

Each factor discussed in this section is integral to the assessment system. Therefore, the outcome of the system will be based on how well each part interacts with the rest of the parts, not on how each part functions on its own. The sum of the parts makes a systems approach to assessment work (Banta, Jones, and Black, 2009; Huba and Freed, 2000). All stakeholders must understand the composition and function of an assessment system; however, senior leadership is primarily responsible for the process of situating an assessment system within the institution, including its processes, timelines, and decision-making procedures (Maki, 2004).

Factors

1. Intentional Assessments
2. Engaged Stakeholders
3. Integrated Database
4. Master Calendar
5. Timely Reports
6. Culture of Evidence

Figure 2.1.   Factors with Institution-Level, Program-Level, and Course-Level Assessment Plans

Factor 1—Provide Intentional Measures for What Is of Value

Importance of Intentional Assessment

A great deal of discussion takes place about what really matters in assessment and how assessment can be more meaningful to institutions engaged in it. Institutions find meaning in claims made, goals or missions stated, and learner outcomes projected. Therefore, in order to achieve meaning in assessment, instruments and measures must be aligned to the claims the institution makes, and data must be used to inform decisions that drive change (Banta, Jones, and Black, 2009; Suskie, 2009).

The construction or selection of intentional instruments requires time and effort. Too often assessment is undertaken to satisfy external entities or cater to the wishes of a new administration, and so the easiest and most direct methods are used to construct or select the measures. Results from such a selection are generally less than meaningful and provide no real evidence to drive change and improve student learning and development (Wehlburg, 2008). Assessment instruments must be tied to where and how the institution finds

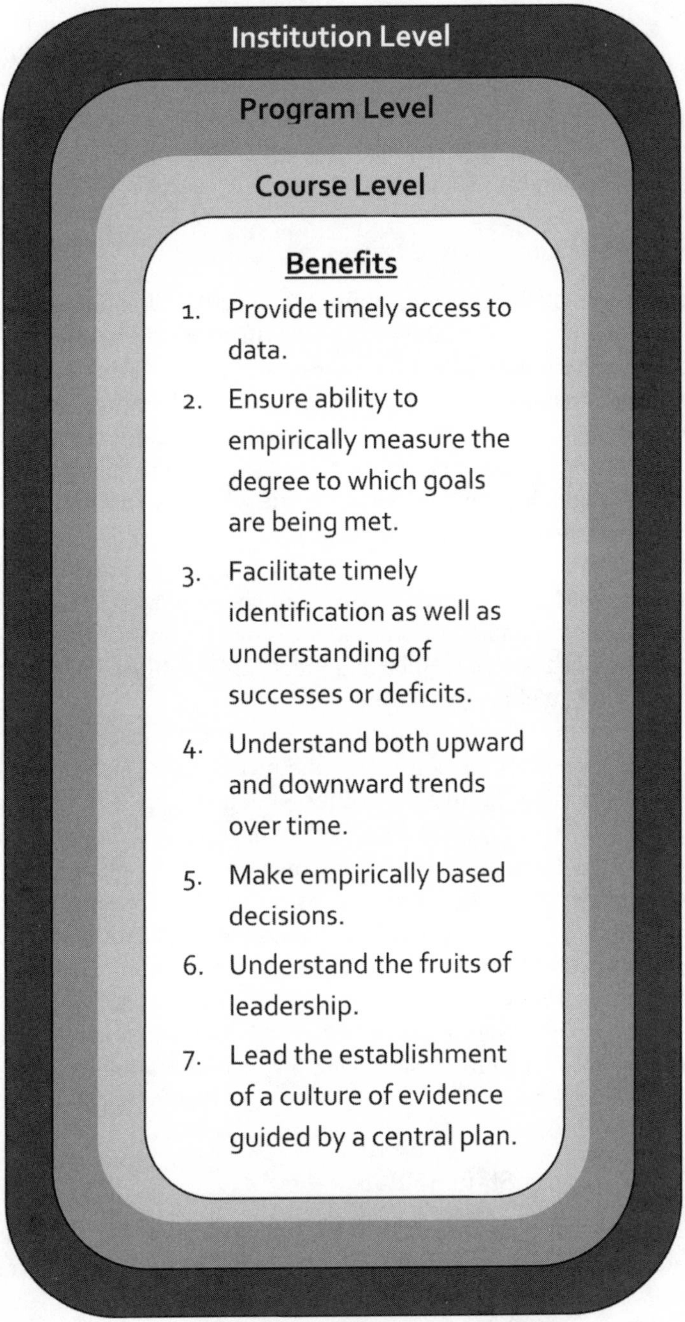

Institution Level

Program Level

Course Level

Benefits

1. Provide timely access to data.

2. Ensure ability to empirically measure the degree to which goals are being met.

3. Facilitate timely identification as well as understanding of successes or deficits.

4. Understand both upward and downward trends over time.

5. Make empirically based decisions.

6. Understand the fruits of leadership.

7. Lead the establishment of a culture of evidence guided by a central plan.

Figure 2.2.   Stakeholder Benefits of a Systems Approach

meaning and purpose; otherwise, assessment will be an exercise in futility. Further, institutions must be able to show that student learning and development are taking place. Statistics related to retention, graduation, the number of full-time faculty, other resources, and so on, are no longer sufficient but must be augmented by direct and indirect evidence of student learning and growth (Bresciani, Zelna, and Anderson, 2004).

Processes for Intentional Assessments

Each campus establishes its own goals and objectives, and the stakeholders, whether faculty members or administrators, will engage in an assessment program more readily if assessment measures focus on the values and objectives that they share. Faculty members, staff members, and administrators will be key in identifying the questions and purposes that will guide the development of the assessment instruments. When these stakeholders are engaged in the assessment system, they will be able to define what should be assessed when developing sustainable and usable measures. Without proper planning, interaction, and communication among stakeholders in the development of assessment measures, a great deal of effort will be spent on assessment without producing any useful data to inform the decisions for program improvements (Banta and Associates, 2002; Huba and Freed, 2000; Miller, 2007; Schuh and Associates, 2009; Wehlburg, 2008).

Peer review is an effective method of ensuring that data are valid and reliable. In fact, peer review is considered the method of choice in higher education for establishing the integrity of research and data; it is very useful in evaluating the trustworthiness of assessment instruments and data. Engaging stakeholders at and outside the institution in a peer review process to evaluate assessment measures is a good way to substantiate the measures and resulting data (Banta and Associates, 2002; Bresciani, Zelna, and Anderson, 2004).

The investment of time and effort to implement intentional or purposeful assessment measures at the institution will be fully returned when decisions no longer have to be based solely on intuition but rather can be supported by real, credible data that confirm the extent to which institutional claims, objectives, and goals are being met (Banta, Jones, and Black, 2009).

Factor 2—Engaging Stakeholders

Of the multiple components of a systems approach to assessment, engaging stakeholders is where the role of leadership may have the greatest influence and importance (Banta, Jones, and Black, 2009). How executive leaders direct and approach assessment and how they engage stakeholders in the process set the tone of assessment for the entire institution. Leaders who engage in active efforts to engage stakeholders are more likely to succeed in assessment endeavors (Banta, Jones, and Black, 2009; Chinyio and Akintoye, 2008; Huba and Freed, 2000).

Without stakeholders' engagement the assessment system has little chance of success (Angelo, 2007; Banta, Jones, and Black, 2009; Palomba and Banta, 1999). In an assessment system, each step is significant, as well as each person or entity. Individual behaviors and properties can influence the whole system, and so each individual who is involved in the assessment system needs to be engaged and supportive. A sustainable assessment program relies on stakeholders' collaboration in designing, delivering, and using the data from assessment (Huba and Freed, 2000).

General Engagement Strategies

Although some negative opinions and stereotypes of assessment may exist among stakeholders, the literature suggests many strategies for assessment leaders to use in engaging these individuals and groups (Angelo, 1999; Banta and Associates, 2002; Banta, Jones, and Black, 2009; Daft, 2008; Huba and Freed, 2000; Maki, 2004; Miller, 2007; Palomba and Banta, 1999; Wehlburg, 2008).

The following general strategies have been used successfully to engage stakeholders. These strategies can be effective regardless of the population from which the stakeholders originate.

- Representation: All stakeholders should be represented and feel they have a "voice" in the assessment system.
- Responsibility: All stakeholders should be given a responsibility in the assessment system.
- Conversation: The assessment system (planning, execution, and use of results) must involve a conversation involving all stakeholders.
- Unified purpose: Stakeholders should view themselves as teammates, united to improve student learning and development.
- Intrinsic motivation and rewards: Stakeholders should be motivated to participate in the assessment system for reasons beyond the requirement of doing so.
- Patience: Successfully engaging stakeholders at the level needed to effectively sustain the assessment system will take time. (Angelo, 1999; Banta and Associates, 2002; Daft, 2008; Huba and Freed, 2000; Kuh and Banta, 2000; Miller, 2007; Wehlburg, 2008)

Though many different groups must be involved in the assessment system at an institution, those who administer the measures (faculty members) and those who respond to the measures (students) are crucial to the success of the assessment program (Angelo, 2007; Banta, Jones, and Black, 2009; Maki, 2004; Miller, 2007; Palomba and Banta, 1999).

Faculty Engagement

Faculty cooperation is vital to the success of an assessment program, as faculty members are responsible for "designing and delivering the curriculum," administering the majority of assessments to students, and participating extensively in making decisions about their programs (Palomba and Banta, 1999, p. 10; see also Angelo, 2007). Because of the importance of faculty engagement in assessment, their possible resistance to and lack of engagement in assessment has garnered much attention (Banta and Associates, 2002; Palomba and Banta, 1999).

Some approaches to engaging the faculty in assessment are not effective because they are not necessarily focused on a "higher" goal or purpose for doing it. Although a decreased workload or added compensation may be enough motivation for getting some faculty members involved, these strategies may not be enough to maintain faculty engagement in assessment over a sustained period of time (Daft, 2008). Rather than relying on such forms of extrinsic motivation, creating intrinsic motivation, such as using assessment to inform teaching and learning of students, will strengthen engagement for a longer period of time and will likely produce more lasting effects for the university as well as in the classroom. As Richard Daft (2008) pointed out, "Intrinsic rewards appeal to the 'higher' needs of individuals, such as for accomplishment, competence, fulfillment, and self-determination. Extrinsic rewards appeal to the 'lower' needs of individuals, such as for material comfort and basic safety and security" (p. 228).

Too often assessment is done for the sake of external entities or extrinsic rewards. As a result, assessment becomes less significant and more difficult to maintain than if it is done for intrinsically motivated purposes such as knowing where to make changes in teaching, courses, and programs to improve student learning and success (Banta and Associates, 2002; Soundarajan, 2004; Wehlburg, 2008). In addition, encouraging faculty members to become intellectually engaged in assessment by trying to answer questions about their students' learning and their own teaching effectiveness creates the potential for the "work to become scholarly—to [become] an avenue of research that advances pedagogy and broadens and challenges what [is known] about what and how students learn" (Driscoll and Wood, 2007, p. 29; see also Angelo, 2007; Banta and Associates, 2002; Van Kollenburg, 2003). If leaders create intrinsic motivation and rewards (i.e., intellectually engaging or scholarly work and opportunities to perform assessment for the sake of student learning), assessment will become more consequential to faculty members because the focus is on something that means a great deal to them—the success of students (Banta and Associates, 2002; Daft, 2008).

The day-to-day needs of the faculty must be considered in addition to factors that help or hinder motivation. Awareness of faculty needs helps those in leadership both in designing intrinsic rewards that fit their faculty and in providing the resources for the faculty to fulfill assessment responsibilities (Daft, 2008). In one of the colleges at a large research institution, assessment coordinators conducted focus groups with faculty members to determine how they could better meet faculty needs regarding assessment. The three main questions asked during the focus groups were:

1. What questions should be answered by the analysis and report of the assessment data?
2. What essential learner and program outcomes should the core/intentional assessments (instruments) address?
3. What recommendations could be made to improve data collection, analysis, and reporting?

Information collected from these focus groups shaped assessments, future reports, and data collection methods. Faculty members were engaged again as the process of developing templates for reporting began. They helped direct and mold the templates so they could be used across multiple academic programs. Asking faculty members what their needs are or what is most useful or important to them—whether through focus groups, survey, or interview—can provide many answers useful in discerning and addressing these needs.

Even when meaningful goals and rewards for assessment are communicated and encouraged, many faculty members may not fully participate. The following suggestions are intended to help combat obstacles, such as time constraints, that may discourage faculty members from becoming involved in assessment:

• Set realistic expectations and create reasonable timelines for assessment (see factor 4, the master calendar).
• Minimize the administrative workload of assessment (providing secretarial or other staff support to alleviate certain tasks).
• Provide the technical support needed for assessment (see factor 3, a relational database that eases the collection, recording, analysis, and reporting of assessment data).
• Provide developmental classes on assessment, enabling faculty members to know where they need help so assistance can be provided and encouraging

them to become more skilled in assessment, thereby reducing the amount of time required to conduct it.

- Link assessment to the program self-study and planning processes that are already in place; since time is already set aside for these processes, a review of the annual assessment report can be included (mapped out in the master calendar).
- Create a "neutral zone"—a time when faculty members can come together and share the positive and negative aspects of their assessment results without worry about negative consequences (Banta and Associates, 2002; Banta, Jones, and Black, 2009; Maki, 2004; Pet-Armacost and Armacost, 2008).

When those in leadership at the institution communicate meaningful goals and rewards for participating in assessment and provide resources to alleviate some of the numerous responsibilities of the faculty, their support of faculty engagement in assessment becomes visible. Without this visible support of the faculty from senior leadership members, the assessment program will not survive in a meaningful fashion (Banta and Associates, 2004; Miller, 2007).

Student Involvement

Another group of stakeholders closely tied to assessment is students. Students can play various roles in the assessment system outside their most obvious roles of test taker or survey respondent. Students can participate in the planning and development of the assessment system by sitting on assessment committees. They can assist in the development of assessment measures, and they should be encouraged to offer comments and feedback on tests and other assessment measures in which they participate. Giving students a voice and letting them know their feedback is important in the assessment system will help engage them in the process beyond completing the assessment measures (Maki, 2004; Miller, 2007; Palomba and Banta, 1999).

Students need to understand the importance of assessment and the benefits assessment has for them. Instruction may include demonstrating to students the benefits of assessment through sharing expected learner outcomes. Communicating the benefits of assessment is often most effectively done through peer-to-peer communication, as "students have the ability to translate the language of the academy into terms their peers will understand" (Banta, Jones, and Black, 2009, p. 3). For example, at a large research university, students were commissioned by the senior university leadership to create an instructional video explaining what expected learner outcomes are and how learner outcomes specifically relate to and benefit students. The video they created was shown to fellow students on the campus during various campus events;

it proved to be an effective medium for peer-to-peer communication of why learner outcomes and consequently assessments are important.

Involving students in discussions about assessment rather than simply giving them feedback from assessment results will help them feel respected and valued, which is necessary for engaging them in assessment (Angelo, 1999). These discussions about assessment results can include mentoring and coaching experiences for students, increasing their motivation to be involved (Banta, Jones, and Black, 2009; Huba and Freed, 2000; Maki, 2004).

A sustainable system of assessment will begin to emerge as stakeholders are engaged and given responsibility in the assessment process. Thus, assessment is more likely to be "ongoing and not episodic" as engaged stakeholders assume active roles in the system (Huba and Freed, 2000, p. 78).

Factor 3—An Integrated Database

A necessary part of any assessment system is having the proper technology to efficiently and effectively collect, store, analyze, report, and distribute assessment data; an integrated database can provide these capabilities (Banta, Jones, and Black, 2009). In the early days of assessment, obtaining accessible, relevant data was a major obstacle to developing an assessment system that was functional and sustainable. Since this time many advances in information technology have enabled universities to better store, analyze, and report their assessment data. Most senior leaders recognize the importance of having a database, but many are not aware of all that a database may accomplish. For example, databases are made more institutionally meaningful by recent developments in access and interpretation of data, availability of data online, varied uses of relational databases, use of power report writers, access to international communities of scholars reviewing data, and in e-portfolios, which as chapter 5 in this volume states, represent the crossroads of assessment and cognitive engagement (see Clark and Eynon, 2009; Schuh and Associates, 2009; Suskie, 2009; and Zubizarreta, 2009, for a further discussion on making databases meaningful).

However, having more data available is not enough; institutions must also be able to compile it in meaningful coherent ways, many times on short notice. This process is complicated when assessment data are scattered throughout the institution in various formats at different locations. This disorganization makes accomplishing assessment tasks difficult, if not impossible (Banta and Associates, 2002; Banta, Jones, and Black, 2009; Bresciani, Zelna, and Anderson, 2004; Ratcliff, Lubinescu, and Gaffney, 2001). In sum, if assessment is to flourish at an institution, an appropriate technical infrastructure must support it (Banta and Associates, 2002).

Advantages of Using a Database

Regardless of the type of data to be collected and stored, several advantages have been found for using a data management system or centralized database. First, putting assessment data in a centralized database makes it easier to locate, navigate, and query the data and to dissect and customize data as required. These benefits of a relational database will also allow key decision makers, such as executive leadership, to customize their own questions and find answers to them in a timely manner (Schuh and Associates, 2009).

Many institutions encounter roadblocks when trying to access existing information to answer assessment questions that will support decision making. "This challenge can be the result of trying to extract information from administrative systems that are designed to manage day-to-day functions and transactions by designing a solid reporting solution that runs beside the administrative system [and that] will save time, money and frustrations" (Schuh and Associates, 2009, p. 40).

Another important advantage to housing data in a centralized database rather than using a different storage mechanism for each cluster of data is that access to accurate and up-to-date information can be quick and succinct, making informed decision making and reporting much more efficient. Because having to access assessment data in multiple locations is burdensome, whether for external or internal reporting, timely reports are more difficult to produce. Many institutions blame their current system of collecting, storing, and reporting data for difficulty in compiling such reports (Banta, Jones, and Black, 2009). Providing a straightforward way to retrieve data "increases the likelihood of the information being used in the academic decision-making process" (Banta and Associates, 2002, p. 41), which is one of the main, if not the main purpose of assessment.

Additionally, a database will increase stakeholders' access to data. Data that are left in hard copy or in multiple electronic files scattered throughout the institution are difficult to use, even when use is specifically encouraged. When data are housed in one centralized electronic location, multiple users can have simultaneous access. Providing users direct access to information through a database facilitates detailed assessment and ongoing use of assessment results not possible if information is disorganized or restricted to a few individuals (Schuh and Associates, 2009).

The college mentioned above as an example of engaging stakeholders (factor 2) developed a database and website to increase the accessibility of their assessment data and reports and make these materials easier to query. Previously this college's assessment data had been stored in multiple files in multiple locations. Accessing data had been nearly impossible for stakeholders—analyzing it even more difficult. To address this problem a database and website were developed to house the assessment data in an organized, usable format. Now stakeholders are able to access all assessment reports through the website and any raw data through the database. Because the database and website house data and reports from multiple assessment instruments regarding student learning and development, stakeholders are able to query the data by semester, program, course, instructor, assessment type, and assessment scores through simple drop-down menus contained in each category column, which then yields a spreadsheet of the requested data that can be exported for further analysis. The website also houses all of the completed assessment reports (in pdf format) for each program in the college over multiple years. Stakeholders are able to access a desired report by navigating to the report page, selecting the year, term, and program from drop-down menus, and performing a find. A list of reports that meet their criteria is then displayed. All of the information contained in the reports and database relate to the college's learner outcomes and claims; thus, access is provided to essential information on student progress, development, and learning. Users can thereby address various accountabilities in a timely manner, which contributes to establishing a culture of evidence at the institution.

Important Considerations in Selecting a Database

To obtain the advantages of a centralized database or data management system, an institution must select a program that best fits its needs. Choosing a program for collecting, managing, and reporting assessment data within the institution, whether commercial or internally created, can be a daunting process. Institutional leadership members must make the commitment to explore emerging technologies capable of advancing, streamlining, and creating greater efficiency within their assessment system (Banta and Associates, 2002).

Necessarily, the first consideration must be to balance user needs with available budget. Forming a committee of stakeholders vested in the assessment system is a good way to begin the process of selecting a database for assessment. At the beginning, the committee must understand the institution's needs. Many questions will have to be answered to find a program that is a good fit for the institution's assessment program and users. A broad array of institutional needs should be considered, including the following:

- What kinds of data are going to be collected, stored, and analyzed?
- Are portfolios or other "senior" type projects being collected that would require the storage of students' electronic files?
- What are the specific data needs of student services and records departments? Do their assessment data needs differ from those of academic departments?

- What resources need to be allocated to purchase and support a new program? (Banta and Associates, 2002; Pet-Armacost and Armacost, 2008; Schuh and Associates, 2009)

The technology that is selected should be sustainable, within the constraints of the budget, for its users and support staff. Users' capabilities and the support staff required for the program are just as important to consider as the cost. It is usually more efficient and cost effective to find software to meet users' needs and capabilities than it is to train and retrain users (Angelo, 2007; Banta and Associates, 2002; Pet-Armacost and Armacost, 2008).

A second important consideration is alignment: The database or data management system must be compatible with the type of data to be stored, and it must be aligned with and integrated into the assessment system. It should also match current systems at the institution (i.e., databases already in place; Banta and Associates, 2002; Pet-Armacost and Armacost, 2008; Schuh and Associates, 2009).

An important aspect of alignment with the wider institution concerns user access and security. To ensure that the technology selected has the capacity to fit the needs of the institution for data security, the planning will require consideration of who will need access to this data and whether access will need to be restricted depending on specific roles of personnel members. Most likely the institution already has policies regarding sensitive information, but these policies may need to be revisited or replaced as applied to access and use of assessment data (Borden and Zak-Owens, 2001; Ratcliff, Lubinescu, and Gaffney, 2001; Schuh and Associates, 2009).

Planning processes must also include the requirements for reporting. Reporting the data is necessary for any assessment system. Many programs have the ability to run reports of data stored in the system; therefore, it is important to ask questions about reporting, including whether analysis or reporting tools will need to be built into the program. Planners should consider how the data are going to be used and at what level and, accordingly, whether the program matches the institution's assessment process and whether it will be able to provide the data in the format necessary to answer assessment questions (Borden and Zak-Owens, 2001; Pet-Armacost and Armacost, 2008; Schuh and Associates, 2009).

Despite the variety of questions that may need to be asked, the following categories will be helpful in formulating considerations specific to the institution's needs:

- Determine the budget—the cost of acquiring a new program and the cost of supporting it.

- Address users' needs.
- Provide support and training to users.
- Understand what type of data will be stored and how data will be retrieved.
- Define current technology that is already in place.
- Provide for keeping sensitive information protected.
- Determine users' rights to data.
- Determine analysis and reporting needs. (Banta and Associates, 2002; Borden and Zak-Owens, 2001; Pet-Armacost and Armacost, 2008; Ratcliff, Lubinescu, and Gaffney, 2001; Schuh and Associates, 2009)

Factor 4—Master Calendar

The fourth component of a systems approach to assessment is a master calendar. It is important to establish a calendar because assessment is not a one-shot attempt at program improvement but rather an information cycle that involves administering the assessment measures, collecting data, recording data, reporting data, and responding to the data. Each stage of the cycle is integral to the next. A calendar maps out a timeline for each major step and provides the direction to ensure that assessment occurs regularly and continuously (Bresciani, Zelna, and Anderson, 2004; Hernon, Dugan, and Schwartz, 2006; Palomba and Banta, 1999).

A master calendar should be worked out before implementation of the assessment measures. Agreement must be reached and maintained on when assessments will be conducted and when resulting data will be collected, analyzed, and reported (Banta and Associates, 2004; Banta, Jones, and Black, 2009; Suskie, 2004): (1) whether it will be annually, biannually, by semester, or monthly and (2) whether every assessment tool in the system will be administered at the same time or whether the tool administrations will vary. Multiple tools may be used in the assessment program, and a timetable will help demonstrate whether the projected use of resources and stakeholders' time is feasible as multiple measures are administered (Banta and Associates, 2004; Maki, 2004).

Benefits of Using a Master Calendar

A great deal of planning goes into creating an assessment system, some of which "requires written guidance on who does what when" (Banta and Associates, 2004, p. 57). The master calendar functions as the map of the assessment system, detailing to stakeholders expectations of the timing by which each stage should be completed. Communicating these expectations clearly may help create collaboration and promote a sense of urgency among faculty and staff "by providing a clear understanding of when tasks need to be started, what must be accomplished, and when tasks should be completed" (Banta and Associates, 2004, p. 43; see also White, 2005).

The master calendar is the heart of an assessment system for the program. Each column of a master calendar may contain dates of when specific phases should be complete, and each is contingent upon the previous column's completion. The calendar collects all stakeholders around the same agenda: setting realistic expectations for and use of assessment data, reporting what is of value to all stakeholders, and enabling them to structure decisions around what is measured.

Function of a Master Calendar in the Assessment System

Specific steps may be taken to secure the use of the master calendar in the assessment program. First, the master calendar facilitates coordination with assessment scheduling of the institution; thus, data should be collected, analyzed, and reported in conjunction with the timetables of institutional planning and decision making (Banta, Jones, and Black, 2009; Wehlburg, 2008). As stated in the introduction, executive leaders are responsible for ensuring that assessment results are "embedded" in the institution's planning and decision-making timetables. However, achieving this goal has been difficult for most colleges and universities because the institution's schedule for planning resources and making decisions often does not coincide with assessment reporting. Consequently, a master calendar that includes timetables for each stage of assessment and ensures that the assessment system corresponds with important institutional dates is vital (Bresciani, Zelna, and Anderson, 2004; Maki, 2004).

Second, the calendar must be somewhat flexible. Because the assessment cycle requires time, timelines need to be realistic and open to necessary adjustment as the cycle progresses. Since the purpose of assessment is to increase the quality of programs, teaching, and learning, the calendar must have the flexibility to accommodate program improvements and adjustments. As the calendar is part of the ongoing process of improvement, it may require replanning and adjustment as changes are made to improve the quality of education that is being offered (Banta, Jones, and Black, 2009; Hernon, Dugan, and Schwartz, 2006; Wehlburg, 2008).

External realities such as accreditation visits, state reporting requirements, or annual accreditation reports are important, and a master calendar should be designed to help in planning for and meeting external deadlines (Palomba and Banta, 1999; White, 2005). If assessment is to be embedded into campus processes, it must coincide with external as well as internal dates and timelines adhered to by the institution.

Assessment should also fit within the everyday functions at the institution. Only when assessment dates fit within regular functions and responsibilities will stakeholders use the results of assessment in the day-to-day decisions they have to make as well as annual reporting requirements. Timing is a crucial piece of any assessment program, and a calendar will help assessment continue past the first attempt into a recurring cycle at the institution (Banta, Jones, and Black, 2009; Bresciani, Zelna, and Anderson, 2004).

Factor 5—Timely Reports; Factor 6—Culture of Evidence

These last two factors of the assessment system are complementary, especially when there is careful and consistent monitoring of the last column of the master calendar, closing the loop with program response (see factor 4 above). Closing the assessment loop is at the heart of the campus assessment plan. Assessment must be perceived as of tangible value, and changes in programs based on the data must have the respect of all stakeholders. Leading assessments on the campus by implementing all the factors above leads directly to decisions informed by measurement data. Assessments are worthwhile only if the results are put to good use, and those uses can take place only after careful consideration and discussion (Suskie, 2009); thus, assessment results must be communicated usefully, clearly, and accurately. Telling the data story and driving decisions from what is measured should be planned as carefully as any other factor of the assessment plan and process. We must determine whether what is measured is of value and thus whether changes based on the measurement data will be of value. If the factors described above are effectively and consistently implemented, then we can recognize that assessments can potentially drive change and improve student learning and development.

But is it that simple? Unfortunately, as Evon Walters, John Gardner, and Randy Swing (2009) point out, "Extensive use of data to inform decisions remains more an aspiration than a reality for most colleges and universities" (p. 14). The research literature asserts that data alone do not drive change (Banta, Jones, and Black, 2009; Bresciani, Gardner, and Hickmott, 2009; Bresciani, Zelna, and Anderson, 2004; Ewell, 2007; Maki, 2004; Suskie, 2004, 2009; Wehlburg, 2008). Yet, accrediting bodies have increased pressure on colleges to use data for decision making, a process often referred to as a "culture of evidence." So, how do campus leaders address these seemingly conflicting assessment issues? While the next section emphasizes the building of a culture of evidence and illustrates this through an institutional model, the section is cautiously introduced by a discussion on return on investments. From our perspective, the best way to address the dilemma as well as create an efficacious culture of evidence is to invest in people first. Data alone do not drive change. People do. Modest investments in people can contribute the following:

- capture and track student learning outcomes;
- turn data into information for decision makers;
- ensure that goals and objectives are measureable and linked to data collections;
- develop a group of peer institutions for benchmarking and comparisons;
- disaggregate reports to reveal differences among subgroups; and
- assist campus leaders to cite data when announcing changes and new initiatives.

In sum, data-driven decision making is not a function of data alone; rather, data should be used to inform decision making. Using data to inform recognizes need and people, gathers data to draw conclusions, prioritizes challenges by developing implementation strategies, and always involves people in feedback and discussion about the data. Data are resources; people are the agents of decision and change. As stated earlier, data ought to be part of the processes of understanding the underlying paradigms governing institutions and of measuring external threats and opportunities.

Since "assessment is grounded in the belief that effective institutions and departments engage in a *systematic* and continuous process of improvement [and change]" to achieve institutional claims (Weiss et al., 2002, p. 63), we have organized this section around important aspects of *leading assessments* on the campus, particularly as applied to building an *intentional* culture of evidence. In particular, we have focused on not only what needs to be in place but also what matters most in creating a systems approach to assessments. The principles of assessment practices and processes described (i.e., a systems approach) are applicable to any campus environment, and they are intertwined with the next section on building a culture of evidence.

CREATING A CULTURE OF EVIDENCE

The research literature emphasizes the need for improvement in leading assessments via a systems approach to measure what matters most and to improve student learning and development programs from what is measured, culminating in a culture of evidence that aligns with the aims and claims of the institution (Angelo, 2007; Banta and Associates, 2002; Banta, Jones, and Black, 2009; Bresciani, Gardner, and Hickmott, 2009; Bresciani, Zelna, and Anderson, 2004; Ewell, 2005, 2007; Maki, 2004; Schuh and Associates, 2009; Suskie, 2007, 2009; Walvoord, 2004; Wehlburg, 2008). Specifically, this section presents constructs to help senior leaders tell their institution's data story. Thus, an intentional culture of evidence becomes meaningful for the institution *only* as a body of knowledge to inform stakeholders, including students, and to *support and qualitatively align* the institution's aims and claims and its processes of assessment.

This section integrates the factors of an assessment plan discussed above, as well as the principles discussed in other chapters, into a working institutional model exemplifying the various strategic notions and plans essential in creating a culture of evidence. In preparation for establishing a campus-wide assessment plan, and thus a culture of evidence, the following questions provide a guide and address issues associated with assessment. Each requires continuous consideration to ensure not only an effective campus culture of evidence but also an institutional planning model that is aligned with institutional, program, and unit claims or mission.

These questions are also addressed in the figures and discussion provided below.

1. Does your institution have a strategic plan for assessment?
2. Does your campus have a shared vision of assessment from the president on down?
3. Are students, their experiences, and their learning central to your assessment plan?
4. How intentional are data collection, analysis, and reporting within your assessment plan, and are they connected to your resource planning and allocation process?
5. Are your assessment activities ongoing, not episodic?
6. How is assessment making a difference on your campus?
7. What is the return on investment for assessment on your campus?
8. What percentage of your institutional fixed costs are allocated directly for assessment?
9. Are campus leaders contributing to the problem or the solution? How? Why?
10. Are indirect and direct assessments connected and providing paths to student graduation and success?

Facilitating cultural change within institutions of higher education is challenging, as indicated by the questions above. A potential model for moving an institution toward a culture of evidence relies on enhanced connectivity between experiences, beliefs, actions, and results (see figure 2.3).

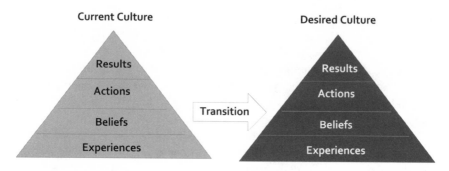

To change current culture to approach an "Ideal Culture of Evidence"

1. Decide what RESULTS you wish to produce.
2. Provide EXPERIENCES that reinforce BELIEFS you wish to create.
3. BELIEFS will reinforce the ACTIONS of the people in your organization.
4. ACTIONS will produce the desired RESULTS of the new culture.

Figure 2.3. Model for Culture Change: Moving toward a "Culture of Evidence"

Source: Adapted from *Journey to the Emerald City* by R. Connors and T. Smith. Copyright © 1999 by Prentice Hall Press.

Overall Perspective

The experiences that individuals have personally or vicariously within their campus environment ultimately shape their beliefs about various issues or movements and subsequently impact their actions and the potential results of any initiative. Therefore, an effective means to transition a campus to an enhanced culture of evidence is to provide new opportunities allowing campus constituents to have meaningful experiences with data, assessment, and the like and thus to genuinely feel they can make a positive difference.

Realizing that experiences shape beliefs that drive actions and subsequent results, leaders in higher education should purposefully instigate varying initiatives that provide such experiences and a resulting culture of evidence. Figures 2.4–2.7 are used in this section to outline and to illustrate the context and steps that a proactive institution takes to build a model for such assessment.

Clearly it is important to consider that moving to a culture of evidence requires sufficient commitment from senior campus leadership and also adequate resources, especially human capital, to facilitate targeted experiences to engage campus stakeholders and constituents. In addition, the reader should consider the following elements to successfully sustain a campus-wide culture of evidence.

• *Commitment and investment.* Effective assessment can support fiscal management at a university, resulting in an increased return on precious

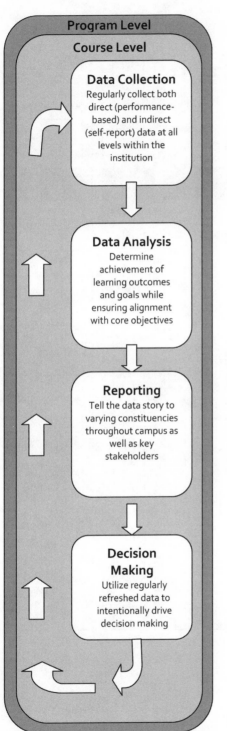

Figure 2.4. Establishing a Culture of
Evidence: A Systems Approach

Figure 2.5. Hypothetical Institutional Strategic Plan: History of Activity

Type	Activity	Cycle	Most Recent 10 Academic Years									Current Year	Next 5 Academic Years				
			-9 Years	-8 Years	-7 Years	-6 Years	-5 Years	-4 Years	-3 Years	-2 Years	-1 Year		+1 Year	+2 Years	+3 Years	+4 Years	+5 Years
Intentional	**Internal Surveys, Questionnaires (Institution Developed Suite of Instruments Mapped to Mission, Aims, Objectives)**																
	Alumni Questionnaire (3yr prior cohort)	Annual	◄	◄	◄	◄	◄	◄	◄	◄	◄	◄	◄	◄	◄	◄	◄
	Senior Survey (Undergraduate)	Annual			◄	◄	◄	◄	◄	◄	◄	◄	◄	◄	◄	◄	◄
	Non-continuing Student	2 yr					◄	◄	◄								
	Advising (Academic/Career)	3 yr						◄	◄								
	Employer	3 yr						◄									
	First-year (Pre-arrival)	Annual								Dev	◄	◄	◄	◄	◄	◄	◄
	First-year (End of Year)	Annual								Dev	◄	◄	◄	◄	◄	◄	◄
	Long Term Alumni Survey	3 year														Dev	◄
	Parent	3 yr										Dev	◄	Dev			◄
	Graduate Student Exit Survey	Annual										Dev	◄	◄	◄	◄	◄
	Others as available, appropriate ...	TBD															
	National Surveys of Student Engagement																
	NSSE (First-year, Seniors)	Annual	◄	◄	◄	◄	◄	◄	◄	◄	◄	◄	◄	◄	◄	◄	◄
	FSSE (Faculty)	3 year			◄	◄	◄	◄	◄	◄	◄	◄	◄	◄	◄	◄	◄
	LSSSE (Law Students)	3 yr			◄	◄	◄	◄	◄	◄	◄	◄	◄	◄	◄	◄	◄
	BCSSE (Entering Students)	Annual										◄	◄	◄	◄	◄	◄
	Higher Education Research Institute (HERI)																
	Faculty Survey	3 yr	◄	◄	◄	◄	◄	◄	◄	◄	◄	◄	◄	◄	◄	◄	◄
	Others as available, appropriate ...	TBD															
	Internal Formal Unit Review																
	Academic Units	7 yr	2	8	8	9	8	8	9	9	9	9	◄	◄	◄	◄	◄
	Educational Support Units	7 yr			3	8	7	7	7	9	9	8	◄	◄	◄	◄	◄
	External Data Reporting																
	IPEDS, Common Data Set, etc.	Annual	◄	◄	◄	◄	◄	◄	◄	◄	◄	◄	◄	◄	◄	◄	◄
	Regional Accreditation Annual Reports	Annual	◄	◄	◄	◄	◄	◄	◄	◄	◄	◄	◄	◄	◄	◄	◄
	Others as available, appropriate ...	TBD															
Reactive	**Ad Hoc Studies (Number Completed in Past Years))**																
	Academic Department	On Demand	2		8	3	3	4	4	2	4	TBD	◄	◄	◄	◄	◄
	Educational Support Unit	On Demand	9	19	26	13	14	10	9	13	9	TBD	◄	◄	◄	◄	◄
	Institutional	On Demand	1		3	3	3	4	8	9	8	TBD	◄	◄	◄	◄	◄
	Total		12	19	37	19	20	18	21	24	21	TBD	◄	◄	◄	◄	◄
	Data Requests																
	From External and Internal Entities	On Demand	◄	◄	◄	◄	◄	◄	◄	◄	◄	◄	◄	◄	◄	◄	◄

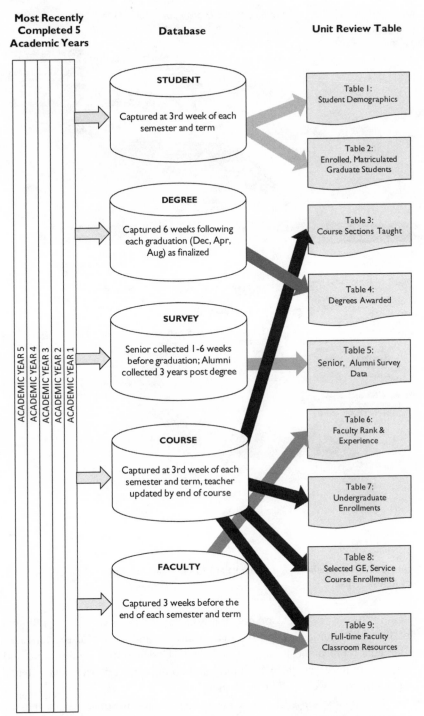

Figure 2.6. Hypothetical Unit Review Data Flow: Degree-Level Assessment

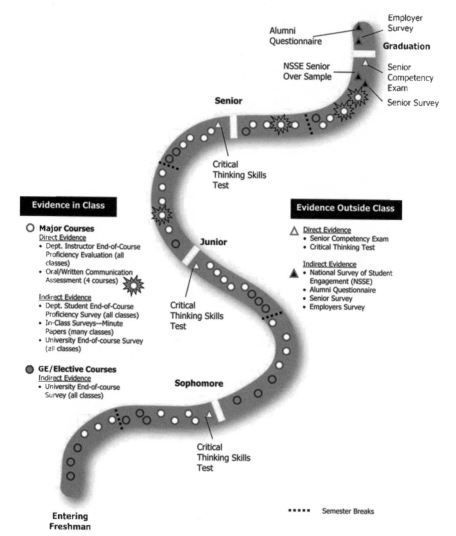

Figure 2.7. **Hypothetical Department Path to Graduation: Timing of Direct and Indirect Assessments**

campus resources. Costs are not simply fiscal but also involve expenditures of financial, human, organizational, political, and symbolic capital (e.g., elements represented in *dollars* and *time*). Considerable commitment and energy are necessary for developing and completing a process that attends to symbolic as well as human elements.

- *Shared responsibility.* Everyone on campus should in some way or another share accountability in an institution's assessment strategy focused toward improvement. Academic units as well as educational support units (e.g., bookstore, library, housing, employment, student life, etc.) contribute to students' university experiences, their subsequent learning, and their perceived return on their educational investment.

- *Strategic plan development.* Strategic plans for assessment are as individual as the institutions that develop them. However, each is a "plan"; they should not be random but rather intentional by design. Potential components of an institutional strategic plan of assessment are presented in figures 2.5, 2.6, and 2.7. An assessment plan must be appropriate for the unit for which it is developed: whether class, degree program, academic unit, educational support unit, college, university, or even system of higher education.
- *Consistent data repository.* Allowing academic units to add questions of their own—mapped to their curriculum, learning outcomes, and so forth—to institutional surveys targeted to seniors and alumni both produces valuable data and helps establish support among these groups.
- *Benchmarking process.* Benchmark comparisons that result from institutional participation in national (external) surveys are an important part of any strategic assessment plan, as they provide context for the data. Thus, leaders of each institution should examine comparatively the content of available surveys and determine which would yield data best suited to their mission, goals, and objectives. It is important to have some outside surveys in the assessment plan to furnish external context.
- *Internal formal unit review.* An institutional strategic plan for assessment should include some form of ongoing internal review of campus units. Perhaps this could be considered a form of "accreditation" and "continuous improvement"—a unit at a time (Banta, Jones, and Black, 2009). Unit reviews benefit from the perspective of an empirical examination over time (possibly the most recent five years), including key indicators that help inform practice.
- *Consistent focus on student learning.* Few would argue that the central purpose of higher education is to foster and facilitate student learning and development, so the focus should be on the students. Accordingly, any institutional assessment strategy must include components capable of adequately demonstrating student learning across the entire curriculum, not just in areas where it seems to fit naturally.
- *Student engagement.* Engaging students in the assessment process can be beneficial. Students can generally get excited about presenting a strong portfolio to potential employers or graduate schools. The interview discussion can go to a dramatically higher level as the graduate advances beyond talking about a list of completed courses to explaining acquired skills as

demonstrated by a portfolio. Units might participate in the National Survey of Student Engagement and implement an oversample of seniors in a given department. The resulting data would provide an opportunity for a department's leaders to learn how their soon-to-graduate seniors compare to national counterparts.

- *Direct plus indirect measures.* Students travel an educational path with many curves and bends as they meander through the educational experience from entering as freshmen to graduating as seniors. Academic departments that systematically utilize direct and indirect assessment tools with students on this path are well equipped to adequately demonstrate student learning. Direct evidence might include faculty-developed proficiency evaluations, writing assessments, departmental competency exams, or even external performance-based standard exams in varying areas such as critical thinking. Indirect (self-report) evidence can be derived from institutional instruments such as surveys of exiting seniors, alumni, employers of graduates, and so on. The direct tools measure *what* is being learned by focusing on kernel concepts of the discipline, proficiency in each of the technical courses, communication skills that cross course boundaries, and critical thinking. The indirect tools provide supporting data on learning specifics but also focus on *how* and *why* learning is taking place. The effectiveness of learning activities, the degree of student engagement, and the impact of various aspects of the learning environment are effectively investigated with these tools.
- *Value added.* As Trudy Banta and Gary Pike (2007) have asserted, standard exams that measure general intelligence are poor measures of value added. Of greater value are exams that measure specific generic skills such as critical thinking. Many accrediting organizations do not emphasize value-added analysis, largely because of its difficulty and because of the possibility that such efforts will divert attention from the more important issue of whether or not learning objectives have been met. Perhaps value added is best examined within individual courses as instructors seek to determine the effectiveness of specific activities through minute papers or other surveys.
- *Continuous progress.* Just as educational processes can continually improve, so can corresponding assessment processes. Effort should be made to improve the use of all of the information provided by assessment tools, along with the efficiency of data acquisition, analysis, and feedback into the learning process. At the same time, academic units should be continually evaluating additional assessment tools for possible adoption into their program. Assessment and continuous improvement will always be works in progress. Obviously each department needs to develop a strategy that fits its characteristics, objectives, and needs.

- *Connections to be considered.* In the spirit of ongoing improvement, every aspect of an institution of higher education has an assessment connection and responsibility. Campus constituents need to genuinely feel that assessment does make a difference and that their individual contributions—individual or aggregated—result in a positive return on their investment.
- *Interconnected levels of student learning focus.* The real reason for institutions of higher learning is for the *students* and their *learning.* All campus functionality should revolve around students—improving their experiences pursuant to their learning.
- *Optimal destination.* The real challenge for the leaders of institutions of higher education is to organize their campuses around an appropriate strategic plan for assessment aligned to their own mission and objectives and to inculcate assessment into the status quo of campus activities from the classroom to the president and everywhere in between.

Establishing an assessment plan that leads to a culture of evidence is thus the best way to arrive at empirically calibrated decision making, which involves measuring what is of value and driving decisions from what is measured. Doing so will enhance productivity by circumventing the pitfalls of unclear expectations, insufficient data, inaccurate data, and arbitrary decisions.

CONCLUSION

As this chapter instructs, to produce a culture of evidence based on what matters most in assessments and to drive decisions from what is measured require leadership, vision, and continuity of the factors or conditions of an institutional assessment system. Catherine Wehlburg (2008) has succinctly pointed out that assessment should not be seen as a process through which external entities act on higher education but rather as a means by which data from intentional assessments (measuring what is of value) are systematically collected to facilitate institutional reflection, renewal, and growth in response to a combination of internal commitments (aligning claims with data) for improvement. When assessments are used to build a culture of evidence to drive change and improve student learning and development, these processes can not only resolve internal commitments but also address societal demands for social and economic salience (p. 84).

The question is not *whether* but rather the *extent to which* assessment is integrated into the institutional fabric of planning and policy. Naturally, as Vasti Torres points out in chapter 3, the assessment process should recognize, include, celebrate, and respond to the full diversity of learners in the institution, both in and out of the classroom.

The challenge is to lead strong, consistent, and significant improvements in student learning and development by building and using a culture of evidence. Unfortunately, the research literature suggests that institutions are hard pressed to do this, at least consistently. Researchers further add that assessments in higher education primarily and consistently reflect external demands for accountability, not significant improvements in academic or experiential learning programs (Angelo, 1999, 2007; Bresciani, Gardner, and Hickmott, 2009; Bresciani, Zelna, and Anderson, 2004; Ewell, 2005, 2007; Maki, 2004; Suskie, 2007, 2009; Wehlburg, 2008). But the promise of this chapter is that leadership matters, especially in guiding a strategic-based assessment framework that not only influences the achievement of institutional claims and continuous assessment of key performance areas but also establishes a culture of evidence from which the institutional narrative or story can be told.

REFERENCES

Angelo, T. A. (1999, May). Doing assessment as if learning matters most. *AAHE Bulletin, 51*(9), 3–6.

Angelo, T. A. (2007, November 6). Can we fatten a hog *just* by weighing it? Using program review to improve course design, teaching effectiveness, and learning outcomes. Materials for a concurrent workshop in the 2007 Assessment Institute, Indianapolis.

Banta, T. W., & Associates. (2002). *Building a scholarship of assessment.* San Francisco: Jossey-Bass.

Banta, T. W., & Associates (Eds.). (2004). *Hallmarks of effective outcomes assessment: Assessment update collections.* San Francisco: Jossey-Bass.

Banta, T. W., Jones, E. A., & Black, K. E. (2009). *Designing effective assessment: Principles and profiles of good practice.* San Francisco: Jossey-Bass.

Banta, T. W., & Pike, G. R. (2007, January/February). Revisiting the blind alley of value added. *Assessment Update, 19*(1–2), 14–15.

Borden, V. M., & Zak-Owens, J. (2001). Measuring quality: Choosing among surveys and other assessments of college quality. A joint publication of the Association for Institutional Research, Tallahassee, Fla., and the American Council on Education, Washington D.C.

Bresciani, M. J., Gardner, M. M., & Hickmott, J. (2009). *Demonstrating student success: A practical guide to outcomes-based assessment of learning and development in student affairs.* Herndon, Va.: Stylus.

Bresciani, M. J., Zelna, C. L., & Anderson, J. A. (2004). *Assessing student learning and development: A handbook for practitioners.* Waldorf, Md.: National Association of Student Personnel Administrators.

Chinyio, E. A., & Akintoye, A. (2008). Practical approaches for engaging stakeholders: Findings from the UK. *Construction Management and Economics, 26,* 591–599.

Clark, E. J., & Eynon, B. (2009). E-portfolios at 2.0: Surveying the field. *Peer Review, 11*(1), 18–23.

Connors, R., & Smith, T. (1999). *Journey to the emerald city*. Paramus, N.J.: Prentice Hall.

Daft, R. L. (2008). *The leadership experience* (4th ed.). Mason, Ohio: Thomson.

Driscoll, A., & Wood, S. (2007). *Developing outcomes-based assessment for learner-centered education: A faculty introduction*. Herndon, Va.: Stylus.

Ewell, P. T. (2005). Power in numbers: The values in our metrics. *Change, 37*, 10–16.

Ewell, P. T. (2007, November). Assessing assessment: Successes, failures, and the future. Presentation given at the Assessment Institute of Indiana University–Purdue University Indianapolis.

Hernon, P., Dugan, R. E., & Schwartz, C. (Eds.). (2006). *Revisiting outcomes assessment in higher education*. Westport, Conn.: Libraries Unlimited.

Huba, M. E., & Freed, J. E. (2000). *Learner-centered assessment on college campuses: Shifting the focus from teaching to learning*. Needham Heights, Mass.: Allyn & Bacon.

Kuh, G. D., & Banta, T. W. (2000). Faculty-student affairs collaboration on assessment: Lessons from the field. *About Campus, 4*(6), 4–11.

Maki, P. (2004). *Assessing for learning: Building a sustainable commitment across the institution*. Herndon, Va.: Stylus.

Miller, B. A. (2007). *Assessing organizational performance in higher education*. San Francisco: Jossey-Bass.

Palomba, C. A., & Banta, T. W. (1999). *Assessment essentials: Planning, implementing, and improving assessment in higher education*. San Francisco: Jossey-Bass.

Pet-Armacost, J., & Armacost, R. L. (2008, May 25). Adapting a systems approach to meet new program assessment challenges. Preconference workshop W-36: 48th Air Forum, Seattle.

Ratcliff, J. L., Lubinescu, E. S., & Gaffney, M. A. (Eds.). (2001). *How accreditation influences assessment: New directions for higher education*. San Francisco: Jossey-Bass.

Schuh, J. H., & Associates (Eds.). (2009). *Assessment methods for student affairs*. San Francisco: Jossey-Bass.

Soundarajan, N. (2004). Program assessment and program improvement: Closing the loop. *Assessment and Evaluation in Higher Education, 29*, 5.

Suskie, L. (2004). *Assessing student learning: A common sense guide*. Bolton, Mass.: Anker.

Suskie, L. (2007, January 4). Understanding and using assessment results. Semiannual meeting of the BYU-Public School Partnership Leaders Associates, Provo, Utah.

Suskie, L. (2009). *Assessing student learning: A common sense guide* (2nd ed.). San Francisco: Jossey-Bass.

Van Kollenburg, S. E. (Ed.). (2003, April). A collection of papers on self-study and institutional improvement. Volume 3: Promoting student learning and effective teaching. Publication prepared for the annual meeting of the North Central Association of Colleges and Schools, Chicago. Retrieved from ERIC database (ED476673).

Walters, E., Gardner, J., & Swing, R. (2009, summer). Making student success a priority. *Trustee Quarterly*, 14–15.

Walvoord, B. E. F. (2004). *Assessment clear and simple: A practical guide for institutions, departments, and general education*. San Francisco: Jossey-Bass.

Wehlburg, C. M. (2008). *Promoting integrated and transformative assessment: A deeper focus on student learning*. San Francisco: Jossey-Bass.

Weiss, G. L., Cosbey, J. R., Habel, S. K., Hanson, C. M., & Larsen, C. (2002). Improving the assessment of student learning: Advancing a research agenda in sociology. *Teaching Sociology*, 30, 63–79.

White, S. H. (2005). *Show me the proof! Tools and strategies to make data work for you*. Englewood, Colo.: Advanced Learning Press.

Zubizarreta, J. (2009). The learning portfolio: Reflective practice for improving student learning. Bolton, Mass.: Anker.

Part Two

BRIDGING LEARNER OUTCOMES: FINDING COMMON GROUND

Chapter Three

Assessment and Student Diversity

Vasti Torres

As the number of students attending college increases, so does their diversity. As a result, colleges and universities are challenged to manage environments that include students of diverse races and ethnicities, genders, social classes, and levels of academic preparation. The reality is that, when a diversity issue rises to the level of senior administrators, it typically appears in the form of a letter or memorandum from concerned faculty members, students, or staff members asking for some type of action to address previous incidents or past inaction. A typical communication may look like this:

MEMORANDUM

Date: Any day, month, or year
To: College President and Leadership
From: Concerned Faculty Members, Students, and Staff Members of Color
Re: The College Plans for Diversification

Within the last two years our college community has felt the effects of several student incidents showing insensitivity to nonmajority cultures, as well as the departure of several faculty members of color who were visibly supportive of students of color. These incidents and this faculty attrition are influencing the campus climate and the morale of nonmajority students, faculty members, and staff members. Our group is greatly concerned that the college leadership is doing little to address these significant negative trends influencing our academic community.

The college's strategic plan, as well as its trustees, expresses a desire to diversify the college community, yet those affected by the negative events of the past two years have observed little such action. As faculty members, students, and staff members of this college community, we believe the college leadership should immediately take certain actions toward meeting the college's diversification goals:

1. Ascertain the rate at which faculty members of color and senior women leave the college and their reasons for leaving. Make special note of whether they find the climate around tenure and promotion to be supportive or negative. Learn about pay equity, both to understand the reasons for faculty departure and to use in recruiting more faculty members from underrepresented groups, thus adding to the diversity of the college faculty. Rather than providing excuses like "personal reasons" for every faculty departure, obtain concrete data to understand specifics behind departure decisions and to guide actions toward dissatisfied faculty.

2. Examine measures of student success that are disaggregated by race and ethnicity, gender, and socioeconomic status—including retention rates, course completion by department, and graduation rates. Not every student is doing well at this college; more focused programs are needed for students who require help. In its recruitment to increase student "quality," the college is forgetting to help the students already enrolled.

3. Increase the amount allotted to grants given students with low income and students of color. Tuition increases have not been accompanied with equivalent financial aid consideration, which hurts the college's ability to attract diverse students. Using university funds to help academically gifted students does not necessarily help diversify the college community.

4. The college's president and provost, specifically and individually, need to publicly address issues of diversification directly with the college community. The college's senior-level administrators have done little to express their interest in or concern about issues important to the college's diverse groups.

These actions should be taken immediately if our college community is to heal from the past two years of negative events and insensitive environment and to address the disparity between the goals the college publishes and the priorities its actions and policies reflect. Our group of concerned faculty members, students, and staff members await your response and look forward to meeting with you soon.

Complaints like this are unfortunately more common than most administrators care to admit. Such memoranda are delivered to someone in university and college leadership every week of the academic year at half of the campuses, at least, in the United States. The underlying request in these communications is for data to prove the point of the concerned group—or, alternatively, to demonstrate that things are not as problematic as they appear to the concerned group. Either way, to dispel negative perceptions or to avoid being called out on issues of equity, colleges and universities are finding they must assess the successes and challenges of diversity in multiple ways.

This chapter focuses on the historical issues institutions face regarding diversity, as well as the struggle to define diversity within any given campus community. Influences of diversity on student learning and the challenges institutions have embracing diverse students should involve decisions driven by institutional data in the interests of concerned students, faculty members, or staff members. Following a brief overview of the history regarding the concept of diversity, this chapter considers the issues involved with assessment and student diversity by explaining the theoretical foundation of the concept of diversity as a positive influence in higher education. A discussion follows concerning the contextual dimensions of defining diversity, the types of diversity assessment institutions should consider, and the issues institutions should consider when embracing diversity with a desire to create change. Finally, the chapter describes some educational practices that can make a difference in student diversity at institutions of higher education.

APPROACHES FOR DEFINING DIVERSITY

Diversity, within any campus contexts, can be defined from many different perspectives. For many institutions, historical and legal elements influence how they approach the issues regarding diversity. Because all institutions consider historical elements, this section will begin with an examination of historical and societal contexts.

Historical Influences

Diversity in the U.S. college student population became prominent with the G.I. Bill and the formalization of financial aid policies that brought an influx of students different from the previous generations of white, mostly male, economically advantaged, academically prepared students. Whether the concern is the first-generation-in-college student who needs assistance in navigating the education system or the multilingual, multiracial student who may struggle with ethnic identity, diversity in higher education is now the norm. A population of diverse students has become commonplace at institutions; however, institutional agents seldom articulate in public forums the associated issues and challenges that come with such a diverse student body.

The widespread assumption is that the operational definition of diversity is broadly focused and includes race and ethnicity, age, gender, and other social identities—such as working class, sexual orientation, or first generation in college. The truth is that most administrators and data collection methods have barely moved beyond the views that emerged during the 1960s as a result of the Civil Rights Act. For many institutions, diversity continues to be focused on counting the number of students by race, maybe including some ethnicity as part of the count. This approach to measuring diversity does not address the different experiences students are having while in college. Although we would like to believe that higher education is accepting of all differences, vast disparities in the higher education experience still exist between whites and underrepresented groups, between those from different socioeconomic levels, and between those with different levels of academic preparation. The ideals of "equal educational opportunity for all students" are still a dream (Ladson-Billings, 2006)—not a reality—as should be evident to most higher education administrators when considering the characteristics of the students entering their institutions each semester.

Foundation Set by the Legal System for Diversity as a Compelling Educational Interest

To consider why diversity has emerged as an important value and topic in higher education requires examination of diversity in both its historical and its current context. Court decisions on affirmative action over the years in many ways chronicle society's views on whether or why diversity should be a compelling interest for educational institutions. The first major legal consideration of diversity as an essential aspect of the educational process was involved with the U.S. Supreme Court decision in the late 1970s in *Bakke* (*Regents of the University of California v. Bakke*, 1977) and more recently in *Grutter* (*Grutter v. Bollinger*, 2003). These decisions expressed the view that a diverse student body is essential for students' appreciation of and exposure to a wide range of people, ideas, and mores (Gurin et al., 2002). This view of the educational value of such exposure, then articulated by the high court and discussed extensively in public forums, is the foundation for the idea of diversity as "a compelling governmental interest" that has provided the justification for affirmative action at selective higher education institutions (Gurin et al., 2002, p. 26).

Although this type of legal justification has been necessary in everyday administrative decisions at only highly selective colleges and universities, this value has set the tone for all institutions: in academic communities, diversity of faculty members and students is important. As a result of these legal cases concerning the influence of race in admissions decisions, a significant body of research has emerged that studies the benefits of racially and ethnically diverse educational experiences (Gurin et al., 2002; Orfield, 2001). Much of this research focuses on curricular and cocurricular efforts to promote positive attitudes toward diversity and reduce racial bias (Denson, 2009). This body of research affirms that the diversification of experiences, ideas, and expression within academic communities is of value. Much less clear is how institutions can promote and assess this value. Before the value of diversity can be assessed, it must first be defined in its context.

Definition in Specific Context

Diversity on the college campus is subjective and highly contextual; thus, the institution's task in developing its own definition of diversity is highly complex. In a nondiverse U.S. state (e.g., Maine), an institution with a 5 percent minority student population could be seen as very diverse, while this same percentage of minority students at an institution in a very diverse state (e.g., California) would be considered very nondiverse. This complexity affects the task of researchers as well. To accommodate the low number of nonwhite students, faculty members, or staff members, many studies combine diverse groups under dichotomous variables of white and nonwhite. While using this type of aggregate variable allows the researcher to run several comparison analyses, it does not provide useful information about the heterogeneous groups of students, faculty members, or staff members in the "nonwhite" category. In addition, this manner of defining diversity does not consider other characteristics that can influence the diversity of the campus, including the first-generation-in-college characteristic, socioeconomic status, and other social identities.

Recent changes to the Integrated Postsecondary Education Data System (IPEDS) enable a more nuanced view of racial and ethnic categories by expanding the number of categories reported. The changes implemented in 2009 provide new categories, yet these also illustrate the difficulty in defining diversity. For example, the new rules require institutions to ask if a person is Hispanic or Latino as a *yes* or *no* question and then to have the person respond to the race question separately. The resulting information can be useful for Hispanic-serving institutions (HSIs), which have high numbers of Latino students, but because only the category of Hispanic/Latino is reported to IPEDS, higher education researchers do not have the same access to these data. With these new rules, colleges are asked to report data in more categories than are actually collected for IPEDS reporting purposes. The new rules ask institutions to report in nine categories, which include two or more races, nonresident alien, and race and ethnicity unknown. What is important about these changes is that they allow institutional leaders to analyze their data in more nuanced ways, rather than in broad, nondescript categories. For more information on the changes in IPEDS's race and ethnicity reporting, see the website of the Association for Institutional Research (www.airweb.org/page.asp?page=1503).

These examples highlight the need to understand the multiple ways diversity assessments can occur. In the memorandum at the beginning of this chapter, the concerned faculty members, students, and staff members say they want data regarding equity in promotion and tenure, use of financial aid funds, and student success measures. How a college or university chooses to report these data can either assist its diversity efforts or hinder its momentum toward diversification.

THREE TYPES OF DIVERSITY ASSESSMENTS

For institutions of higher education, diversity assessments can be grouped into three types, each with slightly different goals and different ways of considering data. For this reason, when an institution begins conversations about diversity assessments it is critical to be clear about the relevant goals.

Structural Diversity

The first of type of diversity assessment focuses on *structural diversity*—the number of students, faculty members, and staff members of color present on the campus (Hurtado et al., 1998). This type of assessment tends to support the position that larger numbers of diverse individuals improve the campus climate. If an institution can illustrate a critical mass of nonmajority students, faculty members, and staff members, these types of assessment are worthwhile and can provide some credibility toward fulfilling diversification goals. Such institutions are likely to be able to provide evidence for learning experiences that can occur with socially and culturally diverse students. Institutions with smaller diverse populations tend to appear less impressive when these types of assessments are used to evaluate diversification goals. The institution's low structural diversity may heighten the visibility of the few minority students on campus, thus forcing this small group to create many diverse learning experiences (Hurtado et al., 1998), exerting pressures on them that can result in a potentially negative environment.

Structural diversity assessments are often done with large data sets where limited nuanced data are available, thus making race and ethnicity the only criteria for diversity. As a result, assessors do not know if all students of color are truly responding in the same way or if the issues are really around males from low-income families. While the data can be manipulated in a variety of ways to make large, diverse institutions look good, the disaggregated data that provide proof will still be requested by groups of concerned individuals.

This type of assessment does not necessarily provide much useful data for the isolated college with limited means of attracting diverse students, staff members, or faculty members. In these settings, diversity in socioeconomic status is often important but is sometimes lost in the national discussions on diversity. For these reasons, assessment efforts for institutions with low structural diversity should include important variables like economic status of students, level of acculturation, generation in the United States for Latino and Asian students, or previous attempts at education for nontraditional students. These other variables can provide more detail about students' actual experiences on campus.

Curricular and Cocurricular Activities

The second type of diversity assessment is focused on curricular and cocurricular activities that influence diversity attitudes and reduction of bias. These types of assessments attempt to measure forms of student learning as a result of participation in the academic community or specific diversity-related activities on the campus. These activities can be required or voluntary, and they typically promote some type of intergroup discussion of issues surrounding diversity. Overall, these assessments do tend to demonstrate that diversity-related activities have some effect (Denson, 2009), although the strength can vary according to program type, intensity and length, and format. These curricular and cocurricular diversity assessment efforts can be particularly beneficial to homogeneous institutions where little structural diversity is found and where the efforts toward student diversity experiences are through programs or academic courses. It is important for institutions to understand that one-shot programs seldom affect any changes in student perception or attitudes; more concerted efforts must be undertaken to influence actual change in student development.

Recent research indicates that college students must experience changes in cognitive development in order to recognize when an attitude or expression is racist (Torres, 2009). For this reason, assessment of interventions should consider the level of development. For example, in a diversity workshop during orientation for first-year students it would be unusual to have a student who understands the complex foundation that comes with societal oppression. It is more likely that first-year students believe that everyone will get along and assume diversity to be present. With this audience a more developmentally appropriate intervention would be to focus on how mutual respect is carried out on a college campus, thus focusing on understanding differences in opinion that can evolve as a result of cultural experiences, respecting those with different viewpoints, and seeking out experiences with different cultures. These elements begin the process of providing the level of disequilibrium that can produce development as the college year progresses and the students experience different cultures.

The best way to assess these curricular and cocurricular initiatives is to create realistic learning objectives during the planning stage. By considering from inception how the success of the intervention will be measured, assessors can more easily gather data after its implementation. By assessing student learning around diversity initiatives, institutions can illustrate both intent and progress toward diversification goals.

Campus Climate

The third type of diversity assessment centers on the *campus climate*, including its effects on students, staff members, and faculty members. Assessment of campus climate measures individuals' perceptions of the campus culture and ways those perceptions may affect learning and other outcomes. Relevant aspects of climate often include the students' perceptions of acceptance on the campus, of campus attitudes toward diversity, or of social experiences that are part of campus life (Hurtado and Ponjuan, 2005). Perceptions of campus climate can have some influence on students' persistence, adjustment, and success in college (Hurtado and Carter, 1997; Hurtado and Ponjuan, 2005; Nora and Cabrera, 1996). Campus climate assessments are helpful when looking at certain student outcomes and when seeking insight into diversity issues for staff and faculty. Often issues surrounding the faculty and staff are less clear than student outcomes, possibly focusing on institutional cultural beliefs and practices that are not as noticeable. An audit of the campus climate may highlight how the institutional culture is viewed by different groups of individuals. Again, disaggregating the data by race and ethnicity, gender, and other variables of interest can provide insight into the differing perceptions that emerge within the college community.

Each of these three types of diversity assessments provides different types of information for campus leaders to consider, thereby enabling interventions and policy changes that are based on more specific information and bring greater certainty that concerns are being addressed. Many institutions consider some form of all three assessment types in order to gain a balanced perspective of perceptions and reality within the campus community. What institution leaders do with assessment data is what really determines if change will be seen and felt.

DISAGGREGATION OF DATA

Perhaps the most visible sign that an institution is embracing the potential of diversity to influence learning and outcome variables is the practice of disaggregating data by gender, race and ethnicity, and socioeconomic status (when available). By considering data through the diverse characteristics that students bring to the campus, an institution can make better decisions about actions that need to occur to affect students' learning. Below are examples of data disaggregation.

Gender and Race and Ethnicity

An example that highlights the need to disaggregate data can be found in the news stories that emerged in the late 1990s about the gender imbalance in higher education—headlined "Where Are the Boys?" (Mortenson, 1999). A disaggregated analysis of this gender imbalance found some interesting trends that would not otherwise have been evident. The cause for concern was not the absence of white, middle-class males; rather, it was actually the gap caused by low-income African American and Latino males who lagged behind their female counterparts (King, 2000). And this lag of African American and Latino men continues today (Ryu, 2009). The assessment of disaggregated data provided a more nuanced view of the phenomenon by illustrating that, although the number of women in higher education had increased, it was the rate at which minority men were attending that lagged behind their counterpart women's attendance, thus creating an imbalance. With this nuanced view, institutions could more accurately orient interventions to help the minority and low-income male students who truly needed assistance.

Evidence of Success Based on Disaggregated Data

The movement to create a culture of evidence on college campuses begins by looking at disaggregated data. Two large initiatives that require the use of disaggregated data to consider student success are the Achieving the Dream initiative (2007), which has examined community colleges and a few universities, and the Diversity Scorecard project (Bensimon et al., 2004). Both of these projects work to increase student success of underrepresented populations by having institutions review disaggregated data and address the achievement gaps that can appear. When institutions take on the attitude that an intervention for all students will eventually help those who actually need the help, the situation that results has the student who needs the intervention

looking for the needle in the haystack. Focusing interventions on the population of students who need the assistance is the more direct manner in which
an institution can truly improve success rates of students; well-intentioned
interventions that are not focused on the problem will likely produce only
marginal gains in student success. By knowing the group of students who lag
behind on specific measures of success, an institution can impact the measurement of success variables and improve its reporting statistics.

As the diversity among students continues to grow in the United States,
more disaggregation will be needed. For example, 12 percent of all undergraduates in the United States are "first generation in the United States"
students (American Council on Education, 2005, p. 28). For these students,
administrators must consider the role of generation in the United States as
well as the specific country of origin. Immigrants from different countries
are grouped together in panethnic terms like Latino or Asian, yet the educational attainment among these immigrant groups by country of origin is very
different (Torres, 2004). A student who is a first-generation immigrant from
Southeast Asia should not be assumed to have had the same opportunities
and experiences as a third- or fourth-generation Japanese American college
student. Similar issues apply to Latino immigrants, the largest minority group
in the United States.

EDUCATIONAL PRACTICES IMPACTED
BY DIVERSITY ASSESSMENT

Disaggregated data have been used to help institutions understand which
students, faculty members, and staff members are not being successful. The
culture of evidence with this view of disaggregated data requires that the
effects of differences not be hidden by the large number of majority white,
middle-class students, faculty members, and staff members. The previously
mentioned Achieving the Dream initiative and Diversity Scorecard (Bensimon, 2004) are helping institutions understand how to use their data. One
example is to consider disaggregated data in gatekeeper courses, discerning
more clearly which students are struggling academically in order to deploy
focused interventions addressing this specific group of students. Thus, student success increases, and the success measures, in turn, make the institution look better. Without disaggregated data an institution ends up aiming at
a nonexistent "normal" in its efforts to improve student success measures. In
this chapter's sample memorandum to the college president and leadership
team, the concerned individuals ask whether the institution has considered

disaggregated data and whether the institution's leaders know if minority students or women are doing better, worse, or the same—fair questions. Although findings based on disaggregated data may lead to sensitive conversations, not having a fuller picture of student success only perpetuates a naive, inaccurate view of the success of the institution.

Other examples of institutions that use disaggregated data to consider student engagement (see chapter 7 in this volume for a further discussion on student engagement) as well as curricular and cocurricular initiatives have been described (Denson, 2009). In these instances, being able to clearly align the institution's goals with the assessment of efforts toward those goals provides much more credible evidence for more productive communications with trustees or concerned members of the community. Evidence that the institution's goals are being addressed through student learning, changed attitudes, or more responsible policies demonstrates that the institution's commitment toward diversification is taken seriously.

While society's views on the value of diversity seem to fluctuate between the public good and private interest, higher education must respond to both sides of the debate simultaneously and adjust policies for institutions so that the changing public opinion does not create a disruptive environment. To weather the uncertainty created by public opinion, most administrators feel they must address two overarching mandates: improve quality and improve equity (Birnbaum, 1996)—but many administrators, unfortunately, see the two as mutually exclusive.

The critical message of this chapter is that these goals are complementary and must be seen as such. Moving toward equity does not require lowering quality. Instead, it requires that institutions evaluate how to serve diverse populations and find ways to help all members of the institutional community succeed—not just the few who have always succeeded. Unfortunately, administrators typically act only when something goes wrong and creates environmental pressure to change the culture. Leaders in higher education can approach the challenge of diversification more effectively, however, with proactive solutions that demonstrate that the campus is dealing with diversification and can provide evidence for several initiatives.

As your institution works to balance its strategic goals, diversity is likely to be somewhere in the mix. The question, then, is not whether diversity is a value but rather what importance the value of diversity has at your institution. An institution's most revealing response to this question may be in whether it acts only after being prodded or takes an assertive, proactive approach to diversity issues. Proactivity creates productive conversations and growth experiences for everyone within a community.

REFERENCES

Achieving the Dream. (2007, October). Success is what counts. Retrieved from www .achievingthedream.org/docs/SUCCESS-counts-FINAL-11.6.pdf.

American Council on Education. (2005). *College students today: A national portrait.* Washington, D.C.: Author.

Bensimon, E. M. (2004, January/February). The Diversity Scorecard: A learning approach to institutional change. *Change, 36*(1), 45–52.

Bensimon, E. M., Polkinghorne, D. E., Bauman, G. L., & Vallejo, E. (2004). Doing research that makes a difference. *Journal of Higher Education, 75*(1), 104–126.

Birnbaum, R. (1996). Administrative commitments and minority enrollments: College presidents' goals for quality and access. In C. S. V. Turner, M. Garcia, A. Nora, & L. I. Rendon (Eds.), *Racial and ethnic diversity in higher education* (ASHE Reader Series; pp. 446–459). Boston: Pearson Custom.

Denson, N. (2009). Do curricular and cocurricular diversity activities influence racial bias? A meta-analysis. *Review of Educational Research, 79*(2), 805–838.

Grutter v. Bollinger, 539 U.S. 306 (2003).

Gurin, P., Dey, E. L., Hurtado, S., & Gurin, G. (2002). Diversity and higher education: Theory and impact on educational outcomes. *Harvard Educational Review, 72*(3), 1–26.

Hurtado, S., & Carter, D. F. (1997). Effects of college transition and perceptions of the campus racial climate on Latino college students' sense of belonging. *Sociology of Education, 70*(4), 324–345.

Hurtado, S., Milem, J. F., Clayton-Pederson, A. R., & Allen, W. R. (1998). Enhancing campus climates for racial/ethnic diversity: Educational policy and practice. *Review of Higher Education, 21*(3), 279–302.

Hurtado, S., & Ponjuan, L. (2005). Latino educational outcomes and campus climate. *Journal of Hispanic Higher Education, 4*(3), 235–251.

King, J. E. (2000). *Gender equity in higher education: Are male students at a disadvantage?* Washington, D.C.: American Council on Education.

Ladson-Billings, G. (2006). From achievement gap to the education debt: Understanding achievement in U.S. schools. *Educational Researcher, 35*(7), 3–12.

Mortenson, T. G. (1999). Where are the boys? The growing gender gap in higher education. *College Board Review, 188*, 8–17.

Nora, A., & Cabrera, A. F. (1996). The role of perceptions of prejudice and discrimination on the adjustment of minority students to college. *Journal of Higher Education, 67*(2), 119–148.

Orfield, G. (Ed.). (2001). *Diversity challenged: Evidence on the impact of affirmative action.* Cambridge, Mass.: Harvard Education.

Regents of the University of California v. Bakke, 434 U.S. 963 (1977).

Ryu, M. (2009). *Twenty-third status report minorities in higher education: 2009 supplement.* Washington, D.C.: American Council on Education.

Torres, V. (2004). The diversity among us: Puerto Ricans, Cuban Americans, Caribbean Americans, and Central and South Americans. In A. M. Ortiz (Ed.), *Address-*

ing the unique needs of Latino American students (New Directions for Student Services 105; pp. 5–16). San Francisco: Jossey-Bass.

Torres, V. (2009). The developmental dimensions of recognizing racism. *Journal of College Student Development, 50*(5), 504–520.

WEBSITE

Association for Institutional Research
www.airweb.org/page.asp?page=1503

Chapter Four

Assessments in Student Services That Foster Student and Program Success

John H. Schuh

MEMORANDUM

Date: Today
To: The President
From: The Campus Assessment Committee
Re: Assessment in Student Affairs

As you have articulated many times, this college is committed to continuous improvement. Among the issues that have surfaced this year is our commitment to better understand our students, with the goal of providing increasingly meaningful experiences for them. Additionally, our committee has been conceptualizing various assessment activities to measure student learning both in and outside the classroom. Because our institutional mission emphasizes the total learning environment, our strategic plan is built around student learning.

Our recent accreditation self-study provided plenty of information about student learning at our institution. As you will recall, the self-study asserted that our programs, activities, and services result in extraordinary student experiences. Our admissions materials reflect our commitment to student learning, and our anticipated capital campaign will be targeted for student learning resources.

With these considerations, we recommend that the institution undertake several initiatives to explore the extent to which our students are learning at the level we desire. Toward that end, we seek your endorsement and support for the following initiatives:

1. We recommend participating in the National Survey of Student Engagement, which measures student engagement along a number of dimensions for our first-year students and our graduating seniors.
2. We desire to administer the College Outcomes Survey to all of our junior students, helping us determine if their perceptions of their experiences align with our published outcome objectives.

3. We recommend increasing participation in the Survey of Academic Advising from every four years to every other year, providing more current data for our faculty and the staff for student affairs.
4. We request that a part-time person be hired to conduct studies of mutual interest to academic administrators and student affairs staff: for example, studies that explore the potency of such jointly administered programs as study abroad, learning communities, and service learning. This individual would report to the provost and vice president for student affairs, helping meet the mandate of the Board of Trustees for increased reporting of data on student learning and program effectiveness.

As you know, our students participate in the annual *Cooperative Institutional Research Program* (CIRP) survey, and we would like for this to continue, as it provides useful information concerning students' perspectives and prior experiences as they enter the institution each fall. We do not support the suggestion that we replace this survey with one of the others identified above.

A budget has not been developed for these initiatives, but we desire to discuss the potential for undertaking them in the next fiscal year or two. We look forward to visiting with you at your earliest convenience.

As a senior leader of your college, you may have received memoranda of this sort. Would you view the request as an issue related primarily to the allocation of institutional resources? Would you view it as one of many such requests that your office receives annually and consider it as you do other resource matters, that is, as a cost-benefit question to be discussed with committee members in those terms. Or might this decision require other considerations? Is it actually part of an institutional commitment to improvement? Could the requested data support your new five-year strategic plan? Could these data respond to the governing board's insistence that the institution meet certain improvement metrics over the next five years? These factors, among others, have contributed to the evolution of assessment in student affairs from an activity perceived as something "nice" but without a central place in the work routine of student affairs to a central activity in student affairs practice (Bresciani, Gardner, and Hickmott, 2009). Such assessment is seen as contributing directly to the success of college students by determining if what students learn is aligned with the learning outcomes of their college or university (See Suskie, 2009).

This chapter examines selected issues related to assessment in student services and student affairs that contribute to student success and, by extension, to program success. A number of books have been written about assessment in student affairs (Bresciani, 2010; Schuh, 2009; Schuh and Upcraft, 2001), so this treatment, due to space limitation, will focus on foundational aspects. The chapter is designed to identify selected contextual issues that frame assessment in student affairs; it will also discuss several theoretical and conceptual foundations of assessment in student affairs. An assessment model will be presented, along with some tools that can be used in conducting assessments in student affairs. The chapter will conclude with some examples from institutions that are engaged in successful assessments in student affairs.

In this chapter, I have frequently used the pronoun *we* because many of the concepts originated in joint projects I have coauthored with Lee Upcraft. We have worked so closely on assessment issues for so long that we cannot identify which ideas originated with whom. So we both use *we* in writing about assessment. In this chapter, I have used a few sources from the literature on evaluation, a close relative of assessment, which have much to contribute to assessment consideration.

CONTEXTUAL ISSUES

Contextual issues that have affected assessment in student affairs have evolved over the past decade or so. Among them are the accountability movement, financial pressures on higher education in general and student affairs in particular, changes in regional accreditation expectations, and the pressure for student affairs units to demonstrate how they contribute to student learning. Each of these issues will be discussed in this section of the chapter, although in many respects they overlap and interact.

External Pressures for Greater Accountability for Higher Education

For a number of decades, external pressures have been accelerating on higher education. While higher education enjoyed a "golden age" (Cohen, 1998) after World War II, toward the latter part of the 1960s and early 1970s campus radicalism and various forms of protest have soured the public and led to increased governmental interest in providing oversight and accountability standards (Thelin, 2004). The successful gubernatorial campaigns of Ronald Reagan in California and James Rhodes in Ohio (Thelin, 2004) illustrate this interest historically. More recently, the report of the Spellings Commission (Secretary of Education's Commission on the Future of Higher Education, 2006) called for higher education to be more transparent in providing information to interested stakeholders, including prospective students, parents, and members of the public. Parenthetically, it should be noted that this interest in accountability is not limited to the United States. Jeroen Huisman and Jan Currie (2004) observed, "Accountability is on the higher education policy agenda in many systems. In a number of countries accountability is

institutionalized and commonly accepted, in others it is a recent phenomenon, and in others it is a contested issue on the higher education agenda"
(p. 529). One response of higher education has been the Voluntary System of
Accountability that "communicates information on the undergraduate student
experience through a common web reporting template, the College Portrait"
(www.voluntarysystem.org/index.cfm). External interest in accountability
has included such topics as persistence and graduation rates, campus crime,
student learning, and the cost of attendance. While much of this information
has been available for years, advocates for greater responsiveness desire to
have it all in one place, easily accessible and, perhaps more important, easily
understood for stakeholders. The role of assessment is obvious: without data
that are collected and analyzed systematically and uniformly, transparency
initiatives would have very limited value, especially to lay audiences.

The future of transparency is difficult to determine. Will systematic evaluations of faculty members appear on institutional websites? Will aggregate
student conduct violations be reported, that is, the number of violations of the
institution's alcohol policy in a given residence hall over the last academic
year? Will the aggregate grade point averages of students from a given high
school at the state university be reported on the websites of both the university and the high school? The answers to these questions are unknown, but
doing such things would reflect greater transparency. How helpful would
they be to institutional stakeholders? Current availability of data has not been
demonstrated to necessarily be of help to students and their parents in developing a precise understanding of the cost of attendance (U.S. Department of
Education, 2003), so a question remains whether even greater transparency
will result in stakeholders actually being able to use the additional information to inform their decisions.

Financial Pressures

While higher education has been spending more, in inflation-adjusted expenditures per student since 1929 (Snyder, Dillow, and Hoffman, 2009,
table 361), recent interest in the rising cost of attendance has placed pressures on institutions to justify their costs. In recent years the published cost
of attendance has increased more rapidly than rates of inflation (College
Board, 2008), and it is not unusual for institutions to publish an annual cost
of attendance of more than forty or fifty thousand dollars. While the net
cost may be considerably less than the published price due to generous financial aid awards (Snyder, Dillow, and Hoffman, 2009, table 336), various
stakeholders have expressed concerns about the rising cost of attendance
(Boehner and McKeon, 2003). In the coming years, colleges will have to

develop a net-price calculator to post on their websites (Brainard, 2009) as one more response to demands for transparency.

Support for state-assisted institutions has declined over the past fifteen years, and given the current financial challenges that most are facing, the future will most likely see additional loss of state support. In some cases, the declines have been severe (e.g., Arizona and Nevada), while in others the decline in state assistance has been steady but not dramatic (Kelderman, 2009).

Accreditation and Professional Standards

In their most recent documents, the six regional accreditation agencies have emphasized the importance of measuring student learning in and outside of the classroom. The Southern Association of Colleges and Schools (2004), for example, asks, "If student affairs personnel are supposed to be sufficiently well qualified to assure the quality and effectiveness of the student affairs program, how are the 'quality' and 'effectiveness' of these services defined?" (p. 14). The Middle States Commission on Higher Education (2006) has also emphasized assessment: "These standards place an emphasis on institutional assessment and assessment of student learning" (p. 6). Though not an accreditation agency, the Council for the Advancement of Standards (CAS; Dean, 2006) has described the elements of more than thirty units or departments in student affairs and identified learning outcomes as well as assessment and evaluation standards for each of them. Beyond the CAS standards are professional organizations that have identified learning outcomes: for example, the emphasis on measuring the effectiveness of academic advising (Cuseo, 2008; Schuh, 2008; Troxel, 2008).

Demonstration of Student Learning

Finally, umbrella professional organizations in higher education have emphasized the profession's commitment and obligation to foster student learning, as included in documents that have been released in the past decade. The American Association for Higher Education, the American College Personnel Association (ACPA), and the National Association of Student Personnel Administrators (NASPA) jointly released *Powerful Partnerships: A Shared Responsibility for Learning*. This document (1998) asserted, "Only when everyone on campus—particularly academic affairs and student affairs staff—shares the responsibility for student learning will we be able to make significant progress in improving it" (p. 1). Released a year later, the book *Good Practice in Student Affairs* emphasized that "out-of-class learning experiences are not ancillary to a liberal education but are central to it" (Blimling and Whitt, 1999,

p. 15). One of the principles of good practice described in this book is that "good practice in student affairs uses systematic inquiry to improve student and institutional performance" (p. 17).

Several years later, in 2004, NASPA and ACPA with other professional organizations released *Learning Reconsidered*, a monograph-length document examining student learning from a variety of perspectives. The document identified a number of student learning outcomes including cognitive complexity, knowledge acquisition, integration and application, humanitarianism, civic engagement, interpersonal and intrapersonal competence, practical competence, and persistence and academic achievement as learning outcomes from the college experience (pp. 21–22). The document provides the theoretical and conceptual basis for this learning, as well as sample experiences that can lead to it. A follow-up document, "Higher Education's New Playbook: Learning Reconsidered," summarizes developments in the understanding of learning as a transformative and integrated process and offers strategies for implementing approaches to teaching and learning based on this understanding" (Fried, 2007, pp. 4–5). Taken together, these documents "represent a single playbook for fostering this type of learning in the classroom, outside the classroom, in the field, and in online environments" (Fried, 2007, p. 7). Whether or not these documents have made any difference in student learning is unknown at this point, but institutions that emphasize student engagement and make student learning a significant organizational priority, as emphasized in these documents, have been demonstrated to have higher than predicted graduation rates (Kuh et al., 2005).

THEORETICAL AND CONCEPTUAL FOUNDATIONS

Assessment can be viewed through a number of theoretical frameworks, but a good place to start may be conceptualizing how institutions can enrich the student experience. An excellent conceptual framework has been provided by Alexander Astin (1985, p. 133), who asserted, "Students learn by being involved," and Robert Pace (1980, p. 169), who noted, "Basically, what students learn is what they study." Astin provided five postulates that comprise his involvement theory:

1. Involvement refers to the investment of physical and psychological energy in various "objects."
2. Regardless of its object, involvement occurs along a continuum.
3. Involvement has both quantitative and qualitative features.

4. The amount of student learning and personal development associated with any educational program is directly proportional to the quality and quantity of student involvement in that program.

5. The effectiveness of any educational policy or practice is directly related to the capacity of that policy or practice to increase student involvement. (pp. 135–136)

If students learn by being involved, then institutions need to determine the extent to which this involvement results from the various programs, experiences, and opportunities in which students participate. For example, does participating in a learning community result in improved rates of student retention? If students study abroad, how is their culture learning enhanced? Does service learning contribute to a greater propensity for civic engagement after students graduate?

Institutional Mission

Joan Hirt (2009), Adrianna Kezar and Jaime Lester (2009), and Margaret Barr (2000) have written extensively about the importance of institutional mission in framing student learning. Institutional mission, in Hirt's opinion, "shapes professional practice for student affairs professionals" (p. 38). Kezar and Lester added that mission helps create meaning for an organization.

Assessment can be helpful in measuring the extent to which student learning is aligned with institutional mission. For example, students at a baccalaureate institution with an emphasis on culture learning may have an array of study-abroad experiences from which to choose. Assessment strategies can measure the extent to which these experiences influence their learning. A metropolitan institution, with perhaps more students who own a home in the institution's service area than live at their parents' home or on campus, may have a special commitment to developing civic leaders. Assessment can be important in determining whether that institutional goal for students has been achieved.

Student Engagement

The value of Astin's theory is its applicability to so many student experiences, curricular and otherwise. In effect, this theory provides a framework for measuring student learning. It also underscores the value of student engagement. Astin (1993) and others (Kuh et al., 2005; Pascarella and Terenzini, 1991, 2005) have found that student engagement can facilitate student success. "What students *do* [emphasis in original] during college counts more for what they learn and whether they will persist in college than who they are or even where they go to college" (Kuh et al., 2005, p. 5).

Good practice in higher education should lead to student learning and persistence, and assessment in this context allows institutions to measure their effectiveness. That is precisely what high-performing institutions do, according to the results of the Documenting Effective Educational Practices (DEEP) project (Kuh et al., 2005). In their study of twenty institutions with higher than predicted graduation rates, George Kuh and colleagues (2005) found that these institutions were data driven, had an improvement-oriented campus ethos, and were never quite satisfied with what they were doing. The authors concluded, "Most DEEP institutions systematically collect information about various aspects of student performance and use it to inform policy and decision making" (Kuh et al., 2005, p. 156). Assessment is central to the data collection process. By conducting assessments in student affairs, institutions can determine the potency of their programs, make adjustments to them as necessary, and sustain their commitment to provide the most robust educational environment possible.

Identification and Measurement of Learning Outcomes

Another important aspect of providing a conceptual foundation for assessment is the development of learning outcomes. Identifying learning outcomes related to student experiences is foundational to the assessment process. If learning outcomes are not designed to be part of a student's experience, assessment may turn out to be not much more than wandering around. Learning outcomes should be tied to the goals that institutions and specific units within them have for their students. For example, if an institutional goal is to help students become self-sufficient and an academic advisement center goal is to help students develop a level of self-confidence and independence so that they are able to select their own courses and develop their own academic schedules, then an appropriate learning outcome for the advisement process could be something like this: "As a consequence of the advisement process, students will be able to select courses appropriate to meeting their academic goals at the college." The assessment, then, would be designed to measure the extent to which the advisement process actually helps students learn how to manage the course selection and program planning process.

In a larger sense, however, learning outcomes can be much more global than students being able to develop an academic schedule. For example, building on the theme of developing skills related to independence, a larger goal for the student affairs division could be "to provide experiences and learning opportunities for our students so that they can become independent, self-reliant members of the larger society." In consideration of that broad goal, specific objectives could be developed for students, with several units being identified to help students develop skills to address the objective. Specific objectives might include students being able to select an appropriate major (academic advisement), manage their financial resources (financial aid), navigate the process of career planning (career planning and placement), thrive in a different culture (study abroad), manage their physical and emotional health (student health services, counseling services, and recreation services), and be of service to the larger society (service learning and volunteerism). With each of these objectives in mind, assessments can be developed to measure the extent to which specific experiences help the students master the objective.

As referenced above in discussing the importance of institutional mission, learning outcomes need to be aligned with the goals and objectives an institution has for its student education, and presumably such outcomes will be used to inform student learning in and outside the classroom. Developing learning outcomes is an initial step in the assessment process. Ultimately, the results (outcomes) of the student experience will be measured by assessment. "Outcomes-based assessment is designed to be a systematic self-reflection process that provides the practitioner with information on how to improve his planning and delivery processes" (Bresciani, 2009, p. 534). What will students learn from serving as a resident advisor, participating in a leadership workshop, or serving as editor of the student newspaper? Presumably students will learn much more than the obvious, and the goal of the assessment process is to capture student learning beyond what might be expected (see, for example, Schuh, 1999).

The results of the assessment of student learning can be used as part of an institutional renewal process. Institutions typically develop a mission statement that guides the identification of learning outcomes that inform the development of programs and other learning experiences. The learning experiences are then assessed to determine their effect on student growth. These outcomes are aligned with the goals of the programs and the extent to which they are consonant with the institution's mission. If the outcomes are inconsistent with the learning outcomes of the institution, adjustments need to be made. If they are consistent with the institution's learning outcomes, then the learning experiences can be repeated.

AN ASSESSMENT MODEL

The American Association for Higher Education (AAHE; 1992) developed a series of principles that can be used to frame the process of assessment. While it has been more than fifteen years since these principles were published, they are still contemporary in undergirding the assessment process. The first and perhaps most important is that assessment begins with educational values. If institutions truly believe that all students who are admitted can be successful, then the role of assessment is to help determine if, in fact, all students at the various stages of their experiences have been successful in what they have learned. If student experiences do not have the desired outcome, then the institution's leaders and faculty members will have to adjust their thinking and modify their approach to the programs and services they offer.

Assessment can be conceptualized as a significant part of a continuous four-step cycle, according to Linda Suskie (2009). In this cycle learning outcomes are established, learning opportunities are provided, learning is assessed, and the results are used to understand and improve student learning. It is important to note that assessment is not an occasional activity (Schuh, 2009) but rather an activity central to the educational process (Suskie, 2009). It is also central to institutional planning and development. Behavior attributed to former New York City mayor Ed Koch illustrates the paradigm. As the story goes, Mayor Koch would walk around the city and ask this simple question of citizens he encountered: "How are we doing?" He would receive feedback from his constituents, and then he and his staff could take appropriate actions. Whether and how often Mayor Koch did this is beside the point. The situation underscores the importance of feedback in responding to the needs of a clientele and of continuously improving.

Upcraft and Schuh (1996) developed an assessment process built on the work of AAHE. As with the AAHE assessment principles, this approach begins with analyzing the situation that brings about an assessment. In an era that is concerned with student learning (see, for example, the Spellings Commission report [Secretary of Education's Commission on the Future of Higher Education, 2006]), thinking about how a program or experience contributes to student learning is where the assessment process begins. If the development of a learning community is seen as a valuable learning experience for students (Barefoot et al., 2005), then assessment can be used to measure the effect of participating in a learning community on a specific campus.

Schuh and Upcraft (2001) and Schuh (2009) developed an assessment model for student affairs based on a sequence of questions. This set of eight questions, augmented by the specific recommendations of Suskie (2009), can be used to measure student learning and development.

What Is the Targeted Issue?

This question is the most important of the set of eight. It encourages the assessor to think about what is going to be addressed by the assessment process.

Could this issue be the influence of a new program on student learning? Are outcomes of interest? What about student perceptions of the learning environment? Will students improve their critical thinking or other skill sets as a consequence of any experience? More time should be spent on sharpening one's thinking about the focus issue than on any other aspect of the assessment process.

What Is the Purpose of the Assessment?

After the issue has been identified, the next step is to narrow the focus of the assessment. The specific purpose will flow directly from the issue under consideration. Are students who participate in a learning community more likely to persist than those who do not? Does living in a residence hall result in students developing a greater appreciation for diversity than students who commute from home? Does study abroad result in enhanced cultural learning for those who participate in programs overseas?

Who Should Be Studied?

The purpose of the assessment helps define who will be studied. Sometimes the population to be studied is obvious. If we want to know about the influence of a learning community on students, those who are members of a learning community will be studied. At times, we might want to do a comparative study. For example, we might compare persistence rates of students who live in residence halls with those of students who live off campus. Or we might want to compare the academic achievement of those students who served as undergraduate research assistants (URAs), as reflected in their grades, with those who did not serve as URAs. And depending on the nature of the study, we might want to study only certain participants, such as twenty-five students who participated in a semester-long service-learning program.

What Is the Best Assessment Method?

A mistake some assessors make is to choose their methodology and then decide on the purpose of the study. This strategy is likely to lead to a failed study. Instead, the assessment methodology should be chosen after the above questions have been answered. Either quantitative or qualitative methods may be chosen depending on the purpose of the project. Since outcomes can be measured qualitatively or quantitatively, the number of students studied may shape the project. For example, if we wanted to examine student learning in a study-abroad project and only a dozen students had participated in the program, a strategy other than administering a questionnaire would be preferred. But if we wanted to look at the influence of participating in a first-year experience course, and one thousand students had been enrolled in sections of such a course, a quantitative approach might be more effective. If time and resources permit, a mixed-methods approach can be especially appealing. Mixed-methods studies take time, broad expertise, and other resources, but they can provide an excellent understanding of the student experience.

One other approach to methodology should also be considered: is the necessary information in an institutional database? For example, if we know the names of students who have participated in a specific experience, perhaps orientation, and the names of those who have not, we may be able to craft a study looking at the potency of participating in orientation by using information we have in the registrar's data files. Existing databases should not be overlooked as sources of information for our studies (Saunders and Wohlgemuth, 2009).

How Should We Collect Our Data?

Data can be collected using many techniques. Again, depending on our methodological approach, we might choose to administer a questionnaire, interview students individually or in groups, have students write reflection papers or journals, mine institutional databases, or use other approaches. If a locally developed instrument is used, then technological support to assist in formatting the instrument, distributing the instrument, and analyzing the responses also needs to be determined. Many commercial resources are available to assist in formatting an instrument as well as collecting and analyzing data.

What Instrument Should We Use?

The development of an instrument refers to selecting a commercially available instrument, developing an instrument using campus personnel, or developing a protocol for interviews or focus groups. Certainly there are advantages to using commercially developed instruments for quantitative studies, but local instruments also have strengths. An added feature of many commercially developed instruments is that they allow for a few items developed locally to be added to the standardized instrument. The instrument selected for implementation should be the one that best meets the needs of the study.

How Should We Analyze the Data?

Data analysis will be driven by the nature of the data and the goals of the project. We may choose to use one or more statistical approaches to analyze our data, or we may choose software that will aid in qualitative data-analysis approaches as discussed below. Typically, the data analysis will flow from the kind of data collected and our goals in undertaking the study.

How Should We Report the Results?

It is highly likely that several forms of reports will be provided from our study. Senior administrators, governing board members, and perhaps others in leadership positions typically have a great deal of information to read and process. Preparing a report that these individuals will actually read is a challenge because they have so much material to manage. Accordingly, a short report, perhaps not much more than an executive summary focused on the purpose of the assessment project, the findings, and the recommendations for practice will suffice. Including graphics will make the report more attractive. Others may want a complete report with a description of the research methods; perhaps this could be posted on a website. If any compromises were made in the methodology utilized in the report, such as using convenience sampling or not conducting a pilot test of a locally developed instrument, these should be acknowledged in the complete report. "No methodology is perfect. There are always shortcomings, and if the evaluator does not acknowledge them, others certainly will highlight them in the public comments that will inevitably follow. But if the evaluator discusses them briefly, the report comes across as being quite professional" (Grob, 2004, p. 608). If any mistakes were made in developing the study, they, too, should be acknowledged.

In addition, an important strategy needs to be developed for using the results in the process by which change is effected. To simply report results and not provide suggestions for improving the student experience would be incomplete. Our view is that recommendations for change should be included in each form of the report. "Recommendations should not be afterthoughts of evaluation efforts but deliberate, empirically based suggestions for organizational action" (Sonnichsen, 1994, p. 542). Such recommendations include aspects of the student experience that can be built upon and enhanced, aspects that should be eliminated, and new elements that should be introduced.

ASSESSMENT TOOLS

As assessment techniques have become more sophisticated, a variety of resources and tools have been developed to facilitate assessment projects. For many projects, technological tools can be used to assist in such areas as instrument development, data collection, and data analysis. In the past, those conducting assessments may have had little more equipment available to them than a reliable typewriter and a mainframe computer; today, the use of technology can expedite assessment projects, making them more sophisticated and more time efficient, capable of providing a much more robust product.

When Upcraft and I published our questions to be used in designing an assessment project (Upcraft and Schuh, 1996), we identified quite a range of assessments. These assessments included measuring students' participation, needs, satisfaction, learning, culture, and so on. These are still important topics, but if we had to identify just one form of assessment that has emerged as being the most critical, we would select measurement of student learning. This current emphasis is due to the reasons cited previously in this chapter. Pressure is on institutions of higher education to report how the experiences, services, and programs they offer enhance student learning. In a challenging economic environment, if student learning is not enhanced, then a legitimate question becomes "why should we spend precious resources on something that does not appear to add value to a student's education?" With that question in mind, we will identify a few tools that can facilitate assessment.

Quantitative Tools

A number of instruments have been developed that target specific outcomes related to the student experience. The sources of these instruments are listed in appendix A. All of them provide the opportunity to add some questions specific to the local situation to the basic set of items. These questionnaires have been developed with care and have excellent psychometric properties.

But at times there are good reasons for an institution to develop its own questionnaire, typically referred to as a *locally developed instrument*. In such a case, technology can still be employed for formatting the instrument as well as collecting and analyzing the data. Appendix B includes several websites for organizations that provide these services. Typically, the cost of using these services is modest, particularly given the potency of the assistance they provide to those conducting the assessment.

A tool that ought to be on the reference shelf of those interested in conducting a quantitative assessment is *The Survey Kit* (Fink, 2003). This set of monographs provides excellent details about conducting a quantitative assessment, ranging from conceptualizing the assessment to reporting results.

Qualitative Tools

A number of software tools are available for those interested in conducting a qualitative assessment. Two that are used commonly for data analysis are NVivo and Atlas.ti. Information about each is available on its website, listed in appendix B. Another particularly valuable resource is *The Focus Group Kit* (Morgan and Krueger, 1998). Similar to *The Survey Kit*, this set of monographs covers everything from when to use focus groups to reporting results.

The Focus Group Kit is an excellent resource for a study that involves interviewing participants, either individually or in focus groups.

EXAMPLES FROM THE FIELD

As institutions engage in the assessment of student learning and determine the efficacy of the programs they offer, they have the opportunity of sharing their reports with audiences on campus and beyond. Several institutional examples of assessment approaches used by divisions of student affairs are presented in this section of the chapter.

North Dakota State University

The Student Life Department at North Dakota State University (NDSU) has identified several programs as "signature programs," which means that the programs teach students important life skills (www.ndsu.edu/student_life). Included in this set of programs are the first-year experience (offered by residence life), the student employee program (offered by dining services), the Volunteer Network and Service-learning Program (sponsored by the Memorial Union), and the Caring Community of Leaders and Problem Solvers (sponsored by Residence Life). These programs and others can be recorded and described in a Student Involvement Transcript that is overseen by the Student Life Department at NDSU. From an assessment perspective, the Student Involvement Transcripts can be reviewed and studied to provide a profile of the developmental experiences of students at NDSU.

University of Nevada, Reno

The Division of Student Affairs at the University of Nevada, Reno, has developed a template for assessing various programs and services, providing uniformity in measuring student learning, growth, and progress (www.unr .edu/assess/model/index.html). Each template includes a mission statement for the unit, various learning outcomes that are designed to be fostered by the unit, performance indicators for each of the learning outcomes, assessment methods designed to measure the performance indicators, a description of how the results of the various assessments will be used, and an implementation plan for the assessment process.

A substantial number of units at the University of Nevada, Reno, have developed these plans. A sampling of them includes the registrar's office, TRIO programs, Greek Life, the student union, the substance abuse prevention program, the office of student conduct, student financial services, and the office of disability services. The strength of this approach is that the mission of each program area frames its learning outcomes, measures have been developed for each learning outcome, and an implementation plan has been devised. This approach has excellent potential for success.

Pennsylvania State University

Pennsylvania State University (Penn State) has had a viable assessment program since 1995. The centerpiece of this program is Penn State Pulse (Pennsylvania State University, n.d.a), a periodic poll of students on a wide range of topics, from an evaluation of civility on campus to first-year programs to student learning outside the classroom. The surveys are administered either by telephone or through the Web. The Penn State studies are particularly useful because the surveys have been conducted over a lengthy period of time, and thus longitudinal data are available. In a typical year four topics are explored, and the results are available on a website. These excellent reports emphasize results and include graphs and charts that are easy to read. Penn State's work in assessing the student experience has been superb over the years and serves as a model for institutions that wish to conduct assessments on a regular basis. Beyond Penn State Pulse, other assessments also are conducted periodically at Penn State (Pennsylvania State University, n.d.b).

Oregon State University

The Division of Student Affairs at Oregon State University (OSU) has developed ambitious plans for assessing the student experience. The division has a very well-developed website (http://oregonstate.edu/studentaffairs/assessment/bestpractices.html) and has adopted a series of questions that can be used to frame various assessments that offices within the division might wish to develop. The questions closely follow those developed by Upcraft and Schuh (1996), ranging from use of services to the student learning outcomes associated with the various programs and services offered by the OSU Division of Student Affairs.

SUMMARY

This chapter has identified selected issues related to the assessment of student affairs programs, services, and experiences that lead to student and institutional success. Contextual issues have been discussed, a theoretical and conceptual foundation has been established for assessment in student affairs, some tools have been identified for the person interested in conducting assessments, and promising assessment programs at several institutions have been described briefly. The chapter ends, as it began, with this assertion: assessment has become a central activity in student affairs. Those student affairs divisions that embrace assessment and conduct assessments on a routine basis will thrive; those that do not, may not.

APPENDIX A: SOURCES OF INSTRUMENTS

American College Testing Program
Two-year college student surveys: www.act.org/ess/twoyear.html
Four-year college student surveys: www.act.org/ess/fouryear.html

College Student Experiences Questionnaire
http://cseq.iub.edu

Higher Education Research Institute
www.gseis.ucla.edu/heri/herisurveys.php

National Survey of Student Engagement
http://nsse.iub.edu/index.cfm

Noel-Levitz
www.noellevitz.com/Our+Services/Marketing+Research+and+Communications/
    Research/The+Research+Toolkit/Instruments.htm

APPENDIX B: USEFUL WEBSITES FOR INTERNET RESOURCES

Sources for Developing Web-based Surveys

Snap Surveys
www.snapsurveys.com/

Survey Monkey
www.surveymonkey.com/

Survey Pro
www.surveypro.com/

Zoomerang
http://info.zoomerang.com/

Sources for Qualitative Data Analysis

Atlas.ti
www.atlasti.com/

NVivo
www.qsrinternational.com/

Sources of Institutional Examples

North Dakota State University, Student Life
www.ndsu.edu/student_life

Oregon State University
http://oregonstate.edu/studentaffairs/assessment/bestpractices.html

Pennsylvania State University
www.sa.psu.edu/SARA

University of Nevada, Reno
www.unr.edu/assess/model/index.html

REFERENCES

American Association for Higher Education. (1992). *Principles of good practice for assessing student learning*. Washington, D.C.: Author.

American Association for Higher Education, the American College Personnel Association, and the National Association of Student Personnel Administrators. (1998). Powerful partnerships: A shared responsibility for learning. Retrieved from www .naspa.org/career/sharedresp.cfm.

Astin, A. W. (1985). *Achieving educational excellence*. San Francisco: Jossey-Bass.

Astin, A. W. (1993). *What matters in college*. San Francisco: Jossey-Bass.

Barefoot, B. O., Gardner, J. N., Cutright, M., Morris, L. V., Schroeder, C. C., Schwartz, S. W., & Associates (2005). *Achieving and sustaining institutional excellence for the first year of college*. San Francisco: Jossey-Bass.

Barr, M. J. (2000). The importance of the institutional mission. In M. J. Barr, M. K. Desler, & Associates (Eds.), *The handbook of student affairs administration* (2nd ed., pp. 25–49). San Francisco: Jossey-Bass.

Blimling, G. S., & Whitt, E. J. (1999). Identifying the principles that guide student affairs practice. In G. S. Blimling & E. J. Whitt (Eds.), *Good practice in student affairs* (pp. 1–20). San Francisco: Jossey-Bass.

Boehner, J. A., & McKeon, H. P. (2003). *The college cost crisis*. Washington, D.C.: U.S. House of Representatives.

Brainard, J. (2009, June 5). Colleges should start planning now for "net price" calculators, experts say. *Chronicle of Higher Education.* Retrieved from http://chronicle .com/article/Colleges-Should-Start-Plann/47299.

Bresciani, M. J. (2009). Implementing assessment to improve student learning and development. In G. S. McClellan, J. Stringer, & Associates (Eds.), *The handbook of student affairs administration* (3rd ed., pp. 526–544). San Francisco: Jossey-Bass.

Bresciani, M. J. (2010). Assessment and evaluation. In J. H. Schuh, S. Harper, S. Jones, & Associates (Eds.), *Student services: A handbook for the profession* (5th ed.). San Francisco: Jossey-Bass.

Bresciani, M. J., Gardner, M. M., & Hickmott, J. (2009). *Case studies in implementing assessment in student affairs.* New Directions for Student Services 127. San Francisco: Jossey-Bass.

Cohen, A. M. (1998). *The shaping of American higher education.* San Francisco: Jossey-Bass.

College Board. (2008). *Trends in college pricing.* Washington, D.C.: Author.

Cuseo, J. (2008). Assessing advisor effectiveness. In V. N. Gordon, W. R. Habley, T. J. Grites, & Associates (Eds.), *Academic advising: A comprehensive handbook* (2nd ed., pp. 369–385). San Francisco: Jossey-Bass.

Dean, L. A. (2006). *CAS professional standards for higher education* (6th ed.). Washington, D.C.: Council for the Advancement of Standards in Higher Education.

Fink, A. (2003). *The survey kit* (2nd ed.). Thousand Oaks, Calif.: Sage.

Fried, J. (2007, March/April). Higher education's new playbook: Learning Reconsidered. *About Campus, 12*(1), 2–7.

Grob, G. F. (2004). Writing for impact. In J. S. Wholey, H. P. Hatry, & K. E. Newcomer (Eds.), *Handbook of practical program evaluation* (2nd ed., pp. 604–627). San Francisco: Jossey-Bass.

Hirt, J. B. (2009). The importance of institutional mission. In G. S. McClellan, J. Stringer, & Associates (Eds.), *The handbook of student affairs administration* (3rd ed., pp. 19–40). San Francisco: Jossey-Bass.

Huisman, J., & Currie, J. (2004). Accountability in higher education: Bridge over troubled water? *Higher Education, 48*(4), 529–551.

Kelderman, E. (2009, February 27). Stimulus bill brings relief to some states but falls far short for others. *Chronicle of Higher Education,* p. A24.

Kezar, A. J., & Lester, J. (2009). *Organizing higher education for collaboration.* San Francisco: Jossey-Bass.

Kuh, G. D., Kinzie, J., Schuh, J. H., Whitt, E. J., & Associates. (2005). *Student success in college: Creating conditions that matter.* San Francisco: Jossey-Bass.

Middle States Commission on Higher Education. (2006). *Characteristics of excellence in higher education.* Philadelphia: Author.

Morgan, D. L., & Krueger, R. A. (1998). *The focus group kit.* Thousand Oaks: Sage.

National Association of Student Personnel Administrators and American College Personnel Association. (2004). Learning reconsidered: A campus wide focus on the student experience. Retrieved from www.myacpa.org/pub/pub_books_services.cfm.

Pace, C. R. (1980). *Measuring outcomes of college.* San Francisco: Jossey-Bass.

Pascarella, E. T., & Terenzini, P. T. (1991). *How college affects students*. San Francisco: Jossey-Bass.

Pascarella, E. T., & Terenzini, P. T. (2005). *How college affects students* (vol. 2). San Francisco: Jossey-Bass.

Pennsylvania State University. (n.d.a). Penn State pulse. Retrieved from www.sa.psu.edu/SARA/pulse.shtml.

Pennsylvania State University. (n.d.b). Student affairs research and assessment. Retrieved from www.sa.psu.edu/SARA.

Saunders, K., & Wohlgemuth, D. R. (2009). Using existing databases. In J. H. Schuh & Associates (Eds.), *Assessment methods for student affairs* (pp. 23–50). San Francisco: Jossey-Bass.

Schuh, J. H. (1999). Student learning and growth resulting from service as an intramural official. *NIRSA Journal, 23*(2), 51–61.

Schuh, J. H. (2008). Assessing student learning. In V. N. Gordon, W. R. Habley, T. J. Grites, & Associates (Eds.), *Academic advising: A comprehensive handbook* (2nd ed., pp. 356–368). San Francisco: Jossey-Bass.

Schuh, J. H. (2009). *Assessment methods in student affairs*. San Francisco: Jossey-Bass.

Schuh, J. H., & Upcraft, M. L. (2001). *Assessment practice in student affairs*. San Francisco: Jossey-Bass.

Secretary of Education's Commission on the Future of Higher Education. (2006). A test of leadership: Charting the future of U.S. higher education. A report of the commission appointed by Secretary of Education Margaret Spellings, U.S. Department of Education. Retrieved from www2.ed.gov/about/bdscomm/list/hiedfuture/reports/final-report.pdf.

Snyder, T. D., Dillow, S. A., & Hoffman, C. M. (2009). *Digest of education statistics 2008*. Washington, D.C.: U.S. Department of Education.

Sonnichsen, R. C. (1994). Evaluators as change agents. In J. S. Wholey, H. P. Hatry, & K. E. Newcomer (Eds.), *Handbook of practical program evaluation* (pp. 534–548). San Francisco: Jossey-Bass.

Southern Association of Colleges and Schools. (2004). *Handbook for reaffirmation of accreditation*. Decatur, Ga.: Author.

Suskie, L. (2009). *Assessing student learning* (2nd ed.). San Francisco: Jossey-Bass.

Thelin, J. R. (2004). *A history of American higher education*. Baltimore: Johns Hopkins University Press.

Troxel, W. G. (2008). Assessing the effectiveness of the advising program. In V. N. Gordon, W. R. Habley, T. J. Grites, & Associates (Eds.), *Academic advising: A comprehensive handbook* (2nd ed., pp. 386–395). San Francisco: Jossey-Bass.

Upcraft, M. L., & Schuh, J. H. (1996). *Assessment in student affairs*. San Francisco: Jossey-Bass.

U.S. Department of Education. (2003). *Getting ready to pay for college: What students and their parents know about the cost of college tuition and what they are doing to find out* (NCES 2003-030). Washington, D.C.: National Center for Education Statistics.

WEBSITES

North Dakota State University, Student Life
www.ndsu.edu/student_life

Oregon State University
http://oregonstate.edu/studentaffairs/assessment/bestpractices.html

University of Nevada, Reno
www.unr.edu/assess/model/index.html

Voluntary System of Accountability
www.voluntarysystem.org/index.cfm

Chapter Five

Documenting Student Learning: Valuing the Process

Kay H. Smith and Raymond D. Barclay

To coherently assess their institutions, leaders on college campuses need to understand and manage complex approaches, vocabularies, scales of operations, disciplinary needs, accreditation pressures, and accountability reports. But they can easily get lost or bogged down in these topics, and the ever-increasing external demands for accountability and accreditation tend to push leaders into focusing on simple inputs and outputs to address student learning and institutional effectiveness. But focusing on these external audiences neglects more authentic documentation and assessment of student learning: what students learn, how they learn, what they can do with their learning, and how this recursively informs instructional design and the creation of academic support services.

PURPOSES OF ASSESSMENT AND DOCUMENTATION

Often the attempt to classify what we are doing in order to demonstrate institutional effectiveness is undertaken at the expense of adopting a deeper, more authentic approach to documenting student learning. Adopting such narrowly conceived approaches is often reasonable because they are easier and are easily applicable to environments struggling to meet budgetary requirements when resources are diminishing or scarce, and faculty and staff members are overburdened with so many competing demands on their time. Additionally, student learning assessment is not easy, and it requires significant time, thought, and resource investment if it is to be done correctly. Assessment also requires a hook that gives careful consideration of how best to tap into and enhance the motivation and intrinsic needs of faculty members, staff members, and students for pursuing this work. Ignoring such challenges, the "external route" will ultimately neglect developing intentional assessment strategies aimed at understanding the phenomena by which learning emerges. In taking a path of less resistance, the institution will have created less rigorous research designs and less useful instructional and program designs—inadvertently undermining its ability to document and present valid evidence of learning.

PURPOSES OF THIS CHAPTER

This chapter will argue that assessment should affect student learning as well as measure it. Further, the chapter will elaborate on the notion that documenting the outcomes of tasks that facilitate and inform learning processes, as well as using coursework and continuous assessment processes within particular learning contexts (academic and nonacademic programs), opens greater possibilities for assessment *for* learning than does course or module examination (Murphy, 2006). In *A Culture of Evidence: Postsecondary Assessment and Learning Outcomes* (2006), the ETS team of Carol Dwyer, Catherine Millett, and David Payne describe this outward focus of much assessment and accountability: "As we outline what a new era in higher education accountability might look like, we will strive to keep in mind two points: the need for clarity and simplicity in the system; and the need for a common language that can be used consistently within the higher education community as well as with stakeholders outside this community" (p. 3). This chapter will argue the opposite: that most faculty members perceive their own disciplines and the learning tasks associated with them as anything but simple or easy to measure in simple terms and that most institutions of higher learning differ from each other in important ways and thus require a more nuanced language to describe the learning that occurs on their campuses, even if that language must be abstracted for a larger audience. Assessment that takes seriously the role of faculty members and students will conversely increase the odds that faculty members and students will take seriously their roles in the learning process and, by extension, in the assessment enterprise. Such an approach closes the student learning loop by giving faculty members and students complex but vital information about the learning task, allowing both groups to make adjustments for continued learning and engaging them more fully. Simplicity and shared terminology may be laudable goals for comparing institutions for purposes of accountability, but these goals rarely have the important effect of going beyond assessing learning to enhancing learning.

The chapter will explain how activities aimed at increasing cognitive and metacognitive processing increase the likelihood of attaining specified competencies related to the disciplines, to general education, and to desired soft skills relevant to the workplace. This chapter will not leave out the student but instead examine processes and programs that have recursive effects: The student is not merely examined by the assessment process but also learns from it. Sound student learning documentation requires capturing information about the outcomes of learning and the process by which learning is pursued. Additionally, assessment processes that both measure and contribute to student learning must have a strong link to faculty development, augmented by other campus offices (e.g., institutional research, assessment, planning, etc.), particularly as they pertain to increasing faculty members' understanding of their role and building their capacity to undertake it. As a natural extension to these arguments, the chapter suggests that campus leaders orient institutional support more intentionally toward the departments where the assessment takes place and invest in instructional and program design support centers and requisite technology, not necessarily toward the traditional accountability functions. In sum, we recommend moving beyond traditional assessment *of* learning to include assessment *for* learning as well.

BEYOND ASSESSMENT *OF* LEARNING

It is understandable that higher education administrators would desire a single measure or a limited number of measures that would present a clear and simple picture of the learning process at their institution. Indeed many faculty members share that desire, particularly if they feel that assessment is something that is imposed from the top and not an integral part of classroom and disciplinary practice. The popularity of competency testing attests to the need to satisfy that desire.

A single test—the Measure of Academic Proficiency and Progress (MAPP), the Collegiate Assessment of Academic Proficiency (CAAP), or the Collegiate Learning Assessment (CLA)—might be the key tool for administrators to communicate student learning to stakeholders, particularly at the state and national levels. Some faculty members might welcome the simple solution of competency testing because they have seen assessment as having little value in their work. Yet the great majority of faculty members at a variety of institutions want assessment that is more closely focused on what they do in the classroom or the curriculum, that examines the pathways of student learning more carefully, and that has some clear value to them in determining how to increase student learning in their courses and in their disciplinary fields (Schilling and Schilling, 1998). Moreover, when student learning or lack of it is demonstrated through a large competency test or other type of institution-wide or multi-institutional assessment, one important constituency, the student, is almost always left out of the subsequent conversations.

For example, students who take the competency tests rarely if ever learn how they performed on the test and what they might do to improve. In fact, motivating student constituencies to take competency tests and other institution-wide assessment efforts seriously when they have so little to gain themselves is a significant problem for such assessments. This is not to diminish the role of these tests as efficient and reasonable metrics for external audiences (e.g., policy makers, accreditation agencies, general public, etc.) concerning broadly defined competencies at the institution. But it is important to recognize that these measures do have significant limitations for understanding how learning emerges in the classroom and that they cannot tell us much about what specific mechanisms impacted the learners or enhanced an approach to the learning process for a faculty member or student.

Assessment *for* Learning

Assessment that affects student learning is undertaken to improve teaching and learning and thus is often seen as limited in scope and situated in the confines of the classroom. Actually, the principles of assessment *for* learning, almost always formative, as contrasted to assessment *of* learning, usually summative, can form the basis of a culture of assessment on a campus and become a guiding model for larger-scale assessment. Figure 5.1 shows how formative assessment (assessment for learning) is part of a process that moves toward accountability. Summative assessment, like competency testing, is often seen as establishing useful comparisons between institutions, as in the Voluntary System of Accountability (VSA).[1] But if summative assessment is put into the context of formative assessment, in a "both/and" as opposed to an "either/or" structure, then each can enhance the other, providing multiple measures of learning (Stefanakis, 2002). Assessment for learning can, in many cases, be aggregated or scaled up to reveal summative patterns, as figure 5.1 illustrates by demonstrating the continuum from learning to accountability.

There are many ways in which performance-based or standardized summative assessments can support learner-centered assessments to improve as well as measure learning. Educational strategies like portfolios, learning communities, internships, and capstone experiences attempt to facilitate cognitive engagement via embedded metacognitive processes (i.e., self-regulation, planning, monitoring) that provide a vehicle for self-evacuation by the learner. They also allow more general insight into the learning process by the institution, which can then be expressed in more specifically crafted accountability measures. Understanding concepts from the learning sciences,

Figure 5.1. Assessment for Learning

like *cognitive engagement,* is key to both understanding how to build assessment that is learner centered and to determining how to create learning environments that not only enhance learning but also support the faculty in developing assessment that contributes to institutionally specific accountability structures.

Cognitive Engagement

How do we get students to exert the considerable mental energy required to persist in a complex learning environment where deeper levels of learning occur through synthesizing, integrating, and attaining strategic knowledge? Leaders in higher education commonly wonder aloud whether students will invest the requisite time and energy to achieve the desired levels of learning just because the institution invests the financial resources to create an authentic learning environment or provide a "takeaway" such as a showcase portfolio or improved résumé. This concern is at least one reason senior leaders often hesitate to invest in these endeavors beyond the "pilot phase" while aspiring to full implementation.

A burgeoning literature in educational research broadly and higher education in particular highlights how specific assessment approaches can have a significant impact on student learning as well as a significant role in motivating stakeholders to participate (Black et al., 2003; Black and Wiliam, 1998; Sutton, 1995; Torrance and Prior, 1998, as cited in Murphy, 2006). Roger Murphy (2006) noted the significant body of literature growing to support this approach, especially in elementary and secondary school classroom research, but asserted, "In higher education we are still at an earlier stage of understanding how effectively this approach to assessment can be developed within different higher education institutions" (p. 43).

To help frame our approach to documenting student learning in postsecondary contexts, we turn to the learning sciences literature, where much scholarly work has been undertaken to address issues related to assessment for learning. Specifically, we will focus on *cognitive engagement*, a concept that emanates from research on motivation that is significantly referenced as a critical component to successfully carrying out and documenting authentic student learning. Essentially, the view is that motivation leads to achievement in learning environments by increasing the quality of cognitive engagement (Blumenfeld, Kempler, and Krajcik, 2006). Content understanding, skill development, and higher-order thinking are all influenced by the degree that students are committed to their learning process and consequently help us assess student learning.

Learning environments seeking to facilitate cognitive engagement among participants attempt to encapsulate more fully the relationship between student effort (*buy-in*) and learning. The cognitive, metacognitive, and volitional strategies employed are intended to increase the likelihood that "learners will think deeply about the content and construct an understanding that entails integration and application of the key ideas for the discipline" (Blumenfeld, Kempler, and Krajcik, 2006, p. 475). These strategies are promoted to increase deeper notions of engagement and learning that influence student motivation, enhance intrinsic values related to learning through fostering situational interest, and ultimately increase the degree of participation in the learning enterprise, thus increasing measurable learning and enhancing learning outcomes.

Notions or levels of cognitive engagement are understood to emanate from superficial and deep approaches to learning. Superficial cognitive engagement includes tasks that rely on elaborative or rehearsed and memory-focused approaches to learning, often those that are measured through competency testing. Deeper notions of engagement facilitate students' reliance on and refinement of metacognitive strategies including the use of intentional reflective mechanisms that help the students establish goals, plan, monitor, and evaluate progress as they iteratively adjust their approach to a learning task (Blumenfeld, Kempler, and Krajcik, 2006). Intentional reflection is an important element in assessment for learning, particularly in learning environments like learning communities (reflection on interdisciplinarity), portfolios (reflection on performance), and senior seminars (reflection on disciplinary understanding). The volitional strategies students employ include self-regulating attention, affective awareness, and effort to overcome various distractions that may be internal (e.g., lack of self-efficacy, insecurity, or insufficient self-confidence) or external (e.g., financial constraints or social pressure).

PRINCIPLES OF COGNITIVE ENGAGEMENT

Specific features characteristic of positive learning environments may contribute to motivation and cognitive engagement if considered in the design of instruction approaches and assessment strategies. Specifically, Phyllis Blumenfeld and colleagues (2006) put forward key features of learning environments that promote construction of strategies for assessment and documentation of student learning. The features or characteristics of such an environment are not mutually exclusive but are facets of its expression. These include authenticity, inquiry, collaboration, and technology.

Authenticity

The concept of authenticity has come into the higher education assessment field through Harry Torrance's (1995) work on formative assessment in teaching and learning. Authenticity in assessment refers to matching the assessment approach to the educational goals of the particular learning context, with a focus on just what is pragmatic or feasible to satisfy the requirement to assess (Murphy, 2006). Authentic assessment is usually achieved by providing reasons for understanding and opportunities to problem solve that are drawn from physical or social examples in the real world (everyday life experiences), as well as discipline or content-related examples that provide opportunities for application within the design of the instructional format, not as an add-on (Newman, Marks, and Gamon, 1996, as cited in Blumenfeld, Kempler, and Krajcik, 2006). Moreover, the authentic assessment process is typically viewed as integrative in that the assessments are chosen because they can be built into the structure of a course or instructional format and, as such, are likely to improve the odds the learning objectives will be met (Murphy, 2006).

By extension, authenticity within a learning context becomes important for motivating students because it gives them multiple opportunities to work with concepts and create artifacts that enable content and skill acquisition that emanate from a relevant question. Students become motivated and subsequently engaged cognitively via the connection of their values to an outcome or set of outcomes with real-world significance. This significance is "situated in questions, problems, or anchoring events that encompass important subject matter concepts so students learn ideas, processes, and skills" (Blumenfeld, Kempler, and Krajcik, 2006, p. 479). Clearly, internships, undergraduate research, field research, peer teaching, and other authentic approaches to learning provide a rich field for meaningful assessment because students are not only invested in the learning process but also motivated to measure their own learning as part of their commitment to the real-world nature of authentic learning activities.

Inquiry

Approaches based on inquiry provide opportunities for autonomous exploration and application, as well as cultivation of or challenge to intrinsic values held by the individual. Blumenfeld and colleagues (2006) highlight that notions of autonomy and value can be enhanced via the type of artifacts being pursued as a function of cognitive and metacognitive tasks (i.e., self-regulate, reflect, synthesize, plan, execute decisions, evaluate information and data, etc.), as well as the roles the student pursues while undertaking the inquiry (e.g., scientist, philosopher, mathematician, historian, etc.). An aspect of most inquiry-based approaches, sharing findings with instructors and others inside and outside the classroom, also increases a sense of autonomy and value. Ultimately, these higher-level approaches to learning will tend to increase students' notions about the value of work being undertaken and enhance their commitments to the learning enterprise, thereby increasing the odds that measurable learning is taking place at a deeper level.

It is important to note that inquiry-based methods must be constructed intentionally and staggered along a developmental continuum from simple to very complex. Moreover, the expectations related to task and performance should adequately match the developmental level for the student. This can be accomplished if care is taken to articulate the requisite skills and desired outcomes related to inquiry and their anticipated expressions for each stage of learning expected in the learning context. This articulation of skills and outcomes simultaneously builds platforms for both learning and assessment. For example, first-year students may not be able to adequately frame questions or utilize inquiry-based methods at a level that would allow them to probe and understand the underlying reasons for poverty in general, in the United States, or in a given city with the same depth as a junior might be able to explore the same sociopolitical issue. Framing an inquiry-based learning task by taking into account issues of complexity as well as notions of autonomy and value may, quite naturally, also establish the framework for assessing learning. And understanding the relationship between framing the task and evaluating the task is of utmost importance in developing meaningful assessment practices. After all, what students learn depends on how they are taught, not just on what they are taught.

Collaboration

Approaches based on collaboration provide opportunities for students to engage with peers, further motivation for them to become cognitively engaged. "Collaborative learning involves individuals as group members, but also involves phenomena like the negotiation and sharing of meanings—including the construction and maintenance of shared conceptions of tasks—that are accomplished interactively in group processes" (Stahl, Koschmann, and Suther, 2006). Collaborative approaches are especially useful for assessment because collaboration lends itself to computer-based learning approaches by which an artifact or the process of discovery can be mapped and feedback can be injected into the learning process for students: for example, portfolios, distance learning and distributed computing environments, telementoring, writing and literacy support efforts, and simulation (Blumenfeld, Kempler, and Krajcik, 2006; Stahl, Koschmann, and Suther, 2006). Also, learning communities have become an approach to education that builds on notions of collaboration, as noted in Jean Lave and Etienne Wenger's work (1991) on situated learning and communities of practice (as cited in Collins, 2006). In a learning community, the goal is to advance the collective's knowledge base, which in turn supports individual knowledge growth and reinforces motivation for the undertaking (Scardamalia and Bereiter, 1994, as cited in Collins, 2006). The role of collaboration in learning and assessment increases personal notions of responsibility and functions as a "hook" that comes about by being associated with others and building an "intersubjective attitude" or "joint commitment to building understanding" and making unique contributions to work (Palincsar, 1998, as cited in Blumenfeld, Kempler, and Krajcik, 2006, p. 483).

Technology

Approaches based on technology are being adopted in institutions across the higher education spectrum. Technologically supported teaching and learning systems enable these institutions to increase implementation efficiency, make student assessment more learner centered, provide motivational incentives for students to participate, and address lifelong learning needs (Collis and Moonen, 2001; Cotterill, Bradley, and Hammond, 2006; Cuthell, 2002; Kimball, 1998; Laurillard, 1993; Lopez-Fernandez and Rodriguez-Illera, 2009; Preston, 2005; Ross, Jordan, and Butcher, 2006; Scardamalia and Bereiter, 1994; Schank, 1997). Shelagh Ross, Sally Jordan, and Philip Butcher (2006) note the importance of feedback, particularly its role in formative assessment, and contend that technological systems typically enable robust approaches for feedback that motivate students to participate in assessment activities. Lessons learned from many of these authors highlight advantages to technologically assisted approaches: (1) supporting self-diagnosis, reflection, and tutoring support that is synchronous and asynchronous; (2) addressing the procedural difficulties of storage and access related to artifacts; (3) providing less cumbersome feedback tools that allow for iterative feedback processes among stakeholders (students, faculty members, and staff members); (4) enabling the use of prompts to assist in the scaffolding required for engaging at various developmental levels; (5) allowing the students to have more control of their own learning pace; (6) assisting a facilitator or instructor to contextualize assignments and assess progress toward learning goals relative to the students' interests, values, and preferred learning approaches; and (7) enabling assessment techniques that can account for cognition in problem-solving processes. In summary, specific assessment approaches can have a significant impact on student learning as well as a significant role in motivating stakeholders to participate. Some key considerations should be kept in view when developing an institutional assessment for learning approach. (See textbox 5.1 for the details.)

PRINCIPLES APPLIED: REFLECTIVE PORTFOLIOS

In considering the issue of increased attention to cognitive engagement in assessing learning outcomes, leaders must seek assessment designs that employ intentional reflective mechanisms in order to ensure that assessment can both facilitate and measure learning. As textbox 5.1 notes, assessment that enhances learning includes desired outcomes of increasing specific content knowledge, building transferable strategic knowledge, promoting motivation, and strengthening self-efficacy. Often assessment that fosters learn-

---

TEXTBOX 5.1
Key Considerations for Documenting Learning for Assessment Activities

Foundations for Cognitive Engagement
- What is the theoretical or disciplinary rationale behind desired proficiencies, and are they clearly articulated at the program or course levels?
- Are the intervention and instructional rationales clearly articulated and linked to desired learning outcomes for programs, services, and courses?
- Are the outcomes related to facilitating cognitive engagement precisely clarified (i.e., metacognition, learning approaches, attitudes, motivation, etc.)?
- How do the curricular and cocurricular intersect to support the developmental path of students?
- What are the modes for facilitating learning, and how do they support the overall instructional and assessment design philosophy as well as documentation needs at the institution and program levels (e.g., reflection, facilitative techniques, technology, collaboration, and inquiry-based techniques).

Informal Assessment Design Decisions
- Is the full set of learning goals covered by the proposed set of assessments?
- To what degree of specificity are the unique characteristics of the population factored into collection, instruction, and analysis?
- Do baselines and postmeasures map onto desired outcomes for the following: specific content knowledge; transferable strategic knowledge (content neutral); and motivation, self-efficacy, attitudinal, and cognitive and metacognitive skills?
- Are the participants adequately trained to reliably score and generalize findings derived from learning activities for assessment purposes at a level beyond an individual student (e.g., capstone projects, reflection and writing prompts, etc.)?
- At the program and campus-wide levels, who are the individuals or offices charged with the actual implementation and documentation strategies, ongoing review of design fidelity, and incorporation of fidelity review into relevant formative and summative analyses?
- Who is responsible for ensuring technology is available, and adapted, and how is it resourced to meet the initiative's facilitative and documentation requirements.

Source: Adapted from "Assessing for Deep Understanding," by S. Carver, in R. K. Sawyer (Ed.), *The Cambridge Handbook of the Learning Sciences* (p. 207). New York: Cambridge University Press. Copyright © 2006 by Cambridge University Press.

---

ing is going to involve the learner in recursive activities facilitated through reflection on practice. The rationale behind this approach is that it enhances content learning and transferable skills while increasing a sense of control (self-efficacy) and strengthening motivation. "The essential way people get better at doing things is by thinking about what they are going to do beforehand, by trying to do what they have planned, and by reflecting back on how well what they did came out" (Collins, 2006, p. 58). Project-based learning, problem-based learning, inquiry-based learning, and collaborative and constructivist learning approaches—indeed, most approaches—to learning that are based on cognitive engagement incorporate some aspect of reflection. In fact, assessment itself might even be defined as "meta-reflection" at a course, program, or institutional level.

This section will concentrate on one of the most accessible and successful applications of the principles of cognitive engagement (authenticity, inquiry, collaboration, and technology), particularly the element of reflection, into assessment activities: the portfolio. Portfolios provide the most efficient way for students to share their findings, and they reinforce important elements of inquiry. Portfolios are containers for products, artifacts, writing, and visual production, among many possible elements, thus incorporating authenticity, a significant element of cognitive engagement (Annis and Jones, 1995; Banta, 2003; Cambridge, 2001; Fink, 2003; Jafari and Kaufman, 2006; Perry, 1997; Zubizarreta, 2009).

Benefits and Capabilities of Portfolios

Even the simplest portfolio frameworks require that students who create them engage in intentional selection and arrangement, reinforcing aspects of autonomy. Portfolios require not only an ordering process but also a simultaneous evaluative process. As John Zubizarreta (2009) points out about the construction of portfolios, "The process of such reflection tied to evidence promotes a sophisticated, mature learning experience that closes the assessment loop from assertion to demonstration to analysis to evaluation to goals" (p. 42). Portfolios may be shared—created or owned by more than one student—allowing students to collaborate in creative ways. Portfolios provide flexibility of scale, with the capability of delineating work in a single class, a particular major, or an entire curriculum. Portfolios can demonstrate the link between general education and the student's major. They can demonstrate the acquisition of skills and their growth over time. Portfolios can be flexible, and they can be revised based on feedback to demonstrate mastery of concepts. Since an increasing amount of the portfolio assessment occurs in a digital environment, electronic portfolios (popularly abbreviated as *e-portfolios*) can incorporate building of technology skills as well as allowing for assessment of the learner's technological capabilities, while enabling collaboration (Banks, 2004; Cambridge, 2001; Jafari and Kaufman, 2006; Stefani, Mason, and Pegler, 2007). In all, portfolios represent the crossroads of assessment and cognitive engagement, employing many aspects of the latter in service to the former.

In his 1998 article "Teacher Portfolios: A Theoretical Activity," Lee Shulman pointed out some of the advantages of using portfolios. His points support the above principles of cognitive engagement, as follows:

1. Complexity and autonomy: "Portfolios permit the tracking and documentation of longer episodes of teaching and learning" (Shulman, 1998, p. 35).
2. Technology and feedback: "Portfolios encourage the reconnection between process and product" (p. 36).
3. Collaboration: "Portfolios institutionalize norms of collaboration, reflection, and discussion" (p. 36).
4. Authenticity: "A portfolio introduces structure to . . . experience" (p. 36).
5. Autonomy: "And really most important, the portfolio shifts the agency from an observer back to the [student]" (p. 36).

Electronic Portfolios

In the comments quoted above, Shulman was primarily describing the use of e-portfolios in teacher education, where they have indeed become the norm. While the National Council for Accreditation of Teacher Education (NCATE) has required e-portfolios in teacher education for some time, more and more institutions are turning to e-portfolios to track a variety of learning processes in a variety of disciplines, including assessment of learning outcomes. A recent survey of Association of American Colleges and Universities (AAC&U) members, conducted by Hart Research Associates, sums up the increase in use of e-portfolios in a graph that shows that 57 percent of the AAC&U member institutions that responded to their survey were using electronic portfolios, 29 percent were exploring the feasibility of using them, and 14 percent did not use them and had no current plans to develop them (Rhodes, 2009). Of those who used electronic portfolios, 42 percent reported that they were using them for assessment as well as other purposes (p. 11). Additionally, Elizabeth Clark and Bret Eynon (2009) note that "the ePortfolio Consortium lists 894 institutional members, nearly 60% of them American colleges and universities . . . across all higher education sectors . . . [evidence that] the use of e-portfolios has tripled since 2003" (p. 18).

Obviously, e-portfolios are gaining in popularity; Clark and Eynon summarized why. These authors described the ease with which e-portfolios may be used for assessment but gave other reasons that emphasize the ways in which portfolios use principles of cognitive engagement—particularly authenticity, collaboration, and technology—to impact the learner and the learning process, not merely to provide evidence for accountability. First, they cited the switch from teacher-centered to learner-centered pedagogies: "Defining students as authors who study their own learning transforms the traditional power structure, asking faculty to work alongside students as co-learners" (Clark and Eynon, 2009, p. 18). They also noted the growth in digital communication technologies and the ease with which millennial students employ these Web 2.0 technologies: "In an age of multimedia self-authoring, student interest in creating rich digital self-portraits has grown exponentially. . . . A digital portfolio for student learning speaks the language of today's student body" (p. 18). Finally, they cited the "increasing fluidity in employment and education" (p. 18). With increasing numbers of students transferring, both from two- to four-year institutions and among four-year institutions, as well as taking courses at multiple institutions, an e-portfolio may become "an educational passport" that students could also take into the employment arena, demonstrating links between their education and their professional aspirations and experiences (p. 19). In an ideal world, lifelong learning might lead to lifelong e-portfolio development, both enriching learners' self-understanding and self-efficacy and also providing ongoing evidence, often hard for institutions to come by, of how student learning has affected professional growth: "The vision of an e-portfolio as a lifelong learning tool that is updated throughout life has considerable institutional implications" (Stefani, Mason, and Pegler, 2007, p. 12).

When students are asked to describe their experience with e-portfolios and process the value of the enterprise, many heartily echo the experts:

> I feel that the process has enhanced my understanding for the overall higher education experience. . . . I have always felt confused and irritated by the lack of connection between my general education requirements and my core department requirements. I think that the e-portfolio is a great way to link the two types of classes. . . . I am a very visual person and the template of the e-portfolio was easy to follow and it truly helped to achieve the goal of linking my personal work to my personal goal. I also believe that this process was very empowering for me. It is easy to get discouraged with work that you complete during classes because you complete a paper, receive a grade, and then that paper is simply stored in a folder on your computer. This process helped me to look back on the work that I had completed in prior classes and place more value on the work that I had created. I was able to value the work because each assignment that I complete I have taken one step closer to completing a personal or professional goal of my own. (Miller and Morgaine, 2009, p. 8)

Rubrics

E-portfolios, along with more traditional material for assessment like timed essays, artifacts, and performances, constitute only the "content" of assessment. The "form" for assessment in these cases is generally provided by rubrics. In some ways, rubrics are much like "scaffolding" in that they provide a description of both the characteristics and levels by which to either achieve or evaluate performance. They increase cognitive engagement by matching expectations for a task or performance with a description of the demonstrated developmental level. Rubrics tell the student and the assessor what performance should look like at each stage or level.

The creation and application of rubrics is often the task of the single professor, who may well use them to not only judge student work but also guide that work, demonstrating expectation as well as evaluating performance. Rubrics may also be the joint effort of faculty members participating in a specific discipline or teaching a specific skill, like writing. Rubrics can provide a structure for assessing general education learning outcomes or institutional goals. The larger the group creating the rubric, ranging from the single professor to the institutional level, the more the rubric reflects consensus about expectations for student learning, but also the more diffuse and general the rubric becomes. Rubrics can be agreed upon by disciplinary bodies and by accrediting agencies as well as by educational organizations seeking to define "fundamental, commonly held expectations for student learning, regardless of type of institution, disciplinary background, part of country, or public or private college status" (Rhodes, 2009, p. 5).

PORTFOLIO-BASED ASSESSMENT PROJECTS

To illustrate the nature and potentials of portfolio assessment, this section will examine in detail two portfolio-based assessment efforts, one national in scope (AAC&U VALUE initiative) and the other institutionally based (University of South Florida's Cognitive Level and Quality of Writing Assessment [CLAQWA] program).

AAC&U VALUE Project

The AAC&U is working with institutions that have a history of successful use of student e-portfolios to develop "meta-rubrics," or shared expectations of student learning, that institutions can apply across fourteen of the AAC&U's designated essential learning outcomes. This project, the Valid Assessment of Learning in Undergraduate Education (VALUE) is developing meta-rubrics or "essential learning outcomes" in the areas of intellectual and practical skills (such as critical and creative thinking, written and oral communication, quantitative and information literacy, inquiry and analysis, and teamwork), personal and social responsibility (such as ethical reasoning, civic and intercultural knowledge, and foundations for lifelong learning), and integrative learning (Rhodes, 2009).

In developing the VALUE project, the AAC&U is basically challenging the arena of competency testing (MAPP, CLA, and CAAP) by creating a scalable assessment process that does not depend on sampling small numbers of students outside their required courses, does not depend on the unmotivated good-will of students, and does not neglect the learning feedback loop to students and faculty members. Instead, the VALUE project is based on locally gener-ated products of student achievement across a wide variety of types, including graphical, oral, digital, and video, since it is based on e-portfolio collections of student work. This project has employed rubric development teams in all of the above areas and tested the resulting rubrics on a range of individual campuses. Researchers are currently in the process of creating national panels to apply, review, and test the usefulness of the rubrics. The three national panels will consist of faculty members who are familiar with rubrics and e-portfolios but were not involved in the development of the rubrics, faculty members who are unfamiliar with the use of rubrics and e-portfolios, and a panel of employers, policy makers, parents, and community leaders (Rhodes, 2009).

The VALUE project argues that faculty members, academic professionals, and public stakeholders can develop and apply national standards of student learning and that those standards should both arise from and be applied to lo-cally produced authentic student learning products. These products would be easily housed in an e-portfolio system but could be compiled in other formats, since campuses that did not gather student work electronically also examined selections of student products and participated in developing the rubrics. This project garnered much attention from the assessment community during its rollout by AAC&U in late 2009 and 2010. However, it is important to re-member that achieving a scale that is sufficient for accountability efforts and for useful comparison of institutions, reflecting consensus about expectations for student learning, can lead to diffuse and general rubrics. Such rubrics can be difficult to link back to the individual classroom, thus having little impact on the individual student and potentially creating problems for scor-ers, resulting in low inter-rater reliability. Participants in the VALUE project are aware that the promise of scale brings with it the problems of scale and have suggested attempting to make the project useful in more specific learn-ing environments:

> The VALUE rubrics, as written, must then be translated by individual cam-puses into the language, context, and mission of their institution. Programs and majors will have to translate the rubrics into the conceptual and academic constructs of their particular area or discipline. Individual faculty will have to translate the rubrics into the meaning of their assignments and course materi-als in order for the rubrics to be used effectively to assess their student assign-ments. (Rhodes, 2009, p. 7)

University of South Florida CLAQWA Project

While it is a promising beginning, the VALUE project will prove useful to produce assessment that affects student learning as well as measures it only if individual faculty members and students are willing to make and value these modifications. It is further enlightening to examine programs that have managed to scale up at least to the institutional level but still have learning impact in the classroom. One such program is the CLAQWA program, developed by Teresa Flateby and her associates at the University of South Florida.

For many years, the University of South Florida had used timed-writing assessments scored with the writing portion of the College Level Academic Skills Test (CLAST), which measured reading, writing, and mathematics skills. The essays produced by the timed-writing assessment were holistically scored by external evaluators. Assessment leaders on campus were discouraged both by the weaknesses revealed about students' writing skills and the inability of the assessment method to identify forms of remediation. As Flateby (2007) wrote, "Although determining the achievement level of our students is important, assessment's major contribution to learning is providing the information needed to enhance student learning outcomes. In addition to having little formative data, our assessment process was further flawed by its lack of inclusion of our faculty" (p. 216).

Around 1999, the University of South Florida began to assess writing with a campus-developed instrument that had originally been created to measure learning in the interdisciplinary portion of the University of South Florida's General Education Learning Community. The instrument, the CLAQWA, incorporated both skills and cognitive-level evaluation, based on the work of Benjamin Bloom. Flateby (2007) explained that it "encourages faculty users to consciously consider the cognitive level expected for an assignment, enables self and peer review, and facilitates a multidisciplinary approach to writing assignments" (p. 214). The CLAQWA uses seventeen writing elements organized into the following categories: assignment parameters, structural integrity, reasoning and focus, language, grammar, and mechanics.

The University of South Florida has trained undergraduate and graduate assistants as scorers who work with faculty scorers to develop consistency in scoring. Most significant, the CLAQWA helps the faculty not only assess assignments but also create assignments; it has also been widely used in peer review activities in which students read and make suggestions for revision of other students' work. Faculty members "found that their students' writing and thinking skills improved . . . with the new CLAQWA adaptation [for peer review]" (Flateby, 2009, p. 135). Indeed, the remarkable thing about the CLAQWA is the way it has impacted instruction significantly while also providing assessment data. In fact, Flateby (2007) claimed that "many faculty

members [who use the CLAQWA rubric for peer review] report improvements in their own writing" (p. 221).

For the AAC&U's VALUE program to have a similar impact, it must pay
considerable attention, as the University of South Florida did, to the local and
the disciplinary uses of its rubrics. Faculty members will value and support
assessment projects that they perceive to have a real and demonstrable relationship to student learning. Students will value and support assessment that
allows them to reflect on their practice and gives them feedback about their
performance. Thus, learning outcomes assessment does not necessarily thrive
in an environment in which the highest priorities are clarity and simplicity in
the system and a common language that can be used consistently within the
higher education community.

Rather than invest in bureaucratic structures of assessment and large-scale
competency testing, which tend to oversimplify and homogenize the task, institutions might see more gains in assessment by investing in faculty development and increasing faculty understanding and pedagogical use of cognitive
engagement practices. Both constituencies, faculty members and students,
might profit from a greater understanding of how a focus on authenticity,
inquiry, collaboration, and technology can increase learning. In *Proclaiming
and Sustaining Excellence: Assessment as a Faculty Role*, Karen Maitland
Schilling and Karl L. Schilling (1998) have listed conditions by which faculty
members, and by extension students, will identify assessment as worthy of
meaningful engagement:

- Assessment must be grounded in significant questions that faculty [and
  students] find interesting.
- Assessment must rely on evidence and forms of judgment that disciplinary
  specialists find credible [and students in that discipline find applicable].
- Assessment must be identified as a stimulus to reflective practice.
- Assessment must accommodate the nature of faculty [and student] life in
  the academy. (p. 85)

When conditions like these are met, both faculty members and students will
value the process of assessment and gain from it.

ORGANIZATIONAL SUPPORT

As noted in the opening section, we argue that assessment processes that
both measure student learning and contribute to student learning have strong
links to faculty development, augmented by other campus offices (e.g., in-

stitutional research, assessment, planning, etc.). Of particular interest is the potential for increasing faculty members' understanding of their role in the "learning sciences," which encompass design-based instruction, research, and assessment. Our argument places the locus of assessment within the actual learning context. To this end, we find it critical that higher education organizations "rethink" their structures for facilitating engagement in processes that improve student learning while measuring learning outcomes.

Faculty members, program developers, and research staff members are keys to constructing a meaningful approach to the design and enhancement of learning environments consistent with these assessment goals. This participation is likely to occur at sufficient levels only when an institution provides the organizational support to advance instructional and program research and design work pertinent to the particular learning context of a content or disciplinary area. Specifically, evidentiary approaches aimed at fulfilling external accountability requirements are necessary but not sufficient for sustained and meaningful assessment work. Rather, institutional-level support must be given to assessment work carried out in departments that generate evidence-based claims about learning that address performance and accountability requirements. Such evidence should simultaneously addresses the contemporary theoretical issues of a particular field and the professional requirements found in a given institution (e.g., tenure promotion). In essence, design-based assessment frameworks at their core should spur the creation of "theoretically inspired innovation" that translates into enhanced practices aimed at addressing outcomes within a particular learning environment (Barab, 2006, p. 155). This engages faculty and research staff members where they live and recognizes the unique and varied contexts of learning in a higher education organization.

An institution that supports such a focus will afford faculty and research staff members opportunities to carefully acquire and utilize the appropriate instructional designs and tools for increasing strategic and content knowledge among students. Further, those engaged in assessment must be able to disentangle the particular conditions under which an interaction or occurrence happens within a particular learning context, recognize the complexity of these iteratively changing environments, and collect evidence pertaining to these variations as it may inform future assessment designs and curriculum enhancements. This work then becomes scalable for the institution's accountability and effectiveness needs and will have a higher likelihood of being efficiently implemented and saving time, energy, and resources. Thus, it may impact curricular practices in similar contexts, enabling faculty and research staff members to address general knowledge development in their fields and fulfilling the external and internal accountability and performance requirements of the current policy environment.

In many respects, the organizational and fiscal support to aid participants in understanding the complexity that exists within a particular learning context, fully appreciating the nuances of discipline-based curricula and providing tools for sound methodological and instructional approaches, might include a variety of campus offices (i.e., assessment and accountability offices, institutional research offices, planning offices, school and college or department assessment functions, teaching or instructional learning centers, instructional technology offices, measurement centers, etc.). Many of the aforementioned offices have important pieces of their operations carved out to support key activities that serve learning design and assessment. But the aggregate effect of this multilayered and distributed approach is imbalance in staffing, budgets, and technical resources as well as inconsistent alignment of work by these offices and their consumers to institutional mission and goals.

Despite these obstacles, many faculty and staff members manage to become deeply engaged in particular assessment initiatives and validate the findings they generate from this work. However, given organizational and funding realities, the support given to faculty members and researchers engaged in design of instruction and assessment is rarely adequate to allow real, systemic connections to discipline- or content-specific requirements that have a direct influence on understanding learning in a given instructional context. As such, the actual professional or disciplinary requirements that call for advancing theory and knowledge in the field for these individuals ultimately gets neglected or diminished. The faculty member or researcher has little incentive for participating, and the institution loses out on a richness of work that would likely have more significant impact if support was better organized and more broadly provided.

In conclusion, campus leaders are challenged to ensure that organizational structures either leverage current funding and support or receive additional funding and support for cultivating work within a specified learning context. Otherwise, the credibility of the enterprise and the campus-wide staff involved centrally in assessment and accountability endeavors will be compromised out of existence. This diminishes buy-in across and within programs and units and also facilitates cynicism and a notion that participants have heard it all before. Additionally, and possibly more important, the nuanced, integrative, and adaptive requirements necessary for the subsequent construction and assessment of specific learning environments might be better supported, enhanced, and managed through synergies developed with an integrated approach that intentionally and consistently solicits department-specific expertise to support this complex of activities. To this end, there is not sufficient evidence in the literature or in practice to support the notion that most campuses are adequately supporting the faculty or research staff within departments or programs with the requisite funding and flexibility required to iteratively design, implement, and assess the effects of a particular learning context.

We contend that a campus that addresses the requirements of assessment for learning in a nuanced and thoughtful manner will simultaneously recognize the accountability and performance demands placed upon it and efficiently address the teaching, research, and methodological support necessary for faculty members and researchers to fully engage in authentic assessment. This approach will yield "theoretically inspired innovation" in a particular field and inform implementation while allowing the institution to say something contextually meaningful about student learning while in the process increasing the odds that the learning will be significant.

NOTE

1. The VSA, developed by university leaders, is sponsored by two higher education associations: the Association of Public and Land-Grant Universities (APLU) and the Association of State Colleges and Universities (AASCU). Initial funding was provided by the Lumina Foundation. For more information, please visit the following url: www.voluntarysystem.org/index.cfm.

REFERENCES

Annis, L., & Jones, C. (1995). Student portfolios: Their objectives, development, and use. In P. Seldin & Associates, *Improving college teaching.* Bolton, Mass.: Anker.

Association of American Colleges and Universities. (2005). *Liberal education outcomes: A preliminary report on student achievement in college.* Washington, D.C.: Author.

Banks, B. (2004). E-portfolios: Their uses and benefits. Retrieved December 7, 2009, from http://ferl.becta.org.uk/display.cfm?resID=8089.

Banta, T. W. (2003). *Portfolio assessment uses, cases, scoring, and impact.* San Francisco: Jossey-Bass.

Barab, S. (2006). Design-based research. In R. K. Sawyer (Ed.), *The Cambridge handbook of the learning sciences* (pp. 153–169). New York: Cambridge University Press.

Black, P., Harrison, C., Lee, C., Marshall, B., & Wiliam, D. (2003). *Assessment for learning: Putting it into practice.* Buckingham, UK: Open University Press.

Black, P., & Wiliam, D. (1998). Assessment and classroom learning. *Assessment in Education, 5,* 7–71.

Blumenfeld, P. C., Kempler, T. M., & Krajcik, J. S. (2006). Cognitive engagement in learning environments. In R. K. Sawyer (Ed.), *The Cambridge handbook of the learning sciences* (pp. 475–488). New York: Cambridge University Press.

Cambridge, B. L. (Ed.). (2001). *Electronic portfolios: Emerging practices in student, faculty, and institutional learning.* Washington, D.C.: American Association for Higher Education.

Clark, J. E., & Eynon, B. (2009). E-portfolios at 2.0: Surveying the field. *Peer Review, 11*(1), 18–23.

Collins, A. (2006). Cognitive apprenticeship. In R. K. Sawyer (Ed.), *The Cambridge handbook of the learning sciences* (pp. 47–60). New York: Cambridge University Press.

Collis, B., & Moonen, J. (2001). *Flexible learning in a digital world.* London: Kogan Page.

Cotterill, S., Bradley, P., & Hammond, G. (2006). Supporting assessment in complex educational environments. In C. Bryan & K. Clegg (Eds.), *Innovative assessment in higher education* (pp. 191–199). New York: Routledge Taylor & Francis Group.

Cuthell, J. P. (2002). MirandaNet: A learning community—A community of learners. *Journal of Interactive Learning Research, 13*(1), 167–186.

Dwyer, C. A., Millett, C. M., & Payne, D. G. (2006). *A culture of evidence: Postsecondary assessment and learning outcomes.* Princeton, N.J.: ETS.

Fink, L. D. (2003). *Creating significant learning experiences in college classrooms: An integrated approach to designing college courses.* San Francisco: Jossey-Bass.

Flateby, T. L. (2007). University of South Florida: General education case study. In M. J. Bresciani (Ed.), *Assessing student learning in general education* (pp. 210–223). Boston: Anker.

Flateby, T. L. (2009). Developments and changes resulting from writing and thinking assessment. In C. S. Schreiner (Ed.), *Handbook of research on assessment technologies, methods, and applications in higher education* (pp. 135–151). Hershey, Pa.: IGI Publishing.

Hart Research Associates. (2009). Learning and assessment: Trends in undergraduate education. A survey among members of the Association of American Colleges and Universities. Retrieved November 15, 2009, from www.aacu.org/membership/documents/2009MemberSurvey_Part1.pdf.

Jafari, A., & Kaufman, C. (2006). *Handbook of research on ePortfolios.* Hershey, Pa.: Idea Group.

Kimball, L. (1998). Managing distance learning: New challenges for faculty. In S. H. R. Hazemi & S. Wilbur (Eds.), *The digital university: Reinventing the academy* (pp. 25–38). London: Springer-Verlag London.

Laurillard, D. (1993). *Rethinking university teaching: A framework for the effective use of educational technology.* London: Routledge.

Lave, J., & Wenger, E. (1991). *Situated learning: Legitimated peripheral participation.* New York: Cambridge University Press.

Lopez-Fernandez, O., & Rodriguez-Illera, J. L. (2009). Investigating university students' adaptation to a digital learner course portfolio. *Computers and Education, 52,* 608–616.

Miller, R., & Morgaine, W. (2009). The benefits of e-portfolios for students and faculty in their own words. *Peer Review, 11*(1), 8–12.

Murphy, R. (2006). Evaluating new priorities for assessment in higher education. In C. Bryan & K. Clegg (Eds.), *Innovative assessment in higher education* (pp. 37–47). New York: Routledge Taylor & Francis Group.

Newmann, F. M., Marks, H. M., & Gamon, A. (1996). Authentic pedagogy and student performance. *American Journal of Education, 104*, 280–312.

Palincsar, A. S. (1998). Social constructivist perspectives on teaching and learning. *Annual Review of Psychology, 49*, 345–375.

Perry, M. (1997). Producing purposeful portfolios. In K. B. Yancey & I. Weiser (Eds.), *Situating portfolios: Four perspectives* (pp. 182–189). Logan: Utah State University Press.

Preston, D. S. (2005). *Virtual learning and higher education.* Amsterdam: Rodopi.

Rhodes, T. (2009). The VALUE project overview. *Peer Review, 11*(1), 4–7.

Ross, S., Jordan, S., & Butcher, P. (2006). Online instantaneous and targeted feedback for remote learners. In C. Bryan & K. Clegg (Eds.), *Innovative assessment in higher education* (pp. 123–131). New York: Routledge Taylor & Francis Group.

Sawyer, R. K. (2006). *The Cambridge handbook of the learning sciences.* New York: Cambridge University Press.

Scardamalia, M., & Bereiter, C. (1994). Computer support for knowledge-building communities. *Journal of the Learning Sciences, 3*(3), 265–283.

Schank, R. C. (1997). *Virtual learning: A revolutionary approach to building a highly skilled workforce.* New York: McGraw-Hill.

Schilling, K. M., & Schilling, K. L. (1998). *Proclaiming and sustaining excellence: Assessment as a faculty role.* ASHE-ERIC Higher Education Report 26(3). Washington, D.C.: George Washington University Graduate School of Education and Human Development.

Shulman, L. (1998). Teacher portfolios: A theoretical activity. In N. Lyons (Ed.), *With portfolio in hand: Validating the new teacher professionalism* (pp. 23–27). New York: Teachers College Press.

Stahl, G., Koschmann, T., & Suther, D. D. (2006). Computer-support collaborative learning. In R. K. Sawyer (Ed.), *The Cambridge handbook of the learning sciences* (pp. 409–425). New York: Cambridge University Press.

Stefanakis, E. (2002). Multiple intelligences and portfolios. Portsmouth, N.H.: Heinemann.

Stefani, L., Mason, R., & Pegler, C. (2007). *The educational potential of e-portfolios: Supporting personal development and reflective learning.* New York: Routledge.

Sutton, R. (1995). *Assessment for learning.* Manchester, UK: R.S. Publications.

Torrance, H. (1995). *Evaluating authentic assessment.* Buckingham, UK: Open University Press.

Torrance, H., & Prior, J. (1998). *Investing formative assessment: Teaching, learning, and assessment in the classroom.* Buckingham, UK: Open University Press.

Zubizarreta, J. (2009). *The learning portfolio: Reflective practice for improving student learning.* Bolton, Mass.: Anker.

Chapter Six

Learning Outcomes, Assessment, and Program Improvement

Russell T. Osguthorpe, Bryan D. Bradley,
and Trav D. Johnson

University administrators must be concerned with the quality of their academic programs so that their institutions can meet requirements for accreditation. They must also find ways to convince the faculty that meeting such requirements will actually improve teaching and lead to increased student learning. Some faculty members wonder if writing learning outcomes is a meaningless exercise to meet an imposed requirement, since some have taught successfully for years without articulating such outcomes. The key to helping these faculty members see the value of learning outcomes is to focus on the assessment of student performance—helping faculty members see that careful course and program design can improve what students learn in their courses. This chapter describes the process and potential benefits of aligning learning outcomes with course, program, and institutional goals. We begin with a case study from an academic department in our university.

A TRUE CASE STUDY

Preparations for accreditation were well underway at a large university in the United States. The central administration had repeatedly stressed accreditation requirements with college deans, and now the deans were working with departments to make sure the needed actions and documentation were forthcoming. One department chair contacted the campus Teaching and Learning Center for help. He explained, "My department doesn't like this learning outcomes stuff. We haven't done a thing. We know that the administration is anxious about accreditation, and we know we have to do something. We don't really know where to start, and many of our faculty are opposed to this idea. Can you give us some help?" This general response is not uncommon.

Many deans and chairs feel confused and overwhelmed when they receive a request to document the establishment, assessment, and steps taken toward achieving learning outcomes.

In this case, the department chair did find help. A consultant from the Teaching and Learning Center responded by requesting to meet with all faculty members in the department to discuss learning outcomes in a way that would be understandable and, hopefully, acceptable to them.

Approaching Unmotivated Faculty

The consultant found the faculty in the department to be every bit as resistant as the department chair had reported. They had no interest in addressing learning outcomes and wanted to get this requirement off their backs as quickly, and with as little effort, as possible. The consultant started the discussion by asking the department faculty what they hoped for in their retirement. Various responses were given, such as sufficient 401(k) funds, resources to travel, time to visit family (especially grandchildren) and friends, and good health. The consultant then asked what they were doing to make sure these retirement goals would be achieved, including how they knew they were on track. Responses were clear and specific.

The consultant then explained to the faculty members that establishing, assessing, and working to achieve learning outcomes works the same way as planning for retirement. The most important thing is to identify their most important goals for students in their courses—what they most want students to learn and become. The consultant explained what he would do to help them once they identified these outcomes. They shouldn't worry about conducting assessments and changing programs at this point; these aspects would be taken care of later with his help.

After this initial meeting, the consultant and department chair decided on the efficient strategy of working with faculty members in one program in the department and then having these individuals help disseminate the important ideas and processes to other department faculty members. The department chair asked that the consultant begin with the most challenging program in the department. The faculty members in this program didn't get along very well with each other and certainly wanted nothing to do with learning outcomes.

Choosing and Organizing Outcomes

The consultant began this application by asking the ten faculty members in the selected program to send him a list of what they wanted most for students to gain from each of their classes. They had to list at least one outcome, but not more than three, for each course they taught. The consultant collected the information and organized it for the next meeting.

The consultant and the faculty members then met to categorize the submitted course outcomes with the established program learning outcomes. (The program outcomes had been written at an earlier date by one person in the department with little input from other department faculty members. This situation was not ideal, but it had to be their starting point.) In this meeting, each participant took three course learning outcomes written by another faculty member, critiqued the outcomes, identified the program-outcome category (or categories) in which the course outcome should be placed, and discussed this analysis with the faculty member who had originally written the outcome. Then the course outcome was written on a strip of paper and taped on the wall under a banner indicating the appropriate program outcome. This process was repeated until all course outcomes were critiqued and categorized under appropriate program outcomes (or under a miscellaneous category).

During this meeting, something happened that faculty members did not expect: they started talking with each other about teaching, student learning, and their goals for students enrolled in their program. The department chair said he had never seen faculty members open up like this in his department, especially in this particular program. The faculty analyzed the course and program outcomes and started to make some decisions on what they wanted most and how their course and program outcomes should be organized. The consultant took the ideas generated by the program meeting and created a new document with outcomes for each course connected with revised program outcomes.

Assessing and Achieving Outcomes

The next meeting focused on how to assess outcomes. This step was particularly baffling to most of the faculty members in this program because they had been teaching courses that relied primarily on professional critique and qualitative judgments; there were few, if any, numbers and a dearth of "hard" evidence. The consultant helped faculty members understand that expert judgment is sufficient, even if it is subjective and qualitative, as long as the conclusions can be supported by clear rationale or supporting evidence.

Finally the group considered how they could maintain an ongoing process for establishing, assessing, and working to achieve learning outcomes without requiring too much work. They decided to begin by making sure course learning outcomes were included in each course syllabus so these would be available to students and faculty members throughout the department. They determined that sample student papers would be used to assess outcomes. A short form was developed that faculty members could use to indicate the

Table 6.1.   A Framework for Linking Student Learning with Program Improvement

	Learning Outcomes	Student Performance	Program Improvement
Worth	Is the outcome worth achieving?	Is the assessment tied to real-life skills?	Is the proposed change worth implementing?
Alignment	Is the outcome aligned with program and university goals?	Is the assessment aligned with learning activities and outcomes?	Do the data provide convincing evidence for the proposed change?
Feasibility	Is the outcome achievable in the time allotted?	Is the assessment cost effective?	Are resources adequate to implement the proposed change?

degree to which the outcomes were met in each course and to determine what changes could be made to increase students' achievement of the outcomes in the future. Periodically, some faculty members would be asked to share their analyses and insights in department meetings. In addition, at the end of each semester, faculty members would submit a manila folder for each course they taught with a list of the learning outcomes, samples of student work that showed the level of outcome achievement, and the completed one-page form analyzing student work.

To disseminate the process throughout the department, three faculty members from this program were selected to share what they had learned with faculty members from other programs. The case study shows that faculty can change their views on the worth of writing learning outcomes. At one point, many faculty members in the department felt that writing outcomes was an exercise administrators were requiring simply for accreditation. Gradually, however, when faculty members came to see how outcomes could be used to redesign their courses and improve student learning, they became significantly more invested in the endeavor. Table 6.1 lists nine related questions that administrators can ask themselves as they attempt to improve student learning, strengthen programs, and prepare for accreditation. At each stage in the process—choosing learning outcomes, developing assessments, and evaluating proposed changes, one might ask questions regarding *worth*, *alignment*, and *feasibility*.

QUESTIONS FOR SELECTING LEARNING OUTCOMES

Is the Outcome Worth Achieving?

The case study shows that, when learning outcomes are written and made public, they often change the way a teacher teaches. In the case study, when faculty members began examining their own outcomes more closely, they found some outcomes to be more defensible than others. They judged some outcomes to be of higher worth for the students to achieve. This question of worth is prerequisite to all other questions. It is an act of human judgment; it can be made at many levels and in a variety of ways, but it must be made before offering a program or creating a course.

Each time a faculty member writes an outcome for a course, he or she must ask the question "Is this outcome worth teaching?" For example, consider the following outcome: "Students will be able to list three events that led to the Civil War." On the surface this appears to be a perfectly worthwhile course objective. But compare the next outcome: "Students will be able to apply accepted standards to conduct interviews and write an oral history." In the first outcome, students are required to memorize factual events. In the second, students have to learn and apply the skills of a historian. Most would consider the second outcome of more worth to the student.

John Biggs and Catherine Tang (2007) state that "good teaching is getting most students to use the level of cognitive processes needed to achieve the intended outcomes" (p. 11). The ultimate goal of education is to help students become proficient at *doing* something they could not do before receiving the instruction. Good teaching, then, demands that instructors help students develop the cognitive processes that are required to *do* the target skill.

Is the Outcome Aligned with Program and University Goals?

A given learning outcome might be worthwhile but not aligned with program or university goals. A University Curriculum Council at our institution reviewed a proposal that would add a "coaching minor" for students who wanted to coach community youth teams but did not wish to certify to teach in the public schools. As university leaders considered the proposal, they first questioned the need for this particular minor, but then the discussion gradually centered on one question: "Should our university be the place where this training is offered?" Leaders agreed that this additional minor would not require allocation of additional resources, that there was a need in the community for such preparation, and that students would enroll. But most agreed that the coaching instruction should likely be offered by another institution rather than by our university. The learning outcomes of this program were worthwhile, but they did not align well with the university mission and goals.

Individual faculty members might also find that certain outcomes in their courses are worthwhile but do not align well with program goals. The case of the department described at the beginning of this chapter illustrates this point. When faculty members began to make their learning outcomes public, they could see that some course outcomes did not seem to fit into program goals as well as they had thought when they were designing the course. This form of scrutiny is one of the central benefits of making our teaching public, as Lee Shulman and Pat Hutchings (2004) have taught so effectively. Sharing learning outcomes with each other as faculty members and administrators also reveals redundancy and sequencing problems in the overall curriculum. All of these issues are related to alignment of outcomes. Accrediting bodies usually place a burden on institutions to defend their programs by showing how each program leads toward attaining university purposes and mission. Thus, the university mission must be clear, program directors and deans must ensure that their curricular offerings fit that mission, and individual faculty members must design their courses in ways that lead to mastery of program goals.

Is the Outcome Achievable in the Time Allotted?

A learning outcome might be worthwhile and aligned with program and university goals but may be impossible to achieve in the time allotted. Most course outcomes must be achieved within a semester or quarter. Program outcomes for baccalaureate degrees must be achieved within four years. The question of feasibility for learning outcomes is not trivial. When students complain about workload when they are asked to rate the quality of courses, they either say that the learning activities were "busy work," which means that they spent time but did not learn from the activity, or they say that the workload was far too heavy and they could not complete the assignments in the allotted time.

While reviewing student comments for a course, the senior author noticed that students tended to complain about the unrealistic amount of time required to complete assignments. A typical comment would read something like this: "This was a two-credit course, and I usually had to spend over ten hours a week to complete the assignments. One assignment that we had one week to complete took twenty hours." When the department chair confronted the faculty member and asked how he planned to deal with the problem, the faculty member defended the workload by saying that he prided himself on teaching "hard" courses. None of the students complained that the assignments were not worthwhile, but most felt that too much was required in too little time.

In another course, students complained that the course did not teach them anything they had not known before taking it. "I don't see why this course is required. I got an A, I did the work, but I don't feel like I learned anything." In the first case, students felt that the assignments were valuable but unrealistically demanding. In the second case, students felt that the outcomes were not worthwhile, so the time they spent was not profitable. As faculty members and administrators design programs, these issues must always be at the center of the discussion.

QUESTIONS FOR DEVELOPING ASSESSMENTS

Is the Assessment Tied to Real-life Skills?

When students praise a course or a faculty member, the most common comments center on *relevance*. When students see how they can apply knowledge from the course, they are naturally more motivated to learn, and the newly learned skill stays with them longer. At the center of most educational institutions' raison d'être is the aim to help students *become* educated citizens who can contribute to the community in which they live. But *becoming* is a lofty goal that constantly shifts. If a student is to become something, he or she needs to acquire new knowledge and develop new skills. This is the "know, do, be" developmental process.

Students who wish to become expert in a foreign language must learn grammar, vocabulary, and cultural practices. They must come to *know* the language and people. But they also must *do* the language. They must become proficient in speaking it and writing it, and proficiency requires actually doing these things—a very different kind of practice than learning grammatical rules. Eventually, the student *becomes* different because of the new knowledge and skills. The student is able to live in a foreign culture and may have developed new attitudes toward a people, toward language learning, or toward learning in general.

Although the teacher may not be able to measure effectively the changes in *being* for a given student, *knowing* and *doing* can be assessed. The point of this chapter is that the more the teacher measures skills that are tied to real-life actions, the more learning and retention will occur. For example, the foreign-language instructor must eventually measure the articulation and writing skills of the student. If the teacher gives tests that ask the student to restate a grammatical rule, it is likely that some students will be able to restate the rule but not be able to use it. Actual performance of the target task is essential if student learning is to be improved. The only way to identify the gap between where a student is now performing and where the student should perform is to measure real-life skills—in this case speaking or writing the foreign language.

One acknowledged shortcoming of higher education is that assessments often rely too heavily on knowledge and not enough on skills. Science courses may place too much emphasis on memorizing terms, history courses on memorizing facts, and math courses on using predetermined algorithms.

When faculty members and administrators engage in conversation about the worth of learning outcomes, the performance measures inevitably emerge. Faculty members usually want their students to learn how to think and act like a scientist, historian, or mathematician, but the measures they use to assess the performance of students often include only items related to *knowledge*. Asking how well assessments measure real-life skills is essential if a faculty member wants to improve student learning or if an administrator wants to improve a program.

Is the Assessment Aligned with Learning Activities and Outcomes?

One of the primary frustrations for college students is that "the tests did not measure what I learned in the course"—an alignment problem. Biggs and Tang (2007) explain that outcomes that are aligned with activities and assessments motivate students and help "ensure that academic activities are meaningful and worthwhile" (p. 37). To illustrate, while pursuing a graduate degree, the senior author completed an introductory programming course in which the final exam did not align with the course learning outcomes. On the day of the final, the professor entered the classroom and said,

> You may not feel prepared to do this, but here is the problem I want you to solve for the final. You have just been appointed the dean of admissions at a large university with selective admissions policies. Your task is to write a program that can be used to determine whether a student will be admitted to the university. You will need to base your admissions decision on as many variables as you see fit, such as ACT scores, high school GPA, personal essay scores, advanced placement course scores, leadership experience, and character reference letters. You will have three hours to complete your program.

As one who was required to complete the exam, I felt unprepared, inadequate, and ill fitted to succeed. During the semester we had never been required to complete a program that resembled the one we were asked to do on the final. But I did my best. I was unable in the time allotted to get the program to run successfully. I did not have time to debug it sufficiently, so I thought I had failed. When grades came out, I received an A. I was so perplexed by the grade, since I had done poorly on the final, I went to see the professor. I asked him, "So why did I get an A in the course if I could not complete the final successfully?" "Well," he responded, "no one in the class actually succeeded on the final, but you did better than the others, so I gave you an A."

My professor had an alignment problem with the outcomes, assignments, and final exam. The learning outcomes and assignments had actually been quite well aligned. Students in the course learned new programming concepts and procedures and then applied them in assignments included in the text. But the final was on a completely different level, perhaps more appropriate for an advanced programming course. This problem is common with university faculty members. Most agree they feel inadequate when faced with the task of developing assessment tools for a course. They have never studied measurement theory or test development, and yet they are required to create valid and reliable measures for their courses.

In addition to course-level assessments needing to be aligned with course-level outcomes, program assessments need to be aligned with program-level outcomes. If administrators are to determine the effectiveness of programs, they must use evaluation tools that are aligned with the program goals (see Banta, Jones, and Black, 2009)—assessment techniques must lead to evaluation practice. To make decisions regarding programs improvement, one needs more than course-level assessment data. Stakeholders (e.g., students, faculty members, administrators, and employers) need to be interviewed for their perceptions of program effectiveness (see Banta, Jones, and Black, 2009). Most institutions administer "senior or alumni surveys" that focus on student perceptions of the programs they have completed. But additional data from other stakeholders are also necessary before program changes are recommended. Alignment with learning outcomes at the program level is just as essential as at the course level.

Is the Assessment Cost Effective?

Assessment strategies must be tied to real-life skills, be aligned with learning outcomes for the course or program, and also be cost effective. For example, someone might recommend that the final papers students submit in their freshman writing course be graded by a panel of three faculty judges. Although the results of such an assessment strategy might be more valid and reliable than having only one reader judge paper quality, it may not be cost effective if there are four thousand freshmen enrolled in the course.

The most important purpose of assessment strategies in a classroom is to provide feedback to students that they can use to improve their performance on selected learning outcomes—sometimes called *feedforward* (see Fink, 2003; Maki, 2004; Swan, 2008; Wiggins, 1998). In a meeting with graduate teaching assistants who were preparing to teach our university's freshman writing course, the senior author asked, "Can anyone give me a learning outcome that you plan to achieve in your course?" One student said, "Yeah, rhetoric." I responded, "Well, the word *rhetoric* by itself may not be a learning outcome. What do you mean by that?" She thought for a moment and then said, "Learning how to write with a purpose." I agreed that learning how to write with a purpose was a worthy goal for such a course.

If "writing with a purpose" is a worthy goal, how would it be assessed? Would students be asked to go to a testing center and complete a multiple-choice exam that included writing examples that they would rate according to how well the author wrote with a purpose? Would students be required to submit three papers, each on a different topic for a different audience, and demonstrate their ability to write with a purpose? If so, who would judge the quality of the papers? Faculty members? Other students? Graduate teaching assistants?

Although the multiple-choice exam would be the easiest to administer and grade, it would likely not be the most effective way to measure "writing with a purpose." To demonstrate this objective the student would need to engage in the act of writing, and then someone would need to judge the degree to which the student had met predetermined standards regarding that outcome. Each option (faculty members, teaching assistants, or other students) has implications for both effectiveness and cost. Faculty members are the most costly and other students, the least costly. On the surface, one might conclude that the faculty members' judgment would be more effective than that of the graduate assistants or peer students. But if graders were given the right training, that might not be the case. Peer feedback can be extremely effective when students are given some sort of checklist with standards for judging the artifact. Peer feedback can meet Dee Fink's (2003) criteria of being "frequent, immediate, and discriminating" (p. 100).

QUESTIONS FOR EVALUATING PROPOSED CHANGES

Is the Proposed Change Worth Implementing?

When the outcomes are judged to be worthwhile and assessments measure real-life skills, gaps between desired and actual performance often emerge. Consider this hypothetical case study. Administrators decide to survey employers regarding their perceptions of the quality of the graduates they have been hiring from the university (see Suskie, 2004). When asked to identify shortcomings of graduates, the employers consistently refer to two weaknesses: (1) students need to become more skilled at collaborating in teams, and (2) students need to be more capable in writing clear proposals, memos, and reports. When faculty members and administrators examine the program being assessed, they notice that students are seldom asked to collaborate and that they are seldom required to write except in their general education courses. Administrators and faculty members decide together to strengthen these two aspects of their curriculum.

As they begin to redesign courses and insert more teamwork and writing outcomes, some begin to question the worth of certain changes; they don't know how far to take the curriculum change. Should more writing and teamwork outcomes be integrated into every course? Or should only the capstone course be changed? Would all courses be strengthened if these two aspects were heightened? Or might the insertion of these two new elements actually weaken certain courses? How many faculty members would need to buy into the proposed change? How would students view the intended changes? In summary, is the change worth implementing? These are evaluative questions—questions that must be addressed by multiple stakeholders. But they are essential questions to answer before moving forward with any proposed change that is intended to improve a program.

Do the Data Provide Convincing Evidence for the Proposed Changes?

We encourage an evidence-based change process. Academic programs are often changed despite the absence of defensible data simply because an administrator or faculty member decides that a change is needed. Two types of data are needed to guide change: (1) assessment of learning outcomes and (2) evaluation data showing program effectiveness (see Suskie, 2004). In the case study regarding students' writing and teamwork skills, the data from employers would not be enough. Once the evaluative data from employers had been gathered, administrators and faculty members would need to examine assessment data to determine what types of writing and teamwork skills had been poorly mastered, where these skills had been taught, and what types of learning activities had been assigned to address these skills.

Even with data from learning assessments and evaluation studies, changes do not define themselves. These data provide the basis on which to discuss ways of improving. For example, assessment data from an introductory science course showed that 20 percent of the students were failing the course each semester. Because this course was required for graduation, the students who failed needed to retake the course. Doing so was difficult for the students and costly for the university. Learning assessment data showed that, early in the course, shortly after the first test, many students dropped the course because they were failing. Evaluative data collected from interviews with students showed that students who dropped or later failed felt that the course was primarily concerned with memorizing new terms and concepts.

When administrators and faculty members discussed the data, some felt that those teaching the course should simply cover less material so that students could digest it more effectively prior to the test. However, another group of faculty members felt that the content should be shifted to a more problem-based curriculum. They felt that, rather than asking students to memorize new terms and concepts, they should ask students to develop the skills to investigate questions in a scientific manner—actually to *do* science. The data alone did not dictate the changes; they showed that changes were needed. The pedagogical and philosophical stances of the faculty members and administrators led to the changes that were actually recommended. They decided to proceed with a more problem-based approach. Failure rates decreased significantly.

Are Resources Adequate to Implement the Proposed Change?

Following an analysis of assessment and evaluation data, one department decided to reduce class size. Classes had typically enrolled eight hundred students per section. This kept costs for the faculty low, but students often felt ignored and expressed frustration in mastering what they were required to learn. When department leaders determined that they would reduce class size, they calculated the cost to the institution for such a change. New faculty positions would need to be added in order to accomplish the goals of the change. Administrators listened to the requests and became convinced that the proposal was worth pursuing. Additional faculty positions were not allotted quickly. However, the department held to the original proposal, and the new positions were eventually granted. Assessment and evaluation data showed that the newly structured classes with smaller enrollments increased student learning.

In an organization that is constantly learning how to improve, data provide the basis for program change. Assessment and evaluation data are essential to inform faculty members and administrators regarding needed improvements in their academic offerings. The example of the department that decreased class size and added faculty positions shows that, even when most may believe that resources are inadequate to implement a proposed change, data can lead to approval when they are convincing enough.

CONCLUSION

We began this chapter by describing the experience of a real department that learned to use outcomes and assessment to improve their academic programs.

We conclude with a succinct set of principles that administrators and faculty members can use as they examine the quality of their current offerings and devise plans to strengthen them.

Principles for Effective Program Improvement

1. Learning outcomes can be an effective foundational tool for strengthening academic programs when faculty members come to see the value of using them to improve student learning.
2. Alignment affects every aspect of program change. Outcomes and assessments must be aligned with each other and with university goals. Proposed changes must be aligned with assessment and evaluation data.
3. Assessment of learning outcomes, combined with evaluative data from all stakeholders, provide the evidence upon which effective program changes are implemented.
4. When faculty members and administrators make public their course and program learning outcomes and assessments, collaborative effort can focus on ensuring that the outcomes and assessments are worthwhile, aligned, and feasible.
5. Relevance of learning outcomes in students' lives and alignment with institutional goals are the primary determinants of the worth of an academic program.
6. Learning outcomes can be categorized into three types: (a) knowing, (b) doing, and (c) being. Outcomes in the *knowing* and *doing* categories are easier to measure than those in the *being* category. If a course focuses only on *knowing* outcomes, students will likely be less motivated and hence will learn less than if the balance shifts toward *doing* outcomes (skills).

REFERENCES

Banta, T. W., Jones, E. A., & Black, K. E. (2009). *Designing effective assessment: Principles and profiles of good practice.* San Francisco: Jossey-Bass.

Biggs, J., & Tang, C. (2007). *Teaching for quality learning at university.* New York: Open University Press.

Fink, L. D. (2003). *Creating significant learning experiences.* San Francisco: Jossey-Bass.

Maki, P. L. (2004). *Assessing for learning: Building sustainable commitment across the institution.* Sterling, Va.: Stylus.

Shulman, L. S., & Hutchings, P. (2004). *Teaching as community property: Essays on higher education.* San Francisco: Jossey-Bass.

Suskie, L. (2004). *Assessing student Learning: A common sense guide*. Bolton, Mass.: Anker.

Swan, R. H. (2008). Deriving operational principles for the design of engaging learning experiences. PhD diss., Brigham Young University, Utah. Retrieved December 21, 2009, from http://contentdm.lib.byu.edu/u?/ETD,1854.

Wiggins, G. (1998). *Educative assessment: Designing assessments to inform and improve student performance*. San Francisco: Jossey-Bass.

Part Three

ASSESSMENTS THAT TRANSFORM
THE LEARNING CULTURE

Chapter Seven

Student Engagement and a Culture of Assessment

Jillian Kinzie

Concern about improving student learning and success in college has never been greater. Legislative bodies, regional accreditors, and the broader public are applying pressure to make higher education more accessible and affordable to a wider range of students, improve graduation rates, and assume more accountability for what students are supposed to learn and how well they are, in fact, learning it. A student population that is increasingly diverse in terms of ethnic identity, age, preparedness levels, and motivations for entering college compounds the pressure and creates a complex context for assessing and improving student learning (Borden and Pike, 2008; El-Khawas, 2005; Ewell, 2002; Suskie, 2004). These demands have shaped campus assessment activities, recasting the meaning of educational effectiveness to require that institutional assessment and improvement strategies ultimately support learning and result in improving it (Ewell, 2008). Accrediting agencies in particular are insisting that colleges and universities use evidence to demonstrate that students are learning. The assessment movement is clearly about change. Against this backdrop, leaders at colleges and universities face a significant challenge to enhance the student experience and demonstrate improvement.

In this complex context of assessment, it is critical to stay focused on activities that lead to improvements in student learning and success, and thus on measuring the processes that lead to student learning. Measurements of the extent to which students engage in educationally purposeful activities—behaviors that research shows influence learning and development—provide fundamental diagnostic information about educational quality that can be used in improvement efforts. Understanding what students *do* in their undergraduate program and how to use this information to improve has been furthered by the emergence of student engagement as an organizing construct for assessment and improvement efforts. Student engagement involves a straightforward focus on the activities that matter to learning and development and also underscores the institution's role in setting up conditions that induce students to participate in meaningful educational activities. Armed with information about what students do, in addition to other more direct measures of learning outcomes including general and specialized knowledge, skills, abilities, dispositions, and values that result from a program of study, campus leaders will be equipped to improve teaching and learning.

Many campuses have made significant advances in assessment practices that drive improvements in student learning and success. While in the early 1990s only about half of college and university administrators surveyed believed that assessment can lead to improvement in undergraduate education (El-Khawas, 1995), more recent reports suggest that the perception of assessment to improve is more favorable (Banta, Jones, and Black, 2009; Kuh and Ikenberry, 2009). For example, according to a recent Association of American Colleges and Universities (AAC&U) report, *Learning and Assessment: Trends in Undergraduate Education* (Hart Research Associates, 2009), the majority of campuses reported that they have a common set of intended learning outcomes for all their undergraduate students and are focused on assessing students' achievement of these outcomes across the curriculum. However, most institutions still find it hard to use evidence for systematic improvement, and few report having well-developed assessment plans to sustain a culture of assessment.

Institutions that have adopted a student engagement framework for assessing and improving the conditions for student success and have made good progress toward educational reform offer instructive and inspirational models of how to advance assessment activities that lead to improvements in learning. In this chapter the lessons learned from twenty educationally effective institutions profiled in *Student Success in College* (Kuh et al., 2005) are reexamined considering information from additional institutions that have advanced a framework for student engagement and success. Some of the new additional institutions were funded by the Teagle Foundation to support improvement of student learning through assessment, while others have been recognized by the AAC&U and Council for Higher Education Accreditation (CHEA) for their assessment work.

This chapter introduces a framework for assessment based on student engagement and success, then highlights nine characteristics of campus assessment activities associated with improvements to student learning. For convenience, characteristics are grouped according to their focus on (1) strong leadership, (2) inclusive involvement, or (3) outcome-based program function. With each characteristic, campus examples are given to illustrate assessment activities intended to achieve what Linda Suskie (2004) identified as the most important goal: to use carefully considered evidence to improve teaching and learning.

A STUDENT ENGAGEMENT FRAMEWORK FOR ASSESSMENT

One keystone for colleges and universities in addressing the challenge of enhancing the student experience and maximizing positive outcomes for student learning has been the emergence of student engagement as an organizing construct for institutional assessment and improvement. Student engagement—as identified with the National Survey of Student Engagement (NSSE) and its two-year counterpart the Community College Survey of Student Engagement (CCSSE)—is a straightforward concept. *Engagement* is the extent to which students participate in educationally purposeful activities and the degree to which institutions allocate their human and other resources and organize learning opportunities and services to induce students to participate in and benefit from such activities (Kuh, 2001). The engagement construct is prominent in assessment work because it focuses attention on what students actually *do* in terms of their investment in effective educational practice, thereby underscoring the role that institutions have in structuring educationally purposeful activities and encouraging students to take part.

Emergence of Student Engagement as an Assessment Concept

The focus on student engagement as a meaningful construct for institutional assessment and improvement has been outlined in several notable publications associated with student success and effective institutional performance, including "Seven Principles for Good Practices in Undergraduate Education" by Arthur Chickering and Zelda Gamson (1987) and *Making Quality Count in Undergraduate Education*, Peter Ewell's synthesis produced for the Education Commission of the States (1995), which fleshes out related factors and conditions in more detail. These publications plainly indicate that colleges and universities have a responsibility to do more to foster student learning. Moreover, George Kuh and colleagues (2005b) assert that "educationally effective colleges and universities—those that add value—channel students' energies toward appropriate activities and engage them at a high level in these activities" (p. 9). Quite simply, the colleges and universities that have the most impact on students engage their students in these effective educational practices. The consistent message across these volumes is that enhancing student engagement should be a central priority at all institutions of higher education.

Engagement is a useful concept for assessing and improving undergraduate education at all types of colleges and universities. Over the last ten years, the framework has been advanced through NSSE and CCSSE, and through the more than 1,400 NSSE-participating colleges and universities that have utilized student engagement in their assessment activities. NSSE results provide diagnostic information about student and institutional performance—process indicators for learning outcomes—to inform campus improvement efforts. Specifically, student engagement data expose strengths and shortcomings in the educational experience and focus institutional attention on areas for improvement in the undergraduate program.

Propositions Underlying Use of a Student Engagement Framework

Information gained through student engagement data is useful in all institutional assessment agendas intent on improving student learning. However, the adoption of a strong student engagement framework for assessment rests on five propositions.

First, a framework built on student engagement and success broadly signifies a commitment to collecting information from students to measure educational effectiveness and to make improvements to enhance student learning. Student input is central to understanding how to enhance student learning. This commitment is grounded in the belief that students' self-reported behaviors and perceptions about the learning environment provide good evidence about the quality of the undergraduate experience. Additionally, what counts in student learning and development is what students *do* in college—not what their entering board scores are or how satisfied they are with their experience. Finally, a critical component of this principle is a belief that what students do is not simply about student volition but rather highly dependent on the conditions that the institution sets up to induce students to do the right things.

Second, a student engagement framework demands consideration of the whole student and appreciates aspects of the undergraduate experience inside *and* outside the classroom that are consistent with good practice in undergraduate education. The framework emphasizes personnel across the university caring deeply about each student's growth as a whole person, which is made evident through efforts to engage, equip, and enable students to succeed in college via educationally effective practices, policies, and programs. Campus leaders must create opportunities for collaboration among students, administrators, faculty members, student affairs professionals, librarians, and community stakeholders for assessment and educational reform initiatives. Student affairs professionals must continue to devise complementary programs and outcome assessments to extend learning into campus environments beyond the classroom and to foster partnerships with academic units to enrich student learning and development.

Third, an important corollary to the emphasis on the whole student is the consideration that engagement is not a one-size-fits-all way of thinking. As the college impact literature shows, engagement has conditional effects: students with certain characteristics benefit more from some educational activities than from others. Because of the variation in engagement among students at an institution, data depicting the "average" student experience can mask noteworthy differences in educational quality. These principles call attention to issues of equity in the student experience, and the implication for the institution is that variation within the student experience must be examined (Kuh, 2008; National Survey of Student Engagement, 2008a). Results must be disaggregated by gender, race and ethnicity, first generation in college status, transfer status, major field of study, and other characteristics that are associated with differences in the quality of the student experience, particularly those differences that perpetuate inequitable educational opportunities and outcomes.

Fourth, a student engagement framework incorporates an all-encompassing definition of student success (Kuh et al., 2007) that is concerned with not only student retention and graduation but also academic achievement; engagement in educationally purposeful activities; satisfaction; acquisition of desired knowledge, skills, and competencies; attainment of educational objectives; and postcollege performance. Student success should not be measured solely by access statistics and graduation rates. Rather, student success must be concerned with the overall quality of students' educational experience. Such a perspective demands that campus leaders appreciate diverse sets of quality indicators and develop valid, reliable measures of student goal attainment, course retention, transfer rates and success, and success in subsequent coursework—to name just a few. For example, measures of success in subsequent coursework are important measures for students who have been historically underrepresented in specific majors and are significant at institutions that provide remedial education. Campus leaders must consider an array of indicators to determine the right course of action to improve student success.

Fifth, to achieve the ultimate goal of improving student learning, the connections between student success and institutional effectiveness must be emphasized. This link is enacted via an ethos of continuous improvement, in which information is used to assess institutional performance, pinpoint where improvement is necessary, inform change strategies, and monitor effectiveness, with the goal of improving student success. Kuh and colleagues (2005b) called this continuous improvement ethic *positive restlessness* to denote the drive for richer, continuous improvements and deeper outcomes. Campus leaders must foster a culture in which data inform decision making and the process is sustained by an intentional focus on creating conditions for all students to succeed.

Over the past decade, many colleges and universities have adopted a student engagement framework and have advanced their assessment activities to improve student learning and success. Assessment and improvement practices were highlighted as essential components of the Documenting Effective Educational Practice (DEEP) project, an in-depth examination of high-performing colleges and universities. These educationally effective institutions, commonly referred to as "DEEP schools," profiled in *Student Success in College* (Kuh et al., 2005b), were identified as operating with a well-developed ethos of improvement, displaying a level of positive restlessness toward change, a deep investment in student success, and an orientation to use data for decision making.

The nine characteristics that follow were distilled from the DEEP schools, plus other institutions featured in funded assessment projects. Recognized by leaders in the assessment movement, these characteristics are proposed as essential lessons for campus leaders striving to operationalize a student engagement framework to advance improvements in the quality of undergraduate education.

CHARACTERISTICS FOCUSED ON STRONG LEADERSHIP

Successful programs begin with strong foundations: committed, supportive leadership that is focused on implementing assessment dedicated to improvement, not satisfied with assessment that merely provides records and fulfills mandates. Leadership is strengthened by ensuring the meaningful involvement of a range of administrators, faculty members, and board members.

Intentional Focus on Improvement

As pointed out in "Never Let It Rest" (Kuh et al., 2005a), institutions that excel at what they do in terms of student engagement and success are characterized by an intentional focus on institutional improvement, beginning with the president and members of the administration. These institutions are bent toward innovation, continuously experimenting with new approaches for improving teaching and learning; to maintain momentum, they monitor what they're doing, where they are, and where they want to go. Leaders at these institutions are confident about the institution and support its values and aspirations; they have the courage to question whether performance matches potential. Supporting this orientation toward improvement is a "can-do" ethic that permeates the campus and reflects willingness to take on matters of substance related to student success. At most of these campuses, visionary executive leaders have pointed the way and actively promoted an improvement agenda. Although executive leaders were instrumental in bringing about some of the changes themselves, more often they motivated, monitored, encouraged, and supported others who were working on assessment and improvement initiatives. In this sense, the influence of campus leadership on advances in assessment that drive student learning cannot be overestimated.

Establishing an ethos of improvement in a college or university is not easy. It requires a deep commitment to educational quality and to the belief that even at the best institutions there is room for improvement. In addition, campus leaders must be curious about and routinely ask questions related to educational effectiveness: How well are students learning? How could we improve the undergraduate experience to enhance student learning and success? Similarly, faculty members, administrators, support staff members, trustees, and students are brought together frequently to collectively explore the answers to these questions and implement improvements in student learning.

Improvement-oriented institutions rely on systematic information to make good decisions. For example, under supportive leadership at the University of Texas at El Paso (UTEP), continuous assessment studies are conducted to assess the quality of the University College and related student success initiatives and to learn ways to become more effective in providing a challenging and productive learning environment for diverse students. The various components of UTEP's Entering Student Program (ESP), a comprehensive campus-wide collaborative effort to address the needs of first-year students through integrated enrollment, orientation, and advising programs, as well as content-based programs, a first-year seminar, student leadership institute, and high-quality tutoring, are evaluated each term by students, faculty members, and peer leaders (Kuh et al., 2005b).

In addition, UTEP's president, deans, and institutional research staff members closely monitor persistence and graduation rates, and student progress indicators such as satisfaction and GPA are incorporated in the review of various programs, along with qualitative data to better understand student perspectives that can help interpret the quantitative indicators. UTEP's priority is identifying what the institution can do to help students succeed and graduate. Leaders support initiatives like the Student Success Project, an externally funded three-year research project, to identify factors related to students' graduating in six years, having left UTEP temporarily and reenrolled, to provide a more nuanced understanding of UTEP students. Leaders at institutions with a strong ethos of improvement do not shy away from data that might expose shortcomings in the educational program; rather, leaders are eager to identify multiple, robust measures and take a hard look at data to understand how to enhance the student experience.

Institutions that enact positive restlessness are places where leaders encourage pedagogical experimentation and support pilot programs to improve student learning and success. For example, campus leaders encourage faculty members to experiment with innovative pedagogy, and they recognize and reward faculty members for doing so. Student affairs professionals and administrators are provided the support to test new programs and policies and then determine the extent to which these initiatives have made a difference to student success. In addition, assessment and institutional research professionals work in partnership with the faculty and staff on evaluation and assessment plans to understand the impact of pilot projects. Most important, faculty and staff members know that their efforts to experiment and take risks will be appreciated even if the pilot does not fully achieve its intended goals.

An example of the kind of experimentation through pilot programs emblematic of an ethos of improvement was displayed at the University of Wisconsin, Green Bay (UWGB). Administrators and institutional research staff members shared NSSE results with a wide campus audience. A team of dedicated faculty members were concerned about first-year student results, which were statistically lower than those of students at similar colleges on virtually all aspects of educational engagement, particularly on the active and collaborative learning and student-faculty interaction benchmarks. These low engagement scores helped prompt a pilot first-year seminar course advocated by a group of committed faculty leaders to improve the quality of the first-year experience (Griffin and Romm, 2008). The UWGB faculty created six sections of freshman seminar, capping each section at twenty-five students to encourage greater student-faculty and peer interaction, and included in their course design an interdisciplinary exercise and cocurricular activities. The faculty team collaborated with the office of institutional research to evaluate the initiative using pre- and posttesting and a control group design (University of Wisconsin, Green Bay, 2009). The final assessment revealed that freshman seminar participants were significantly more engaged across a variety of indicators than their peers who were not in the seminar.

The UWGB freshman seminar pilot received the necessary support from campus leadership; the team was provided resources for course redesign and faculty development through the UW system Office of Instructional and Professional Development, and participants were encouraged to disseminate their findings at conferences. Administrative leaders at UWGB used results from the pilot to increase the number and variety of freshman seminars. Results also reinforced the importance of partnering with the Office of Student Life to promote greater involvement in cocurricular activities. Since the thirteen new seminars were implemented, UWGB leaders have been closely monitoring NSSE results and other measures of first-year student persistence and success. They have been pleased to see an uptick in the key indicators of active and collaborative learning and student-faculty interaction and 6 percent increase in retention, suggesting that the new seminars are having the intended effect (Bartel and Ritch, 2010; University of Wisconsin, Green Bay, 2009).

Assessment that is conducted in an ethos of improvement focused on student learning and success demands continuous monitoring of the conditions for student success, decision making informed by data, and involvement of a range of stakeholders in assessment. Leaders at UTEP have a well-developed sense of data-informed decision making, and they continuously assess the impact of their initiatives on key student success measures. As at UWGB, campus leaders ensure that pedagogical experimentation and pilot projects are encouraged and rewarded. Positive restlessness is engendered and sustained when the faculty and staff do not fear that a low course evaluation or a decline in program participation will negatively influence instructor evaluations and annual reviews and when campus leaders demand evidence of effectiveness to make decisions, using data to continuously monitor and direct improvements in the undergraduate experience.

Strong Administrative Leadership

Once the priority on student learning has been established and the faculty and staff feel secure in experimentation, administrative leaders must encourage widespread involvement and provide strong support if assessment and improvement efforts are to be effective. Strong presidential leadership, chief academic officers and deans who make student learning assessment a priority, and faculty members dedicated to discovering how well their students learn and who implement pedagogical practices that improve student learning are critical to assessment. To unify the efforts of faculty and staff members, leadership including presidents, provosts, vice presidents, and deans must reaffirm the importance of assessment results. Additionally, leaders must surround themselves with talented colleagues—especially senior academic and student affairs personnel—who work well together to implement policies and practices that realize the institution's mission. For example, at Miami University of Ohio, academic and student life administrators speak with one voice in campus publications and forums to remind faculty and staff members of their commitment to collaboration on behalf of student success.

Formalizing the linkage between academic units and student affairs on assessment activities can be particularly beneficial. Colorado State University (CSU) operates a campus-wide continuous improvement system known as PRISM (Plan for Researching Improvement and Supporting Mission) that exemplifies an effective formal collaborative arrangement (Colorado State University, 2007). The emphasis the university places on collaboration between students and academic affairs is symbolized by the participation of nearly all CSU academic programs and student affairs units in the PRISM online database, with established assessment plans, explicit outcomes statements, reported results, and documented improvements. CSU claims that the structured, transparent collaborative assessment planning among academic and student affairs units reduces the insular state of some student affairs units and furthers the impact of assessment information by reaching a wider audience (McKelfresh and Bender, 2009). The structured arrangement also facilitates joint action by students and academic affairs units to conduct more in-depth explorations through student focus groups and interviews to examine disconcerting results and cull solutions related to student engagement.

Expanded Board Involvement

In *Making the Grade* (2006), Ewell makes the case for greater involvement of boards of trustees in the heart of the academic enterprise—the quality of teaching and learning. Ewell advises trustees to require that learning outcomes be spelled out, to demand that their institution develop meaningful assessments of student learning to document actual results, and to insist that what is learned from assessment activities inform efforts to improve student learning and success. Trustees should monitor educational performance as keenly as they monitor financial performance.

Former Harvard president Derek Bok (2005) urged college and university trustees to consider student engagement data, advising trustees to inquire, "Does the college participate in NSSE? If so, what steps are taken to act on the results?" Administrators at dozens of institutions report positive effects from sharing their NSSE results with trustees. Presentation of survey results to the Academic Committee of the Carroll University Board of Trustees reinforced proposed initiatives to improve the first-year experience and to increase faculty and staff accessibility to students. The president at Eckerd College regularly shares results with the board; results showing that Eckerd students' scores exceeded scores at comparison institutions on many meaningful learning activities have reinforced trustee confidence in the quality of learning at the institution. At other institutions, results have been shared to advance institutional priorities. For example, Allegheny College (in Pennsylvania) shared NSSE results on the quality of diversity experiences extensively with faculty members, staff members, and trustees to document the need to enhance campus diversity initiatives. Some institutions also feature NSSE data as part of their institutional accountability reports to trustees. For example, Swarthmore College (also in Pennsylvania) shared results from specific NSSE items that are central to the institution's mission as feedback to the trustees and the president's staff regarding the extent to which they were fulfilling their institutional mission.

Board members can demonstrate their support for collaborative, integrated programs and services by reviewing the quality of academic and campus life policies and functions together and asking how various initiatives complement one another. To ensure that such reviews occur, the board should assess its committee structure to confirm that one of its committees is responsible for monitoring key indicators of student engagement. As Kuh (2005) advised, college and university presidents should work intently to share meaningful assessments of educational quality with their trustees and collaborate with trustees to help hold the institution accountable for improved performance.

CHARACTERISTICS FOCUSED ON INCLUSIVE INVOLVEMENT

One of the most important lessons from decades of research on student persistence is that retention is not the responsibility of admissions or student affairs and that it cannot rest on the efforts of a lone "retention coordinator." Student retention is everyone's business, a shared responsibility on campus (Tinto, 2006). Assessment and improvement initiatives in a student engagement framework should be inclusive efforts: faculty members, staff members, students, and even representatives from other campuses should be involved in collaborative efforts.

Campus-wide Involvement in Assessment

Although educationally effective institutions usually assign specific individuals or groups the responsibility for efforts to assess and improve student learning and for monitoring the status and impact of improvement initiatives, the success of these efforts demands widespread investment by all members of the campus community. The involvement of a range of stakeholders in assessment and improvement must begin with creating the assessment plan, continue through collecting evidence and interpreting results, and culminate in using student learning evidence to guide improvement activities.

Assessment in a student engagement framework is an inclusive endeavor. Widespread involvement helped a small private university in the Midwest (Midwestern University [MWU]—pseudonym) make sense of assessment results and improve the conditions for student success. NSSE results revealed that students' scores on measures of academic challenge—specifically the amount of time students spend preparing for class and their perceptions about the institution's emphasis on studying—were significantly below those of students at comparable institutions. Members of the president's cabinet suspected that something about the MWU experience lessened the amount of time students spent studying. Focus groups with students and faculty members, interviews with campus staff members, and evaluations of campus space were conducted to elaborate on the results and determine how to enhance the student experience.

Findings revealed that students were rarely studying in their residence halls; however, science faculty members and custodians reported that students were using classroom space in the science center after class hours for group and individual study. Although the building was supposed to be closed in the evenings, students found the science center convenient for studying, convening groups to complete projects, and watching movies on a big screen. Sharing assessment results with a range of campus stakeholders—including students, physical plant staff members, campus safety officers, faculty members, and librarians—led to a collective effort to understand and improve access to students' preferred study space and to enhance the environment for studying in the library and residence halls. As with these stakeholders at MWU, nearly everyone at an institution has a role in decisions about educational quality and should be involved in assessment and improvement plans.

The promotion of whole campus involvement in assessment and improvement further emphasizes the importance of placing the responsibility for student engagement on faculty members, staff members, and administrators. Quite simply, because engagement is defined as a measure of institutional quality, institutions must be intentional about creating educationally engaging learning environments. Shaun Harper and Stephen Quaye (2009) offer practical guidance for institutions willing to accept their responsibility for engaging all students. When all members of the campus community start asking how well our students are learning, it becomes evident that improving learning requires a team effort. Both the principles of embedding assessment in institutional practice and making assessment everyone's concern demonstrate that assessment to improve student engagement and learning should never be the sole responsibility of a single office or position.

Meaningful Student Involvement in Assessment

As students are the main stakeholders in the assessment process (Suskie, 2004), special efforts must be made to be sure that they are extensively and meaningfully involved. Perhaps the most obvious example of meaningful assessment for students is the assessment of their performance at the classroom level. This evaluation provides students with important information about how they are doing, exposes difficulties, provides students with a measure of their mastery of knowledge and skills, and allows them to understand their improvement over time. Involving students in assessing their own learning increases their self-efficacy, engagement, and learning, as well as reduces their reliance on grades as the sole measure of their performance (Banta and Palomba, 1999; Suskie, 2004). Alverno College's innovative abilities-based, assessment-as-learning approach to education (see www.alverno.edu/about _alverno/ability_curriculum.html) is a strong example of involving students in the assessment of their learning via the use of self-assessment and portfolios.

Students should also be involved in the broad accountability and improvement activities of the institution. The most fundamental type of student involvement in institutional assessment is as survey respondents or as learning outcome assessment test takers. While this level of involvement is obviously essential to gathering information about student learning, it is sometimes the most challenging to achieve. Advice about increasing student participation in surveys and noncompulsory assessment activities abounds (Porter, 2004). Certainly, there is great variation in institutional student survey response rates. For example, in 2008 the average institutional response rates on NSSE was 37 percent, with a large majority of institutions ranging from 20 to 60 percent (National Survey of Student Engagement, 2008b).

Most institutions must dedicate considerable attention to increasing student participation in assessment activities. By examining their campus culture, administrators can determine appropriate methods to reach their students. A good place to begin is with the recommendations of survey research expert Don Dillman (2007), who found that participation is associated with the perceived importance of the survey (value to the student and perceived legitimacy), the level of interest students have in the topic, respondent trust, perception of rewards for participation, and (low) perceptions of respondent burden. In addition, publicity about assessment activities should help send a message to the whole campus that the data are valuable for institutional improvement. All this contributes to building a culture of assessment in which students have a stake.

An example of an approach that was successful in increasing students' stake in assessment is from the University of Louisville (UofL). A public, metropolitan research university, with more than twenty thousand students, UofL is committed to continuous self-assessment, ranging from programs for student engagement to campus climate opportunities. Inspired by a strong Kentucky legislature interested in improving universities and increasing the number of postsecondary degree holders in Kentucky, UofL launched a comprehensive undergraduate-quality initiative designed to achieve excellence in undergraduate education (University of Louisville, 2001).

With assessment information and institutional effectiveness activities as the foundation for their plans, UofL's Office of Academic Planning and Accountability set a specific goal to increase student participation in assessment activities as reflected on NSSE. For the spring 2009 NSSE administration, the university launched an extensive campaign to increase student participation by emphasizing the importance of students' views in enhancing the undergraduate experience. UofL created a marketing plan, coordinated by a core team of eight, including faculty members, institutional research administrators, assessment professionals, and marketing experts. Many forms of advertisement were used, including outdoor banners, yard signs, posters, website banner ads, newspaper ads, and a dedicated website. The central message of the campaign was that every student voice matters, advanced via the slogan "Every Card Counts"—a wordplay on their mascot, the cardinal. To promote the survey, advertisements emphasized this theme, and undergraduates were quoted with such statements as "My voice matters. This February I'm taking the NSSE survey to let UofL know about my undergraduate experience." Through these efforts, in 2009, UofL doubled its NSSE response rate from 2007. By obtaining a greater investment of students, faculty members, and staff members in NSSE, UofL is changing the culture of assessment on campus and laying firm groundwork for a successful culture of evidence.

Students should also be involved in more in-depth and long-range assessment and improvement initiatives. For example, Boston College (BC) administrators were curious about the nature of seniors' responses to the Higher Education Research Institute's College Senior Survey (CSS) items related to diversity and campus climate. BC seniors reported fewer experiences with diversity, such as socializing with someone of another racial or ethnic group during the past year or attending a racial or cultural awareness workshop, and indicated lower perceptions about their ability to get along with people of different races and cultures and their knowledge of people from different races or cultures. To explore what might account for these results, the director of assessment worked with the staff in residence life to conduct interviews with seniors concerning their diversity experiences. By adding student voices and specific examples of institutional practice, faculty members and other educators on campus had more information to plan approaches for increasing students' experience with diversity.

Buffalo State College, a member of the State University of New York (SUNY) system, conducted an in-depth assessment initiative with students. Administrators used their NSSE results to identify areas that were of concern to campus educators and then invited students to "student stakeholder forums" to explore what the college could do to support and enhance their success related to these issues. Nearly two hundred students participated in a series of forums that required them to reflect on their experience and to contribute information to the college's ongoing planning efforts. The forums were structured so that each participant had an opportunity to give voice in a facilitated group to needs and concerns related to his or her experience. Nominal group techniques were used to report concerns to the group, followed by large group sharing and identification of key priorities. Faculty members, staff members, and senior-level administrators, including the president and provost, were present and engaged in dialogue about the topics raised at the forums. Student stakeholder feedback enriched the survey data collected by the college; both are being used to guide student and academic affairs in seeking ways to improve the student experience (Student Stakeholders Assessment Project, 2008). The seriousness with which the students approached the activity and their constructive suggestions for improvement suggested to administrators that students are committed to obtaining the best possible learning experience while attending Buffalo State. Most notably, participation in the stakeholder project helped students believe the college cared about them and their ideas, creating an immediate and tangible sense of engagement.

Campus leaders must seek out students' views and appreciate their perspective to truly understand how to enhance the undergraduate experience. At the same time, institutions must establish routines for tapping students' views, consulting with students, honoring their opinions, and considering this information in efforts to optimize the learning environment.

Collaborative Assessment

Collaboration in businesses and organizations is positively associated with innovation, quality improvement, and knowledge sharing. As the earlier section on campus-wide involvement in assessment illustrates, assessment activities at most campuses depend on collaboration among a variety of campus stakeholders. Several recent initiatives that have been effective in advancing assessment and improvement in student learning have capitalized on collaboration across institutions and fostering a commitment to a process of assessment to drive change.

Collaboration among small groups of institutions on assessment, particularly for improving student learning, was the approach of the Teagle Foundation when it launched a series of grants for assessment initiatives within "collaboratives." Integral to the project was Teagle's insistence that colleges collaborate by establishing joint working groups composed of faculty members and administrators to develop faculty-led projects to assess student learning. Conceptually, a major benefit of participating in a collaborative is the collective support provided for campus leaders in planning, implementing, and sustaining assessment activities. The collaboratives provide campus leaders with a peer group to support, to dialogue about assessment results, and to consider implications from findings (Kinzie, Buckley, and Kuh, 2007). Peggy Maki (2004) noted that establishing new or different kinds of relationships and opportunities for dialogue is essential to building a collective commitment to assessing student learning. She suggested creating learning circles or inquiry groups to track student learning over time and establishing neutral zones to share institution- and program-level results, such as "good news and not-so-good news, to collectively reflect on results, and to propose innovations in practice or modifications in current practice" (p. 6).

Although the collaborative model enacted by the Teagle consortia seemed to foster interinstitutional learning and the structure to work collectively on assessment goals, collaborative approaches are inherently challenging in higher education because of hierarchical and bureaucratic functioning, as well as departmental silos that create barriers to cross-divisional work (Kanter, 1994). Adrianna Kezar (2005) observed, and Jillian Kinzie and colleagues (2007) for the most part affirmed, that collaboration follows a model that includes an initial phase of developing a shared purpose for collaboration, followed by a commitment to partnerships, and lastly a final stage of sustaining the collaboration. During the initial phase of building a commitment, a compelling and shared purpose for the collaboration is essential. Because transitioning to collaboration can be difficult, the external pressure and support from the Teagle Foundation was valuable in helping its grant recipients overcome institutional inertia. Once dialogue about collaboration is begun, having both relationships and trusting partners helps facilitate the developmental process of advancing these partnerships. Finally, to sustain the collaboration, senior leaders need to place priorities on these ventures as the last stage involved, offering rewards and integrating structures to support collaborative efforts.

Faculty members and administrators working in Teagle collaboratives benefited from having colleagues at peer institutions with whom to process new assessment experiences, more resources to draw from when making assessment decisions, and examples when considering the implications of results. Participating in a collaborative with other schools provided institutions with opportunities for comparison, along with peer pressure to compel action. A dean from a private liberal arts college stated that the value of having a common project is the leverage it provides: "If I can say 'other schools in our Teagle consortium are trying this,' it always helps me at my institution. It gets faculty on board, and then they tend to be more willing to reconsider their practice" (Kinzie, Buckley, and Kuh, 2007). The chances that changes in policy and practice will succeed tend to increase when campus teams are formed and institutions work together in consortial arrangements on topics of mutual interest.

Another demonstration of the power of collaboration on assessment is found among the two dozen institutions selected for the Foundations of Excellence® in the First College Year Project, a comprehensive, guided self-study process grounded in decades of research on first-year student success. Institutional teams spend the year assessing and discussing what works and what doesn't work about students' first-year experiences and synthesizing this into aspirational standards reflective of best practice. As a participant in the Foundations of Excellence® (www.fyfoundations.org/) in the First College Year Project, Buena Vista University (BVU) identified performance indicators and developed a strategic action plan for campus improvement. The plan emphasized, for example, revised goals and outcomes for the BVU First-Year Seminar (FYS), along with a linked cocurricular advising program to assist students in their transition to BVU and to support the academic mission of the university. The Foundations of Excellence® project raised important questions about consistency in communicating academic expectations, connecting students with faculty members and other students, and connecting new students with learning support resources. In addition, the project provided an opportunity to consider how academic and student affairs can develop enhanced opportunities to collaborate for student success and to develop a structure for reflecting on best practice in the first year of college.

CHARACTERISTICS FOCUSED ON
OUTCOME-BASED PROGRAM FUNCTION

Effective programs that apply assessment to improvement in student learning within a framework of student engagement require strong, committed, well-prepared leaders and a broad base of participants, including individuals from all areas of campus involved with student experiences. With a strong basic focus and committed multifaceted groups of participants, productive programs can be designed and sustained. Following are some functional characteristics that have been demonstrated as contributing to effective assessment and change.

Explicit Learning Goals

Making learning goals explicit to students is central to promoting learning and success. When learning goals are explicit and visible, students know exactly what will be expected of them. Of more concern, students tend to miss important information if they are not directed to it, and keeping goals hidden does nothing to help students learn. The high-performing institutions profiled in *Student Success in College* (Kuh et al., 2005b) make plain to students what they need to do to succeed. Students are shown what to expect and what success looks and feels like. Making learning objectives plain to students increases coherence among learning experiences leading to student success and helps students bring meaning to their college experiences.

An exceptional example of making learning goals and assessment explicit to students is found at Indiana University–Purdue University Indianapolis (IUPUI). In 2006 CHEA recognized IUPUI with an award for Institutional Progress in Student Learning Outcomes to acknowledge the institution's outstanding progress in developing and applying evidence of student learning outcomes as part of the ongoing evaluation and improvement of college and university programs. Beginning in the late 1990s, IUPUI established six Principles of Undergraduate Learning (PULs) to implement a coherent institution-wide program of general education (Hamilton, Banta, and Evenbeck, 2006). As a central feature of undergraduate education at IUPUI, PULs are explicitly integrated and assessed throughout the undergraduate program and are documented in each academic major through the inclusion of evidence of student mastery of the PULs in department annual reports.

It is important that PULs are made explicit to students during their first interactions on campus. These principles are introduced at orientation, printed on laminated bookmarks, painted in bold red letters on the classroom and stairwell walls, and listed in course syllabi. The goal is to guarantee that every student is exposed to and able to understand PULs and has opportunities to improve and achieve a high level of performance in core undergraduate learning outcomes. As the PULs have increasingly become ingrained in the curricular and cocurricular culture of IUPUI, students are more able to demonstrate what they know and can do in terms of specific learning outcomes.

Motivated by a Northwest Accreditation standard that all learning outcomes need to be published for students, Brigham Young University (BYU) embarked on several innovative projects to increase student awareness of and involvement in outcomes assessment activities. BYU students participate on the assessment and accreditation task force. These students created a video explaining what learning outcomes are, discussing their purposes, and previewing what students can expect to learn in their programs. They also created a wiki site (http://learningoutcomes.byu.edu/) to electronically publish information and solicit feedback on learning outcomes. During the first year, they had more than one thousand students offer feedback. One important by-product of the student comments is that the feedback increased faculty members' interest in assessment.

Although more institutions are reporting that they have a common set of learning outcomes for all students and are communicating these outcomes in a variety of ways, administrators acknowledge that many students still lack understanding. In fact, among those institutions that say they have learning outcomes for all undergraduates, only 5 percent report that all students understand these intended learning outcomes, and nearly half (49 percent) say that only some students understand (Hart Research Associates, 2009).

Assessment Embedded in Institutional Practice

If assessment is to be systematic, it must be knit into institutional governance and policy structure. Assessment within the College of Arts and Sciences and for the general education curriculum at Ohio State University (OSU) has been slowly embedded into policies and routine initiatives. For example, the approval process for course revision now requires specification of student learning outcomes. Thus, if a department wants to change a course or alter the requirements for the major, an outcome and assessment plan is required. Similarly, every program review now requires assessment and outcome plans. Attention to assessment and learning outcomes has been cycled in through established processes to OSU, furthering efforts to increase faculty and administrative understanding of assessment and its value to improving student learning and success.

Albany State University also adopted an embedded approach to increasing assessment of student learning outcomes. The entire reporting system of the university was revised so that every required report incorporates information about student learning outcomes. For example, the departmental assessment plan required every two years is based on student learning outcomes, and department annual reports require specification of student learning outcome results. One important component of the annual report is that departments must detail how they have implemented their assessment findings by enhancing their activities to produce student learning outcomes. The streamlined reporting makes assessment seem a little bit less painful for faculty members, program coordinators, and department chairs because they are required only to focus on updating how they have met their learning outcomes.

Another way of getting more faculty members engaged in assessment is to tie assessment to faculty governance activities. For example, the assessment committee at St. Olaf College had been making slow, steady progress on assessing learning outcomes working out of the office of the director of assessment. Then, under a governance restructuring process, the assessment committee became a subcommittee of the influential faculty curriculum committee. Under this arrangement, the work of the assessment subcommittee is directed and vetted by a faculty committee that reports directly to the dean, carrying greater weight and significance at the institution and, more important, increasing faculty awareness about assessment activities.

Variation in Student Engagement

The concept of student engagement is a powerful way to envision a high-quality undergraduate experience that fosters student success. However, it is in no way a universal conception of the undergraduate experience. It falls short in attending to issues of quality of educational activities and in examining the extent to which all students benefit in the same ways from engagement. For example, NSSE results show that less than 10 percent of the total variation in effective educational practices is attributable to differences between institutions (National Survey of Student Engagement, 2008b). Most of the variation in engagement is among students within institutions. Attending to institutional comparisons can distract from the important variation that exists among students within an institution.

Campus leaders are urged to look beyond their average score and instead "look within" to examine the variation in the student experience—consider how student experiences differ by major or by groups of related majors, or by demographic or enrollment subgroups. Leaders might ask, "Who are the least engaged students?" (those at the lowest ends of the engagement distribution) and "What can be done to improve their experience and narrow that gap between our least and most engaged students?" This strategy brings attention to students who might be most at risk of premature departure or who are just not getting the most out of their education—providing institutions a more specific target for improvement initiatives.

The University of Virginia (UVa) explored the variation theme using their NSSE data and other student information to determine whether minority and low-income students were doing as well as others. They found few differences in the quality of student engagement when comparing the responses of African American, Asian American, and Hispanic American students to nonminority students at UVa. However, UVa was particularly interested in responses of African American seniors since in the past this group had been somewhat less satisfied with the university compared to their peers. UVa had invested in programs and other initiatives aimed at improving the overall climate and experience for African American students and realized a steady improvement over a six-year period in these students' satisfaction with their overall UVa experience (University of Virginia, 2009).

Campus leaders at UVa also used student engagement results in their ten-year plan to evaluate AccessUVa, a financial aid program that limits debt (or eliminates it altogether) by offering loan-free packages for low-income students, caps on need-based loans for all other students, and a commitment to meet 100 percent of need for every student (see www.virginia.edu/financialaid/access.php). The student engagement results for high-need and middle-income students were compared to results for peers not on financial aid and to low-income and middle-income students who did not receive the benefits of AccessUVa's no-loan and loan-cap programs. Specifically, leaders were interested in knowing how well the cohort of 2008 seniors with high need performed after benefitting from four years of the no-loan program. Evidence is being used to determine the extent to which AccessUVa is supporting student engagement among low-income students. Preliminary analyses suggest that engagement levels of low-income students are increasing, especially in the area of cocurricular activities, and AccessUVa appears to be a factor in this improvement.

Average scores mask important variation in the student experience. Assessment activities should examine differences to get at more targeted improvement activities. Results about subpopulations and under-engaged students were used at DEEP schools to tailor efforts to meet student needs. Each institution set standards according to what is reasonable for its students' experiences and aspirations and provides the support—remedial, supplemental, or enrichment—that students need to meet these standards. Specifically, Harper and Quaye (2009) offered fresh strategies for addressing some of the shortcomings of engagement and reversing problematic engagement trends among diverse college student populations.

CONCLUSION

To develop an assessment culture that fosters student learning and success, senior campus leaders should consider the following questions in relation to the nine characteristics:

1. *Intentional focus on improvement*: To what extent does your institution value and foster innovation, experimentation, and risk taking? Are faculty and staff members encouraged to experiment with pedagogical approaches and new policies that promise to foster student learning and engagement? Do they have resources to assess the impact of their innovation? Are they

supported for trying? To what extent are individuals and offices account-able for collecting and using reliable and valid data and for using results to inform improvement efforts?

2. *Strong administrative leadership*: Do administrative leaders routinely champion assessment and improvement for student learning? Do formal structures for assessment (committees, online assessment databases, ac-creditation committees, etc.) require participation from student affairs, library staff, and faculty members from all departments? Are these struc-tures collaborative and transparent in their design and activities?

3. *Expanded board involvement*: To what extent are trustees involved in as-sessment and in ensuring that the institution is measuring student learning and using results to improve?

4. *Campus-wide involvement in assessment*: To what extent and in what ways do academic affairs staff members, student affairs staff members, faculty members, librarians, and instructional technology profession-als—and their policies, programs, and practices—reflect and support assessment? To what extent do these groups collaborate? To what extent is commitment to student learning a criterion for selecting and rewarding administrators, faculty members, and staff members?

5. *Meaningful student involvement in assessment*: How are students mean-ingfully involved in assessment activities? How does the institution dem-onstrate that student input is valued?

6. *Collaborative assessment*: To what extent is collaboration fostered among departments on assessment initiatives and improvement of student learn-ing? How has the campus invested in collective efforts to improve student learning and success through grants and projects such as NSSE Consor-tium or the Foundations of Excellence® project?

7. *Explicit learning goals*: To what degree are students aware of and do they understand the institutions' goals for learning?

8. *Assessment embedded in institutional practice*: Are student learning out-comes specified and assessment activities required in routine reports and other standard institutional practices?

9. *Variation in student engagement*: Are assessment results disaggregated for underrepresented student populations? How are these results used to narrow the student engagement gap?

Campus leaders are urged to reflect on these questions to enhance their capacity to operationalize a student engagement framework to advance as-sessment of and improvement in student learning and success. The instructive lessons and institutional examples described in this chapter show the potential in using assessment to drive change in higher education.

Assessment and improvement are linked practices. Although many institutions have increased their assessment activities, there is little evidence of results being used to guide improvements in student learning and success (Banta, Jones, and Black, 2009; Suskie, 2004). Student engagement provides a useful construct for focusing attention on the processes that lead to learning and for guiding institutions in structuring educationally purposeful activities and encouraging students to take part. We need to ensure that assessment really leads to improved student learning and that college and university leaders are ready to address the complex demands for doing this effectively.

REFERENCES

Banta, T. W., Jones, E. A., & Black, K. E. (2009). *Designing effective assessment: Principles and profiles of good practice.* San Francisco: Jossey-Bass.

Banta, T. W., & Palomba, C. A. (1999). *Assessment essentials: Planning, implementing, and improving assessment in higher education.* San Francisco: Jossey-Bass.

Bartel, D., & Ritch, D. (2010). Get with the (First-Year Seminar) program: Creating connections to promote engagement. Presentation at the Annual Conference on the First-Year Experience. Denver, CO.

Bok, D. (2005, December 16). The critical role of trustees in enhancing student learning. *Chronicle of Higher Education, 52*(17), B12.

Borden, V. M. H., & Pike, G. R. (2008). *Assessing and accounting for student learning: Beyond the Spellings Commission. New Directions for Institutional Research, Assessment Supplement 2007.* San Francisco: Jossey-Bass.

Chickering, A. W., & Gamson, Z. F. (1987). Seven principles for good practice in undergraduate education. *AAHE Bulletin, 39*(7), 3–7.

Colorado State University, Administrative Communications, Office of the President. (2007). Accountability: How are we assessing institutional performance? *Comment Quarterly, 2*(1).

Dillman, D. A. (2007). *Mail and Internet surveys: The tailored design method 2007 update with new Internet, visual, and mixed-mode guide.* Hoboken, N.J.: Wiley.

Education Commission of the States. (1995). *Making quality count in undergraduate education.* Denver: Romer.

El-Khawas, E. (1995, August). *Campus trends 1995: New directions for academic programs* (Higher Education Panel Report 85). Washington, D.C.: American Council on Education.

El-Khawas, E. (2005). The push for accountability: Policy influences and actors in American higher education. In A. Gornitzka, M. Kogan, & A. Amaral (Eds.), *Reform and change in higher education: Analyzing policy implementation.* New York: Springer.

Ewell, P .T. (2002). An emerging scholarship: A brief history of assessment. In T. W. Banta (Ed.), *Building a scholarship of assessment* (pp. 3–25). San Francisco: Jossey-Bass.

Ewell, P. T. (2006). *Making the grade: How boards can ensure academic quality.* Washington D.C.: Association of Governing Boards.

Ewell, P. T. (2008). Assessment and accountability in America today: Background and context. In V. Borden & G. Pike (Eds.), *Assessing and accounting for student learning: Beyond the Spellings Commission.* San Francisco: Jossey-Bass.

Griffin, A. M., & Romm, J. (Eds.). (2008). *Exploring the evidence, Volume 4: Reporting research on first year seminars.* Columbia: University of South Carolina, National Resource Center for the First-Year Experience and Students in Transition. Retrieved from www.sc.edu/fye/resources/fyr/pdf/MExpEvid_IV.pdf.

Hamilton, S. J., Banta, T. W., & Evenbeck, S. E. (2006). Principles of undergraduate learning: The not-so-easy road to writing and committing to them. *About Campus, 11*(4), 9–17.

Harper, S. R., & Quaye, S. J. (Eds.). (2009). *Student engagement in higher education: Theoretical perspectives and practical approaches for diverse populations.* New York: Routledge.

Hart Research Associates. (2009, April). Learning and assessment: Trends in undergraduate education (A survey among members of the Association of American Colleges and Universities). Washington, D.C.: Author. Retrieved from www.aacu .org/membership/documents/2009MemberSurvey_Part1.pdf.

Kanter, R. M. (1994). Collaborative advantage: The art of alliances. *Harvard Business Review, 4,* 96–108.

Kezar, A. (2005). Redesigning for collaboration within higher education institutions: An exploration into the developmental process. *Research in Higher Education, 46*(7), 831–860.

Kinzie, J., Buckley, J., & Kuh, G. (2007). Using assessment to cultivate a culture of evidence on campus: Evaluation of six Teagle Foundation–funded collaboratives. Bloomington: Indiana University Center for Postsecondary Research.

Kuh, G. D. (2001). Assessing what really matters to student learning: Inside the National Survey of Student Engagement. *Change, 33*(3), 10–17, 66.

Kuh, G. D. (2005). Seven steps for taking student learning seriously. *Trusteeship, 13*(3), 20–24.

Kuh, G. D. (2008). *High-impact educational practices: What they are, who has access to them, and why they matter.* Washington, D.C.: Association of American Colleges and Universities.

Kuh, G. D., & Ikenberry, S. (2009). More than you think, less than we need: Learning outcomes assessment in American higher education. National Institute for Learning Outcomes Assessment. University of Illinois and Indiana University, Bloomington.

Kuh, G. D., Kinzie, J., Buckley, J., Bridges, B. K., & Hayek, J. C. (2007). *Piecing together the student success puzzle: Research, propositions, and recommendations.* ASHE Higher Education Report 32(5). San Francisco: Jossey-Bass.

Kuh, G. D., Kinzie, J., Schuh, J. H., & Whitt, E. J. (2005a). Never let it rest: Lessons about student success from high-performing colleges and universities. *Change, 37*(4), 44–51.

Kuh, G. D., Kinzie, J., Schuh, J. H., Whitt, E. J., & Associates. (2005b). *Student success in college: Creating conditions that matter.* San Francisco: Jossey-Bass.

Maki, P. (2004). *Assessing for learning: Building a sustainable commitment across the institution*. Sterling, Va.: Stylus.

McKelfresh, D. A, & Bender, K. K. (2009). Colorado State University. In M. Bresciani, M. Gardner, & J. Hickmott (Eds.), *Case studies for implementing assessment in student affairs* (New Directions for Student Services 127; pp. 13–19). San Francisco: Jossey-Bass.

National Survey of Student Engagement. (2008a). *Promoting engagement for all students: The imperative to look within*. Bloomington: Indiana University Center for Postsecondary Research.

National Survey of Student Engagement. (2008b). Response rates. Retrieved from http://nsse.iub.edu/NSSE_2008_Results/response_rate_summary.cfm.

Porter, S. R. (Ed.). (2004). *Overcoming survey research problems* (special issue). New Directions for Institutional Research 121. San Francisco: Jossey-Bass.

Student Stakeholders Assessment Project. (2008). *Report of group responses*. Buffalo, N.Y.: Buffalo State College Student Affairs.

Suskie, L. (2004). *Assessing student learning: A common sense guide*. Bolton, Mass.: Anker.

Tinto, V. (2006). Research and practice of student retention: What next? *Journal of College Student Retention, 8*(1), 1–19.

University of Louisville. (2001). Meeting the challenge: A status report on the University of Louisville's Challenge for Excellence. Retrieved from https://louisville .edu/institutionalresearch/files/key-information-data-files/Challenge%20-%20 Status%20Report.pdf.

University of Virginia. (2009). NSSE 2008: How UVa fared. Report on Office of Institutional Assessment and Studies website. Retrieved from www.web.virginia .edu/iaas/reports/subject/nsse/2008/report2008.htm.

University of Wisconsin, Green Bay. (2009). Report on the Office of Institutional Research website. Retrieved from www.uwgb.edu/OIRA/reports/nsse2008/index.asp.

WEBSITES

Alverno College
www.alverno.edu/about_alverno/ability_curriculum.html

Foundations of Excellence®
www.fyfoundations.org

AccessUVa, Student Financial Services
www.virginia.edu/financialaid/access.php

Chapter Eight

Assessment in the Disciplines

John Muffo

Previous chapters have emphasized the importance of senior system and campus leaders understanding the major principles of assessment for the purpose of leading a system or institution. This chapter involves a conceptual shift of sorts, moving in a slightly different direction without contradicting anything in prior chapters, for assessment in the disciplines in most cases presupposes simultaneous institutional assessment. It just takes the focus a level or two closer to where the learning takes place, at the college, school, department, or unit level.

An understanding of disciplinary assessment is important to a senior leader, particularly one with major academic or academic support responsibilities, because the leader may spend a great deal of time and energy dealing with such matters in the course of his or her career, especially if the assessment program in place is mandated externally, for example, by the state or federal governments or by professional or specialized accreditation. (Additionally, most academic assessment matters involved in institutional accreditation take place at the unit level first and are then aggregated upward.) Thus, comprehending the assumptions behind the processes and methods employed in disciplinary assessment and the related area of disciplinary accreditation can only enhance one's effectiveness as a senior leader in higher education. The fact that many decisions resulting from these processes have major budgetary implications, some of which may differentially impact academic and administrative units, only heightens the importance of comprehension.

In a number of situations, issues of assessment and accreditation have been utilized in budget negotiations. For instance, units have been known to use the threat of loss of disciplinary accreditation to leverage more resources, putting units within the same institution that do not have accreditation requirements at a competitive disadvantage. The situation is especially difficult for the senior administrator when the accrediting agencies involved are related to state licensing of professions in fields such as law or medicine in which graduation from an accredited program is often a precondition for sitting for the state licensing examinations. Many state-mandated assessment programs involve financial repercussions of one kind or another, which are likely to focus on the disciplines. In some cases, the two even intersect: for example, one of the state-mandated assessment measures can be the number or proportion of academic programs that earn disciplinary accreditation.

DEFINITIONS AND DISTINCTIONS

One might begin by asking how assessment in the disciplines differs from assessment at the institutional level. It might seem reasonable that, if a college or university is assessed at an institutional level, assessment has been completed and nothing else is necessary. Point 1, then, is to distinguish between the various levels of assessment and discuss the institutionalization of assessment in one form: the structure or process known as accreditation.

Assessment versus Accreditation

In accreditation, the focus of the review at the institutional level is on institutional effectiveness, that is, accountability as well as appropriateness of organization and operations. Depending on the agency, stronger emphasis might be placed on certain aspects over other aspects, but in virtually all cases there is great concern regarding such matters as institutional financial viability (i.e., whether or not the organization has the economic wherewithal to provide the services promised to the students) as well as the quality of those services. Normally, there is also concern about the minimal academic standards as they apply to admissions, faculty appointments, learning resources, and courses that impact most or all students; in traditional American higher education this is often called *general education*. Beyond these areas, an accreditation team, by its very nature, cannot deal with every academic specialization offered by the institution, especially if the institution is large and complex, since the team itself must have a number of administrative experts to cover the various institutional-level specialties that need to be addressed. Consequently, an institutional accreditation must focus on issues of institutional accountability, paying limited attention to matters of minimal academic standards as they impact most students.

How, then, have the disciplines sought to guarantee some kind of minimal academic standards and hopefully encourage academic excellence?

The answer in many fields has been to develop professional standards for disciplinary accreditation, though this is only one aspect of assessment in the disciplines, and not all disciplines have accrediting bodies.

To place the situation in context, it is important to emphasize that assessment and accreditation are not necessarily the same thing. Many assessment efforts take place voluntarily or under some mandate from federal, state, or other external bodies unrelated to accreditation. In fact, these efforts are commonly criticized because they tend to duplicate preexisting accreditation requirements. Accreditation is mentioned here because it tends to demonstrate well the distinction between the institutional and disciplinary levels, which holds true whether assessment is due to federal or state mandate or to accreditation requirements. The kinds of activities that take place at the institutional level for accountability are distinctly different from those that take place at the disciplinary level, normally for a combination of accountability and quality improvement. Efficiency is often a concern as well, particularly in times of especially tight fiscal constraints, such as have been experienced in recent years.

To increase potential confusion, much that has been written recently about assessment seems to be at either the highest level (i.e., national and state policy levels, since these matters have the greatest number of legal and budgetary implications) or the lowest level (the individual classroom, because that is the most tangible place, with the most people who are interested in getting practical assistance). Consequently, less has been said or written about the collection of classroom experiences up to the course through curriculum or program level within the discipline. In the end, however, what is most important to the individual, though in many cases no single person takes responsibility for it, is the collection of all the courses into the unified whole of the curriculum within the discipline. That is the role of assessment of the discipline and its institutional, structural process— disciplinary accreditation: to guarantee the quality of the academic program and to encourage its improvement.

Disciplinary Accreditation

As noted above, disciplinary accreditation, widely referred to as professional or specialized accreditation, is not competitive with regional or national accreditation but rather complementary to it. (Traditionally, nonprofit colleges and universities have relied primarily on regional accreditation, while for-profit institutions have used national accrediting agencies. This pattern has shifted in recent years now that regional accrediting bodies have recognized many for-profit institutions.) In fact, as noted above, most disciplinary accrediting bodies require regional or national accreditation as a precondition for candidacy for disciplinary accreditation. (As an aside, regional and national accreditation is also a precondition for accessing federal student financial aid and grant funds.) However, some faculty members tend to get the two confused or place heavier emphasis on disciplinary accreditation. This is especially true at large, complex universities where regional accreditation in particular is assumed, though such assumptions have proven problematic, especially in the Southern region where several large universities have been placed on probation in recent years.

In certain professions, disciplinary accreditation is critical to practicing in the field, though most of these are limited to postgraduate areas such as law, medicine, dentistry, and so forth. In some states, one must graduate from an accredited program to sit for a licensing examination at the undergraduate level as well; licensing laws seem to vary substantially from state to state and from one professional or specialized accreditor to another in this regard.

The strongest and most common benefit across all fields for disciplinary accreditation, the most widely held among all faculty members, is that of perceived quality: being an accredited program constitutes recognition of high quality by professional peers. The difficulty of achieving such status and the evidence required to prove that the programs meet accepted (or "minimum") standards provide sufficient credibility to make the process acceptable to a broad range of faculty with high standards. A list of disciplinary accrediting groups can be found at www.chea.org/Directories/special.asp.

Disciplinary accreditation developed from the professions, that is, the groups of educated individuals who deal with the public and as such have responsibility for protecting the public. Some of the better-known professions and their respective professional accrediting bodies include the following:

- Architecture: National Architectural Accreditation Board (NAAB)
- Business:
  - AACSB International (formerly American Association of Collegiate Schools of Business)
  - Association of Collegiate Business Schools and Programs (ACBSP)
  - International Assembly for Collegiate Business Education (IACBE)
- Dentistry: American Dental Association (ADA)
- Education (K–12):
  - National Council for Accreditation of Teacher Education (NCATE)
  - Teacher Education Accreditation Council (TEAC)
- Engineering: ABET, Inc. (formerly Accreditation Board for Engineering and Technology)
- Law: American Bar Association (ABA)

- Medicine:
  - American Medical Association (AMA)
  - American Osteopathic Association (AOA)
- Nursing:
  - American Nurses Credentialing Center (ANCC)
  - Commission on Collegiate Nursing Education (CCNE)
  - National League for Nursing Accrediting Commission (NLNAC)
- Pharmacy: Accreditation Council for Pharmacy Education (ACPE)
- Theology: Association of Theological Schools (ATS)
- Veterinary medicine: American Veterinary Medical Association (AVMA)
- Others: for example, medical technologies, optometry, and nutrition

Each of these bodies has its own accrediting organization with its own organizational structures (some of which include multiple agencies), its own accrediting procedures, its own accrediting standards, and specified outcomes and measures appropriate to the field. The mature accrediting group for engineering, ABET, Inc., is an example of an effective program. Its structure is unusual, made up of individual scientific societies (e.g., of electrical engineers, civil engineers, mechanical engineers, etc.)—a "society of societies." Individual academic programs are accredited, not the college or school of engineering; ABET is the umbrella group under which the individual societies operate. Another unusual practice is that up to half of the members of the teams that visit colleges and universities are from outside of academe. The standards are limited primarily to undergraduate programs, and most of the current standards are nontechnical, a surprise (and challenge!) to many engineering faculty members who are used to the old input counting-oriented standards. As engineers, they expect the outcomes to be specified and measurable, with demands for hard evidence of progress toward those identified learning outcomes.

A wide range of other professional accrediting bodies exists outside of the traditional professions. Some of these bodies accredit programs in a comprehensive, thorough manner, while others are less rigorous; standards do vary considerably from field to field. For example, AACSB,[1] the business accrediting body, one of the largest in terms of students impacted (www.aacsb.edu), accredits colleges or schools of business (unlike ABET). It is now an international organization, accrediting business programs outside of North America. (An office was recently opened in Singapore to serve its Asian and Pacific Region members.) In addition to AACSB, there are at least two other business accrediting organizations, mainly accrediting programs at smaller institutions. As can be seen from the (above) list of professional accrediting bodies, nursing is another field with at least three such organizations competing with one other. A review of all accrediting bodies recognized by the U.S. Department of Education would further evidence the number of disciplines with multiple accrediting bodies. Despite the wide range of disciplinary accrediting bodies, including regional and national accrediting bodies in the United States and a large number of international and national accrediting bodies in other countries, consensus seems to be developing on the basic principles involved in conducting sound assessment work. Linda Suskie of the Middle States Commission on Higher Education, in her summary entitled "What Is 'Good' Assessment? A Synthesis of Principles of Good Practice" (2006), demonstrates five basic dimensions of good assessment practice: (1) there are clear and important goals; (2) the process is cost effective; (3) it is valued by the entire community; (4) the results are reasonably accurate and truthful; and (5) the results are used for improvement purposes. Suskie came to these conclusions by scanning a number of statements of principles of good practice in assessment by national organizations and individual scholars. Included in the summary are "Principles of Good Practice for Assessing Student Learning," one of the earlier statements of principles published by the now defunct American Association for Higher Education in 1991, and "Student Learning Principles," put forth by the Council of Regional Accrediting Commissions in 2004. Another seventeen statements of principles are included in this summary as well. Her 2009 volume is an even more comprehensive guide to assessment practice (Suskie, 2009).

Virtually all disciplinary accrediting bodies, regardless of discipline, begin with institutional mission as the basis or starting point for their reviews. Academic programs must reflect institutional missions and cannot be outside of them or contradict them. This is one basic way in which the disciplinary accrediting bodies complement and reinforce the institutional accreditation process.

Disciplines without Accreditation

Many disciplines, particularly traditional liberal arts and sciences groups, do not have accrediting bodies, although they have professional scholarly and scientific societies. Thus, they have not had the long traditions of accreditation typical among the professions, perhaps because specialists in these fields are not responsible for protecting the public as are physicians, attorneys, engineers, architects, and others involved with public health and safety. But this does not mean they do not have high professional standards and long-accepted norms for research and ethical behavior. For example, the work of Anthony Biglan and others have verified the numerous ways that faculty members in different disciplines follow distinct norms in their research and other behaviors and have noted that these vary significantly from discipline to discipline (Biglan, 1973a, 1973b; Muffo and Langston, 1981; Stoecker, 1993).

At a practical level, some argue that a lack of disciplinary accreditation puts these fields at a disadvantage in competing for resources within institutions of higher education. Individuals in the professions can often earn high salaries outside of academe; thus, colleges and universities must pay higher salaries in order to be competitive for the best faculty members. Additionally, threats of losing disciplinary accreditation can eventually lead to resources being taken away from liberal arts and sciences faculty and given to faculty in the disciplines with such accreditation. This is particularly true if graduating from an accredited program is a precondition for sitting for a state licensing examination, as for law and medicine.

Another drawback is that those who have not had exposure to disciplinary accreditation in the past may be unfamiliar with accountability issues and procedures, such as assessment, while those with such experience can be more comfortable with these matters due to their long traditions of accountability. This does not always hold true, however, as Bernard Madison (2006) shows that certain faculty members in mathematics have experience and success with assessment in mathematics. At the same time, Kathryn Martell and Thomas Calderon (2005) and William Kelly (2008) demonstrate the advantages to the disciplines of business and engineering of having had long exposure to disciplinary accreditation.

THE ABET CRITERIA AS A MODEL

Regardless of why a discipline is undergoing assessment, whether for accreditation, by state or national mandate, or simply from the conviction that it is the right thing to do, one of the best models available is that developed for engineering (www.abet.org/), particularly for applied fields, but for others as well.

Advantages of the ABET Criteria

The ABET criteria are attractive for many reasons:

* The focus is on student learning outcomes.
* The criteria are broadly applicable to a wide range of institutions and disciplines.
* The starting point is institutional and program missions.

- The criteria are comprehensive.
- The assumed approach is bottom up and faculty driven.
- The outcomes must be realistic given the society in which the institution operates.
- The criteria are value driven.
- The criteria have now been tested for nearly a decade and have been found to be sound in practice.

Criterion 3, Program Outcomes, covers the overarching outcomes that apply to all engineering fields regardless of major. Known as A–K for their lettering in the original document, they are as follows:

A. An ability to apply knowledge of mathematics, science, and engineering
B. An ability to design and conduct experiments, as well as to analyze and interpret data
C. An ability to design a system, component, or process to meet desired needs within realistic constraints such as economic, environmental, social, political, ethical, health and safety, manufacturability, and sustainability
D. An ability to function on multidisciplinary teams
E. An ability to identify, formulate, and solve engineering problems
F. An understanding of professional and ethical responsibility
G. An ability to communicate effectively
H. A broad education necessary to understand the impact of engineering solutions in a global, economic, environmental, and societal context
I. A recognition of the need for, and an ability to engage in, lifelong learning
J. A knowledge of contemporary issues
K. An ability to use the techniques, skills, and modern engineering tools necessary for engineering practice (www.abet.org/)

Since the A–K criteria cross all engineering programs at a college or school of engineering level, they can as well be considered to be roughly analogous to general education outcomes at an institutional level, only these apply at a college or school of engineering level. So there are also outcomes that exist for each program level such as civil engineering and chemical engineering. These vary in specificity.

ABET Criteria Considered Individually

How have the new ABET criteria changed the way that engineering is taught and learned and by inference ways engineering is practiced in North America? And how can those who are not engineers learn from this experience? A review of each of the criteria can demonstrate these lessons.

Criterion A—An Ability to Apply Knowledge of Mathematics, Science, and Engineering

Traditionally this is one of the central, core areas of engineering assessment. In the past, this criterion was emphasized in accreditation over most of the other criteria, almost to the exclusion of the rest of the subject matter. In the past, accreditation in this area was based on a rigid auditing approach to course detail on paper, with little attention to student learning. Inputs were emphasized over outputs, counting over comprehension. Now the emphasis is on broader mathematical and scientific principles and the students' ability to apply those principles in a broad range of situations, as opposed to rote memorization and mechanical application of formulae.

Examples of how similar criteria might be observed in other fields include the tools such as accounting, economics, statistics, and so on, for the field of business, or a tool such as geographic information systems (GIS) that is used in geography, planning, and other fields of study.

Criterion B—An Ability to Design and Conduct Experiments, as Well as to Analyze and Interpret Data

Traditionally this would include assessing how well students are able to design experiments on paper and in the lab, conduct those experiments, analyze the results, and interpret the meaning of those results. Currently, emphasis is also placed on discerning student flexibility in terms of designing and conducting experiments under different conditions, interpreting the data under a variety of circumstances, and so forth. In other words, can the students perform well under nonstandard conditions? Have they learned sufficiently well to apply what they have learned to new situations? Similar criteria might be observed for assessing student learning in other contexts, as in the examples below:

- Case analyses in business
- Quasi-experimental designs in the social sciences
- Critical analysis in the humanities
- Ability to distinguish a sound city plan from a poor one

Criterion C—An Ability to Design a System, Component, or Process to Meet Desired Needs within Realistic Constraints Such as Economic, Environmental, Social, Political, Ethical, Health and Safety, Manufacturability, and Sustainability

The point of this criterion is quite simple—the most elegant design from an engineering standpoint is useless if it is not feasible in the society in which it is intended to be used. This is a reminder that engineering does not operate in a vacuum; it is not about things in themselves but rather about things for people. The list of constraints to be assessed has grown and can continue to grow. For instance, *sustainability* is a relatively new constraint but one that must now be considered in any society. Including this list in assessment also reminds faculty members that they need to be considering such constraints when teaching students engineering principles, since students will be expected to be sensitive to constraints once they leave academe.

Similar criteria might be observed for assessing student learning in other contexts, ensuring that other disciplines such as architecture, law, education, business, dentistry, nutrition, and so on, all of which are embedded in the societies in which they operate and reflect the values and cultures of those societies, incorporate the values of those societies into their academic disciplines. The same should be true for the arts, humanities, social sciences, languages, and so forth.

Criterion D—An Ability to Function on Multidisciplinary Teams

This criterion has been suggested by industry, where teamwork is so critical and where the teams often include people with a variety of expertise. The challenge in this criterion is for programs to demonstrate that students are learning how to operate successfully on such teams, not just having the experience of being on such teams. It is difficult for faculty members who have not been taught how to operate on such teams themselves to teach students how to do this successfully. Often such attempts are haphazard, unsuccessful, and frustrating, but these difficulties are themselves learning experiences. Thus, consideration of such change can be considered part of the assessment process.

Examples of how similar criteria might be observed in other contexts include examining ways in which programs are embedding projects requiring teamwork, multidisciplinary if possible, in a number of courses in the curriculum, with student evaluations and grades tied to performance of those teams. Student input into the performance measures and evaluations would be necessary for such a process to be successful, since students need to have the experience of setting the standards as well as evaluating their peers. They also need to have confidence in whatever evaluations result from group exercises; helping to set the standards and determine the outcomes enables them to build that confidence. Often that process is not comfortable. Consequently, manifestations of discomfort and ways of handling it might be included in the evaluation process.

Criterion E—An Ability to Identify, Formulate, and Solve Engineering Problems

Although somewhat similar to criterion A, criterion E focuses more on the knowledge of engineering principles, while criterion A emphasizes the basic mathematical and scientific knowledge involved. Obviously, this is a core area of knowledge for engineers; due to its comprehensiveness, assessment for this criterion is focused more on the latter part of an undergraduate program.

Similar criteria might be observed in other contexts by examining mastery of the knowledge base of the advanced courses in the discipline, focused on the latter part of the program after undergraduate students have addressed the basics. For a biology student, for example, this criterion would be appropriate after the basic science courses are completed; for a business student, the first courses in accounting and economics would need to be passed before the individual would be adequately prepared for evaluation. In any field of study, a criterion of this sort involves moving from simple to more complex problem-solving applications, with higher-order thinking processes and skills. Developing ways of measuring such knowledge and skills presents some of the most challenging and interesting tasks in assessment.

Criterion F—An Understanding of Professional and Ethical Responsibility

Traditionally, ethics has not been considered a major subject in engineering, as it does not involve science and mathematics; thus, it has not been an area that has been assessed systematically. When ethics has been discussed, views among undergraduates in engineering, as in many fields, have been somewhat simplistic at first, with most answers being considered black and white, yes or no, right or wrong, with little room for areas of gray. More recently, case studies enhanced with guest speakers from such organizations as NASA, engineering consulting firms, and so forth, have been revealing to students that the ethical issues likely to be addressed in an engineering career are not so easily categorized. Criterion F now assesses such opportunities offered by the programs.

In other contexts, similar criteria might be observed by examining how programs use case studies and guest speakers from other disciplines and from society in general (e.g., the courts, public agencies, different levels of government, the military, nonprofit organizations, etc.). When programs include such strategies, examples of real-life situations that have occurred can reveal many of the challenges involved with professionals attempting to balance the many pressures involved in making what they hope to be the best decision. Students learn about weighing the costs and benefits to the persons involved and to society in general on both sides of the issues. Examples drawn from various economic crises might be especially relevant.

Criterion G—An Ability to Communicate Effectively

Difficulties in oral and written communication may be the most common complaint of employers in all fields, whether of technical or nontechnical employees and regardless of level. The tendency among engineers has been toward breakdowns in oral and written skills as opposed to technical communication: in many instances, engineers have been known to communicate with flow diagrams and mathematics better than in spoken or written modalities. Within assessment and accreditation this may be one of the more obvious areas in which to evaluate competency, particularly by examining samples of student work. The challenge is in identifying and reporting precisely what it is that is supposed to be communicated and how.

Many disciplines have continually evolving standards for oral and written communication. Assessing those standards remains challenging and often time consuming. For those disciplines for which communication criteria have not been identified or standardized at a national level, likely those without disciplinary accreditation procedures, local assessment efforts have been attempted. These sometimes incorporate various forms of portfolios, including electronic portfolios, and other sampling techniques to draw student work for assessment purposes. The volume by Marie Paretti and Katrina Powell (2010) suggests a variety of ways for doing this.

Criterion H—A Broad Education Necessary to Understand the Impact of Engineering Solutions in a Global, Economic, Environmental, and Societal Context

Though difficult to demonstrate, this criterion requires that the program prove that students understand via the curriculum that not all engineering solutions work equally well in all places, economies, environments, and societies. One way to do this would be class exercises or experiments in which different scenarios are run using variations of location, economics, environment, society, and so on, including student results. Written test questions with variations of these themes would also provide examples of such learning. Student competitions are also evidence of this criterion, especially if a high percentage of students participate.

Other curricular areas might demonstrate this criterion with simulation exercises and written variations on test questions. For instance, business schools need to show that their students understand that accounting standards vary significantly by country or that marketing practices are affected a great deal by the society in which they take place. There are also classical examples of multicultural marketing mistakes, a notable one being the Chevrolet Nova, which means "no go" in Spanish. The arts and humanities can demonstrate that their students are able to recognize that even humor, through newspaper and magazine cartoons, for example, varies widely by culture.

Criterion I—A Recognition of the Need for, and an Ability to Engage in, Lifelong Learning

This criterion has been challenging to a number of engineers since the inception of the standards. How can one prove that undergraduates recognize at the age of twenty that they need lifelong learning? What seems to have evolved as an acceptable answer is to give evidence of whether or not the programs have inculcated their students with a sense of a need for lifelong learning, an understanding that what they have learned as undergraduates is just the beginning of their learning process, and that they know where to go for their continuing education, which frequently means their professional association.

Transferability of this criterion to other contexts and other fields can be quite direct and can be accomplished in several ways. How can assessors tell whether students understand that they have just begun their educational experience? The best way is to ask them. Do they know where to go for their continuing educational needs? Do they expect to do this? Asking them can be done quickly and efficiently during a site visit. Since many students may not yet be settled on a career path, to know that they will someday need some form of lifelong learning may have to be sufficient at this point.

Criterion J—A Knowledge of Contemporary Issues

Here, too, the transferability of this criterion to other disciplines is quite direct and can be accomplished in a variety of ways. Do students know what the major issues are in engineering generally and in their specialty area within engineering? Do they have a good sense of where the field is headed in the next few years and what the major trends are? What evidence can be presented to show this knowledge? Questions like these address this criterion in a disciplinary area, in contrast to more general contemporary issues in society, though those should not be ignored.

As with criterion I, the transferability of similar criteria to other fields and contexts is quite direct. To the extent that students in any discipline can understand and demonstrate that they understand the issues of the day in their field, they meet this criterion directly. An art, English, or physics major should be knowledgeable regarding the contemporary issues in the discipline, at least at a bachelor's level of understanding, and should be able to demonstrate this knowledge through an assessment process.

Criterion K—An Ability to Use the Techniques, Skills, and Modern Engineering Tools Necessary for Engineering Practice

In engineering one must be competent in the use of a variety of tools and techniques in order to be competent in the field, and required tools have changed over time. Whereas forty years ago or more a slide rule might have been a tool "necessary for engineering practice" (and thus for assessing student learning), now a laptop computer with graphics software and several programming languages is more likely to be needed. Different programs require different tools, so this criterion is quite specific to the discipline and even to subdisciplines in some instances. This is probably the most technology dependent of the criteria, and it will continue to evolve over time.

Virtually all other fields likewise use tools and technology of some kind and therefore require assessment of technological capacity and tool capabilities as well. Determining students' expertise in accessing and using those tools is basic to assessment of any academic program and can best be done through direct evidence. It is rare that a field is not affected by tools and technology; thus, it is the degree to which the discipline is affected rather than whether or not the discipline is affected that must be assessed. As with many other criteria, direct observation of student learning is the most desirable way of demonstrating knowledge.

FUTURE TRENDS

Pressure from the federal government, in addition to the marketplace—including the marketplace of ideas—research and scholarly activities, drives disciplinary as well as regional and national accreditation. If the federal government should withdraw recognition of a regional or national accrediting body, this action would have substantial repercussions in terms of the ability of its members to offer federal student financial aid. Those with licensing authority, affecting virtually all of the professions, also need that recognition for their survival as licensing bodies. Thus, institutions of higher education tend to be quite sensitive to the forces of recognition from the federal level. The other accrediting bodies tend to be driven along with the rest to avoid the embarrassment of losing federal recognition held by their colleague organizations. So, the federal government's efforts to enforce accountability in accreditation, along with its emphasis on the need for verifiable outcomes, is likely to continue to produce pressure on the accrediting agencies to incorporate accountability and continuous improvement measures into their accreditation criteria, even at the disciplinary accrediting agencies with programs in federally accredited colleges and universities.

As the federal government is strongly encouraging increased accountability in accreditation, the states and other societal agencies are also promoting improved quality of education through the use of institutional effectiveness measures. Many states have assessment programs in which state-supported colleges and universities are required to participate in order to qualify for state funding, and some have private institutions that participate if there is state funding of programs for in-state student tuition assistance or similar incentives. There are states like Ohio that have thorough review processes for both public and private institutions for all new academic programs that incorporate institutional effectiveness measures. As at the federal level, all of these are in response to public concerns about program quality and protection of the public from poor quality programs.

While federal and state responsiveness to citizen concerns about program quality is likely to continue (although some at the institutional level consider this to be interference in college and university academic affairs), large areas of the curriculum do not have formal disciplinary accreditation and hence feel less direct pressure for reform from among their colleagues. Large disciplinary areas such as English, foreign languages, the biological sciences, physics, history, sociology, and so on, have professional societies but no accreditation, and they are unlikely to have accreditation in the near future. Consequently, they are unlikely to have formal site visits, disciplinary criteria developed by professionals in their own field, formal reviews with written reports, and a determination of pass or fail along with a series of recommendations for improvement. Thus, these disciplines are on their own at the disciplinary level, though not at the institutional level if there are mandated assessment systems in place for institutional accreditation or state-required assessment reporting. This means that such disciplines will likely continue to be the more difficult ones to work with, on average, in doing assessment, since they will have less experience and guidance from their own disciplines. This is unlikely to change soon, though leadership in some of these fields can help by providing models to assist their colleagues in moving forward.

CONCLUSION

Some faculty members and administrators have been hoping for a couple of decades now that assessment will go away. This is not likely to happen anytime soon, for society's investment in time and money is so great that some observable return on the investment is required; assessment is a way of measuring societal return on investment in terms of student learning. This chapter has suggested the ABET criteria as one approach to structuring a set of assessment criteria that can apply to virtually any discipline with a bit of adjustment. Building and testing a set of criteria around the ABET A–K set is one way to ensure that students are getting a thorough academic experience at the undergraduate level in a discipline and to enhance student success in general.

Disciplinary assessment, as shown in this chapter, can be successful quite often through the auspices of disciplinary accreditation such as the system used in engineering via the A–K criteria. That is because it engages the faculty in that which they already care about so much, their academic disciplines and learning in their own disciplinary field. The engagement of the faculty in something that they care about deeply is the key to successful assessment of learning outcomes.

The major benefit of employing criteria such as the A–K discussed above utilized by engineers is that they use empirical data that can be shared with external as well as internal audiences. It is the empirical data that take the discussion to a higher level than just the reputational ratings. These also can serve as a baseline for future improvements, since measurements can be made over time to see if conditions are improving.

One of the reasons the A–K criteria have become widely accepted in engineering, and similar criteria should work in other fields, is that they measure what is important to those in the field, that is, they measure what matters. In the case of engineering, the wide acceptance of the criteria gives the foundation to the assessment process. This acceptance is based on the fact that they were developed by an inclusive, painstaking process that sought widespread input over a long period of time. As a consequence, engineers have tended to accept the results, even in cases where they don't particularly like them. In addition, the criteria tend to be aspirational as opposed to being merely minimal standards and can reflect changing times easily.

A final advantage of the A–K criteria worth pointing out is that they set a road map for action but, at the same time, allow for local values to shape responses to the criteria. As a result, the measures at one institution appropriately can be quite different from those at another based on institutional mission, for mission drives measurement as it should in all good assessment. The A–K criteria allow for, even celebrate, institutional differences; one size is not expected to fit all.

In conclusion, this chapter has outlined an approach to disciplinary assessment that depends on disciplinary accreditation. It is an approach that is working well for one discipline and that can be adapted to others. This is a prime example of where we can learn from each other.

NOTE

1. The full name is AACSB International: The Association to Advance Collegiate Schools of Business.

REFERENCES

Biglan, A. (1973a). The characteristics of subject matter in different academic areas. *Journal of Applied Psychology, 57*(3), 195–203.

Biglan, A. (1973b). Relationships between subject matter characteristics and the structure and output of university departments. *Journal of Applied Psychology, 57*(3), 204–213.

Council for Higher Education Accreditation (CHEA). (2008). Programmatic accrediting organizations 2008–09. Retrieved from.

Kelly, W. E. (2008). *Assessment in engineering programs: Evolving best practices.* Tallahassee, Fla.: Association for Institutional Research.

Madison, B. L. (2006). *Assessment of student learning in college mathematics: Towards improved programs and courses.* Tallahassee, Fla.: Association for Institutional Research.

Martell, K., & Calderon, T. (Eds.). (2005). *Assessment of student learning in business schools: Best practices each step of the way.* Tallahassee, Fla.: Association for Institutional Research.

Muffo, J. A., & Langston, I. W. (1981). Biglan's dimensions: Are the perceptions empirically based? *Research in Higher Education, 15*(2), 141–159.

Paretti, M. C., & Powell, K. (Eds.) (2010). *Writing in assessment.* Tallahassee, Fla.: Association for Institutional Research.

Stoecker, J. L. (1993). The Biglan classification revisited. *Research in Higher Education, 34*(4), 451–464.

Suskie, L. (2006). What is "good" assessment? A synthesis of principles of good practice. Retrieved August 21, 2009, from www2.acs.ncsu.edu/UPA/assmt/resource.htm#suskiegood.

Suskie, L. (2009). *Assessing student learning: A common sense guide* (2nd ed.). San Francisco: Jossey-Bass.

WEBSITES

AACSB International
www.aacsb.edu

ABET, Inc.
www.abet.org

Chapter Nine

Assessment That Transforms an Institution

Peter J. Gray

"Assessment is grounded in the belief that effective institutions and departments engage in a systematic and continuous process of improvement in order to better achieve their goals and objectives" (Weiss et al., 2002, p. 63). When this belief is shared by faculty and staff members in an institution or department, then what is sometimes called a *culture of assessment* exists. Of course, it is debatable whether or not this belief is true. What is known from the literature on planned change and innovation is that certain conditions contribute to the likelihood that improvement will occur and persist and that the process of assessment can be important among those conditions.

Given unrelenting internal and external pressure for improvement and accountability, higher education institutions and departments are constantly in the process of transformation. Consistent with the definition that transformation means "undergoing total change—to change completely for the better" (Encarta Dictionary, http://encarta.msn.com/dictionary_1861721459/transformation.html), Peter Eckel, Madeleine Green, and Barbara Hill (2001) provide the following insight: "To distinguish transformation from other types of changes, we developed the following definition: Transformation (1) alters the culture of the institution by changing underlying assumptions and overt institutional behaviors, processes and structure; (2) is deep and pervasive, affecting the whole institution; (3) is intentional; [and] (4) occurs over time" (p. 5). However, we know that change is incremental and that at any given point the smallest change is the most likely change. Therefore, it is only through the systematic gradual accumulation of many small positive changes over a long period of time (with numerous setbacks in between) that a culture is transformed. While this may be a source of frustration for some, the true leader sees the wisdom in the observation that "change can look like a failure from the middle. The work not yet accomplished often is more visible than the changes made" (Eckel, Green, and Hill, 2001, p. 27).

This chapter will define assessment not in terms of *tests and measurement* but rather as a generic process that provides *a means of systematic inquiry in support of continuous improvement and accountability*. This process is grounded in the mission and goals of an institution, department, or program; focuses on academic and nonacademic practices and procedures; uses qualitative and quantitative methods to answer important evaluation questions; and, based on the results, provides feedback for improvement and accountability (see figure 9.1).

The *process of assessment* is a means for guiding systematic, incremental positive changes that over time add up to the *transformation of institutions or departments* in order to better achieve goals and objectives and meet the demands of accountability. And when assessment is an integral part of the change process, it too becomes embedded in the institutional culture and, in this sense, is also transformative. However, while assessment is not an end in itself but rather a vehicle for educational improvement and accountability, it is new to most people on campus, and, therefore, it does have to be treated as an innovation. In this way, it can serve as a model for the introduction of innovative teaching and learning practices.

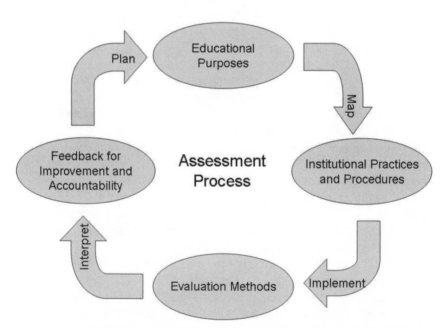

Figure 9.1.   Assessment Process

The purpose of this chapter is to describe a way of conceiving and implementing assessment so that it becomes embedded in the culture as a systematic and continuous process of improvement and as a way to provide valid and reliable information for accountability. This involves designing meaningful, manageable, and sustainable assessment practices that help institutions and departments fulfill institutional priorities, especially related to their educational purposes, as well as meet accreditation and other standards regarding institutional effectiveness.[1]

MOVING ASSESSMENT FROM INNOVATION TO INSTITUTIONALIZATION

In order to move the process of assessment as *a means of systematic inquiry in support of continuous improvement and accountability* from innovation to institutionalization (i.e., embedded in the culture), faculty and staff members must first see it as *meaningful*. Second, its structures and procedures must be *manageable* so it does not become a one-time effort that collapses under its own weight. Finally, thoughtful, persistent, and sensitive campus leaders must link assessment to current conditions and introduce it gradually as part of a long-term planned change process it order to make it *sustainable*. Of course, these characteristics are intertwined and reinforce each other, as is evident in the following discussion.

Making Assessment Meaningful

Assessment will be judged as meaningful only if it helps faculty and staff members better achieve their educational purposes. Five questions must be answered to help faculty and staff members see the assessment process as meaningful (based on Senge et al., 1999, pp. 166–167).

- What is this *change*, in this case, assessment?
- Why is it urgent that the assessment occur?
- What are the intended benefits of adopting assessment?
- Where do people stand in relation to adopting assessment?
- What are the important questions that can be addressed by assessment?

What is this change, in this case, assessment? In simple terms, what do we mean by assessment? As noted above, this chapter defines assessment as a generic process that provides *a means of systematic inquiry in support of continuous improvement and accountability*. Clarifying the principles of assessment enables an academic community to define what assessment means within its own local culture and in its own terms. This is the first step in embedding assessment in the local culture and, thereby, transforming it into a culture of assessment.

The following *9 Principles of Good Practice for Assessing Student Learning*, developed under the auspices of the American Association for Higher Education (AAHE) Assessment Forum (1992), provide a structure for creating a meaningful local definition of assessment.

1. Assessment begins with the educational values of the local community.
2. Assessment is most effective when it reflects an understanding of learning as multidimensional, integrated, and revealed in performance over time.
3. Assessment works best when institutions and programs have clear and explicitly stated purposes related to learning.
4. Assessment requires attention to outcomes but also equally to the academic and nonacademic procedures and practices that lead to those outcomes.
5. Assessment works best when it is ongoing, not episodic.
6. Assessment fosters wider improvement when representatives from across the educational community are involved.
7. Assessment makes a difference when it begins with issues of use and illuminates questions that people really care about.
8. Assessment is most likely to lead to improvement when it is part of a larger set of conditions that promote change.
9. Through assessment, educators meet responsibility to students and to the public.

The guiding principles of assessment from Winthrop University, represented in textbox 9.1, provide an excellent example of adapting the principles of assessment to the local culture.

Why is it urgent that the assessment occur? There are many pressures involved in adopting assessment in *support of continuous improvement and accountability*. By identifying the most significant pressures, administrators can *make a case for assessment* that is locally relevant and compelling.

Faculty members commonly desire to be effective teachers who foster desired learning by their students. Instructors are always seeking better textbooks, adapting their syllabi, and trying out different teaching methods and techniques in order to improve teaching and learning. Assessment is a way to provide both direction for and evidence of such efforts.

Instructors engage in assessment every day when they ask questions, stimulate discussion, and review assignments, quizzes, and tests, not only to grade students but also to determine which areas students have grasped and

TEXTBOX 9.1
Winthrop University, Principles of Assessment

The assessment program strives to incorporate all aspects of student learning and development, including skills, knowledge, and attitudes related to college readiness (entry level), general education, majors, career preparation, and personal growth and development.

1. The primary reason for assessment is to improve student learning and development.
2. The assessment program is designed primarily for internal use in making decisions that seek to improve programs, instruction, and related services.
3. Assessment program initiatives must include training and related resources for the faculty and student support personnel who are responsible for assessment activities.
4. Participation by the faculty in student assessment activities should be appropriately supported and recognized by the university.
5. The development of an effective, valid assessment program is a long-term, dynamic process.
6. The assessment program seeks to use the most reliable, valid methods and instruments of assessment.
7. Assessment must involve a multimethod approach.
8. The technical limitations of the respective data will be considered during subsequent decision making and delineated in assessment reports.
9. Assessment results are not intended to be used punitively against students or faculty members.
10. Assessment of student learning and development is a process that is distinct from faculty evaluation.

Source: Winthrop University. Principles of assessment. Retrieved October 6, 2009, www.winthrop .edu/accountability/default.aspx?id=6875.

which areas seem to require additional effort. This information is then used immediately to guide changes in subsequent instruction. This urgency to improve is a primary motivator for assessment.

In addition, faculty members are often held accountable for teaching and learning through an annual review process as well as the institution's promotion and tenure process. By having documented evidence of assessment activities, including both systematic data collection and data-driven improvements in teaching and learning, a faculty member can respond satisfactorily to these routine accountability requirements.

At the department or program level, one of the most immediate pressures for assessment can be the need to attract and retain students in the face of economic uncertainly and increased competition. In addition, local and other administrators often apply pressure on institutions, departments, and programs to justify their existence or explain their strengths in relation to similar entities. They are asked to show that they are effective and efficient in accomplishing their goals and aligning themselves with current priorities and conditions.

Current and potential students, their parents, and the public in general seek information about the quality and effectiveness of educational programs in order to make decisions about enrollment as well as funding and other support. Professional organizations, state education agencies, and other accreditation and funding bodies are increasingly holding programs and institutions accountable for assessment that supports a *systematic and continuous process of improvement.*

By considering these various sources of pressure, a local educational community can identify those that are most relevant and, through the development and implementation of a systematic process of assessment, devise meaningful responses.

What are the intended benefits of adopting assessment? There are many potential benefits of adopting an assessment process to better achieve educational purposes that may be relevant to different members of an academic community. For instructors, this process can help clarify what is to be taught and how it is to be evaluated. When this information is shared with students, they have a better understanding of what is to be learned and tested. For both instructors and students, clarifying goals and objectives reveals the big picture: it demonstrates how all of the curricular and cocurricular teaching and learning practices contribute to achieve the mission and goals of the institution, department, or program mission, vision, and purpose. Thus, assessment can provide the basis for communication across the institution and with external audiences. The benefits of assessment include the following.

Assessment can help the faculty and staff

- clearly identify what to teach,
- coordinate what is taught and what is evaluated,
- provide the basis for communication about learning outcomes, and
- direct cocurricular programs.

Assessment can help students

- see the big picture regarding their education,
- know what they are expected to learn,
- prioritize their studying,
- complete assignments and projects,

- prepare for exams, and
- communicate to others what they have learned.

Assessment can help a program or institution

- reach consensus on educational purposes,
- ensure that mission, core values, and learning outcomes are consistent,
- specify and coordinate learning outcomes throughout the program or institution,
- evaluate learning across the program or institution, and
- report to various constituencies the accomplishments of educational purposes and student learning.

Assessment can help the public

- understand a program's or institution's educational purpose,
- make a choice of which institution to attend or support, and
- feel confident that the program or institution meets the quality standards and requirements of state education agencies and professional and regional accreditation agencies.

Where do people stand in relation to adopting assessment? No matter how long the idea of assessment has been circulating within higher education in general, or even within an institution, it must be treated as an innovation whenever it is introduced to an individual or group. (It could be argued that assessment has been extant for ten, twenty, thirty years, or longer.) One can guide the movement of assessment from innovation to institutionalization by drawing on the adoption of innovation and planned change literature (Gray, 1997).

By knowing where faculty members individually and collectively stand in relation to assessment, administrators can tailor the change process to address their specific questions. The questions in the following list, which relate to the adoption of an innovation like assessment, provide a structure for making assessment meaningful and lay a foundation for making it manageable.[2]

1. Awareness/nonuse
   - What is assessment in general?
   - What does assessment mean in my context?
2. Information/orientation
   - What are the expectations for assessment?
   - Am I not already doing assessment?
   - How does what I am already doing fit into assessment?

3. Application/preparation
   - What kinds of assessment are others in my local educational community doing?
   - How are others in my discipline responding?
   - What examples demonstrate good practice in my discipline?
4. Management/mechanics
   - What do I have to do differently?
   - What are the steps that I have to follow, or is there a template?
   - What support is available (consultation, release time, summer stipend, graduate assistants, etc.) for doing assessment?
5. Outcome/progression
   - What are the benefits to me and my department?
   - Where does the department or institution want to be five years from now?
6. Collaboration/integration
   - What links exist among academic departments and between academic departments and administrative units?
   - How can assessment be coordinated across courses, programs, and the institution?
7. Refocus/renewal
   - What is the long-term impact of assessment likely to be?
   - How can our educational programs and our assessment efforts be continuously improved?

What are the important questions that can be addressed by assessment?
To be meaningful, assessment must address important questions, generally about educational purposes and specifically about teaching and learning. For example, the following questions might guide an assessment:

- What should students get out of our educational programs or experiences?
- Have we structured our courses and curricula as well as cocurricular activities in ways that enhance learning and development?
- How can we document student learning and development?
- How well are we doing in achieving our educational purposes?
- Based on what we have found, what should we change to get better?

These common questions are often asked on an ad hoc basis throughout an institution. When assessment is being introduced, faculty and staff members must have an opportunity to ask even more specific questions so they can immediately relate the assessment process to their own concerns. This will make assessment meaningful.

Making Assessment Manageable

In making assessment meaningful, administrators must establish its value as a means of improving the achievement of educational purposes. To make it manageable, they must provide a plan for success; an interconnection with other structures and practices; and communication, communication, communication.

To plan the successful introduction of assessment as a *means of systematic inquiry in support of continuous improvement and accountability*, the following common negative perceptions of educational innovations should be addressed (Rogers, 1968):

- low compatibility with current values and past experiences;
- low relative advantage over existing approaches;
- high complexity due to its structured nature, technical aspects, and unique jargon;
- lack of manageable stages that can be adapted to local conditions and tried on a limited basis; and
- low visibility of positive results, many of which may take place incrementally over many years and may be confined to individual efforts.

Compatibility with Current Values and Past Experiences

Building a foundation for assessment perceived as meaningful to the local educational community is the first step in making assessment manageable, since it helps people understand the role of assessment in achieving their educational purposes. In addition, many successful changes that have taken place in a program or institution typically provide elements that can serve as models for the adoption of assessment. By developing an inventory of existing practices, such as periodic internal program reviews and external accreditations, as well as informal systematic change efforts, administrators can demonstrate that assessment is not such an extraordinary activity.

Relative Advantage over Existing Approaches

However, this question often arises: if we are already engaged in efforts similar to assessment, why should we adopt this new approach? One answer is that similar efforts are often ad hoc and isolated within a program or unit of the institution, a situation that can render results incompatible with other efforts. When a standardized process of *systematic inquiry* is established across a program or institution, it is more likely to generate reliable and valid findings that can be used to answer important questions about teaching and learning as well as questions about other institutional procedures and practices. When existing practice is used as a point of reference, the advantages of a *systematic* and *consistent* approach to improvement that is compatible with current values and past experiences can be developed.

Structured Nature with Technical Aspects and Unique Jargon

While the structured nature of assessment may have its advantages, it does come with some elements that put off many faculty members. Even scientists, mathematicians, engineers, and others who use quantitative and qualitative research methods in their own scholarly work may shy away from assessment. One reason is that they may misunderstand assessment as *tests and measurement* rather than a *means of systematic inquiry*. Thinking of assessment in terms of tests and measurements, with their technical psychometric jargon and demands for reliability and validity, makes many faculty members uncomfortable because they have not been trained in these areas.

Another issue is that assessment seems to be based on a philosophy of education with which some faculty members do not agree: that learning can be determined in advance and can be measured through a structured process. Many faculty members take a more constructivist view of learning, by which teachers and students learn together as they make meaning through guided reflection on shared experiences. In addition, some faculty members balk at the notion of the measurement—that is, the quantification of learning outcomes—since "not everything that can be counted counts, and not everything that counts can be counted" (from a sign hanging in Einstein's office at Princeton, quoted in Harris, 1995).

Third, concerns about control are raised by the contemplation of assessment. Requirements for assessment are often seen as *bureaucratic overhead* and as managerial tools of the administration or, even worse, as an infringement of academic freedom. In essence, assessment is all about language and power, that is, how assessment is described and who controls the process (Ewell, 1989). Therefore, assessment must be introduced in ways that are compatible with the local culture, use locally relevant language, and connect with existing approaches that have been successfully adopted to guide improvement and accountability. The seeming complexity of assessment can be reduced by having those who have been engaged in assessment-like activities describe their experience in familiar terms using relevant local examples of successful implementation.

Manageable Stages That Can Be Adapted to Local Conditions and Tried on a Limited Basis

The assessment process is less overwhelming if it is broken down into its component parts, as shown in figure 9.1. In this way, individuals and groups can experiment with describing their educational purposes, mapping them to practices, developing and implementing evaluation methods, and using the results to make changes, with plenty of support from internal and external colleagues and consultants. In fact, adopting assessment should be seen as a long-term process taking at least five to seven years from initial introduction to routine implementation. And even at that point, new people and groups who, for one reason or another, have not worked through the initial stages of adoption (awareness, orientation, and initial application) will need to be brought along with the same deliberation as the early adopters.

Visibility of Positive Results

Of course, success breeds success; the results of these trials can be shared to illustrate the utility of assessment and provide models for others to follow. Having credible examples provided by local opinion leaders is essential in disseminating assessment throughout a program or across an institution. Such a tangible demonstration sends the strongest possible signal that assessment is important and thus should be the cornerstone of a communication strategy intended to foster a culture of assessment.

A major error that leads to the failure of transformation efforts is that the importance of the change, the plan for the change, and the interconnectedness of the change with other institutional structures are undercommunicated by a factor of ten (Kotter, 1990). Therefore, the key to the successful adoption of assessment is strong, consistent, and sensitive communication over time by leaders throughout an institution.

Making Assessment Sustainable

To paraphrase *The Prince*, "It must be considered that there is nothing more difficult to carry out, nor more doubtful of success, nor more dangerous to handle, than to [initiate a new order of things]" (Machiavelli, 1999, p. 21). It is only through effective leadership—within a department, across departments, and throughout an institution—that an innovation like assessment can be moved from an innovation to institutionalization.

Leaders need to do five things to create a climate for change and, ultimately, for the institutionalization of a culture of assessment (Curry, 1992):

• prepare for change,
• define and shape issues,
• build a community,
• act as sponsors, and
• provide incentives

Prepare for Change

Leaders begin the change process by reminding the campus community that theirs is an institution where innovation and change can and have taken place (Peterson and Spencer, cited in Curry, 1992). Whether they are course leaders for a multisection course, department heads, deans, provosts, or presidents, they provide a rationale and promote a sense of urgency for change by referring to the sources of pressure noted above. In doing so they develop an overarching vision and strategy that they share with the community and thus answer the sometimes unspoken question "why change?"

Define and Shape Issues

As noted by Dean Phillips in his letter to the reader quoted at the end of this chapter, at some point he finally *got* the message from "key leaders who understood how to effectively change the culture behind assessment and keep the focus on asking the big questions about student learning." By actively participating in discussions about the principles of assessment as well as both why and how to do assessment, leaders influence the perceptions and attitudes of the faculty and staff.

Their involvement in defining the language of assessment puts leaders in an important position to address issues of power and control. Using language familiar to the local educational community and pointing to other examples of efforts aimed at improvement and accountability, they are able to allay some of the fears of the faculty with the ultimate goal of building a community that can facilitate the adoption of assessment

Build a Community

"Communication leads to community, that is, to understanding, intimacy, and mutual valuing" (May, 1972, p. 247). Barbara Curry (1992) provides a number of important insights regarding a leader's efforts to build community. Through persistent and sensitive communication, leaders "define and shape community issues such as competition and politics that are manifested in the academy in the form of alliances, power, identities, and control" (p. 22). In building a community, leaders manage (1) the *attention* of the campus community with a focus on assessment over the long term, (2) the *meaning* of assessment and its manifestations in the campus community, (3) the *trust* of the campus community that members will be listened to and that their opinions will be respected related to the use of assessment outcomes, and (4) *self* through awareness of their own strengths, weakness, and limits (Bennis cited in Curry, 1992, p. 20). According to Curry (1992), "Skillful leaders know their limitation and do not work in isolation" (pp. 22–23). Instead, they "involve other members of their organization in designing, implementing and institutionalizing change." This is crucial, since "mobilizing resources in any social system depends upon the ability of leaders to direct the behavior of others" (Rosen cited in Curry, 1992, p. 20).

The successful leader uses multiple means to build a community around assessment (Curry, 1992). These include

- promoting participation in *assessment* activities,
- identifying new and existing coalitions that have a stake in *assessment*, and
- gathering and sharing information about *assessment* with the broader community.

Thus, leaders can "mobilize human, material, and symbolic resources toward the adoption of assessment" (Rosen cited in Curry, 1992, p. 20).

Act as Sponsors

Perhaps the best way that a leader can release the energy needed to move assessment from innovation to institutionalization is to actively sponsor assessment. Sponsoring involves sharing leadership with other formal and informal leaders in the community and developing a collaborative environment that promotes faculty and staff participation and creates a critical mass of support (Curry, 1992).

In a professional organization such as a college or university, resources needed for change are mobilized within a network of complex relationships referred to as *collegial*. Rather than having a hierarchical structure or "chain of command," higher education institutions have an inverted structure allowing the power over governance, as well as the actual work of the organization (teaching and learning), to be largely controlled by the faculty (Curry, 1992). Therefore, as noted above, in order to build a campus-wide community where assessment is embedded in the culture, leaders must identify new and existing coalitions that have a stake in assessment, such as those under external pressure from accrediting agencies for assessment. In the end, the ultimate "measure of organization members' commitment to assessment is the extent of their participation in decisions governing the change process" (Curry, 1992, p. 25).

Provide Incentives

Making assessment manageable is facilitated by connecting it not only to existing assessment-like practices but also to larger institutional structures such as

- faculty governance,
- faculty roles and rewards,

- institutional planning and resource allocation, and
- institutional renewal.

For example, the assessment process may be embedded in the faculty governance structure in the form of a standing committee of a faculty senate with responsibility for coordination and oversight similar to that of a faculty curriculum committee. Such a structure will, first, give the faculty an opportunity to define assessment related to the local context and culture, making it meaningful. Second, the structure will make assessment more manageable since it will be part of an existing structure with familiar procedures. Third, as part of an acknowledged element in institutional governance, assessment is more likely to be sustainable.

In order for the faculty to view assessment as meaningful, manageable, and sustainable, they must perceive it as valued by the institution. The importance of assessment can be demonstrated by making it a topic in the hiring process, an element in the annual review process, and a factor in the merit pay and promotion and tenure decision processes. For example, including an item on the annual review form that asks instructors to describe and document assessment activities and explain their contribution to continuous improvement would provide the basis for short-term and long-term decisions, thus helping to make assessment part of the institutional culture. In addition, other tangible support may include stipends to cover individual faculty members' time and the resources needed to develop and implement assessment, as well as funding for assessment support staff and consultants and for travel to attend conferences or other training opportunities. Such extrinsic incentives are essential, but so are intangible incentives. These include the intrinsic rewards that come from recognition and celebration of accomplishments. Giving faculty members internal and external visibility for their good work related to assessment is important to the institutionalization process.

Intrinsic and extrinsic incentives must extend beyond the initial start-up phase of adopting assessment. Faculty and staff members who can be characterized as innovators and early adopters are the ones most likely to be involved during this period. Often, funds, events, and recognition are focused on the first three years for pilot and other such projects, and none is given to sustaining the ongoing efforts needed to spread assessment throughout an institution, which involves the majority of faculty and staff members. Understanding what motivates the majority of faculty to adopt an innovation should form the basis of a long-term plan for sustainability. A substantial chasm exists between the adoption of an innovation by the innovators and its implementation by the majority of faculty members (Geohegan cited in Gray, 1997). This chasm results

TEXTBOX 9.2
Contrasts between Early Adopters and the Early Majority

Early Adopter	Early Majority
Revolutionary	Evolutionary
Visionary	Pragmatic
Project oriented	Process oriented
Risk takers	Risk adverse
Experimenters	Advocates of proven practices
Self-sufficient	Need support
Horizontal	Vertical
Connected	Connected

Source: Geohegan, cited in Gray, 1997, p. 12.

from the substantial differences, shown in textbox 9.2, between early adopters and the early majority that must be taken into account when attempting to move an innovation from initial implementation to institutionalization (Gray, 1997).

If individual faculty members are to be expected to spend the time and energy needed to include assessment in their local course, program, and department practices, comparable procedures must be implemented at the institutional level so they see it as an institutional value.

A systematic process of inquiry, such as that shown in the assessment model in figure 9.1, can provide not only the basis for sound local planning and decision making but also the foundation for determining institutional effectiveness and guiding institutional renewal. By using a systematic assessment process to address important institutional issues, the administration can demonstrate its commitment to assessment and can model the type of behavior expected of faculty and staff members at the program and department levels. In other words, the institutionalization of assessment will be complete when it encompasses both academic assessment of student learning outcomes and institutional assessment as the foundation of strategic planning and institutional renewal.

In summary, faculty ownership and leadership support are both crucial to making assessment part of the institutional culture. Faculty members must have ownership of the assessment process in order to maintain their commitment over time and ensure that the results are used to make a difference. In addition, the assessment programs must have strong leadership in order to remain flexible and adaptable to changing needs, not merely ad hoc efforts (Middle States Commission on Higher Education, 1996).

FOCUSING ON EDUCATIONAL PURPOSES: USING ASSESSMENT TO TRANSFORM A CAMPUS CULTURE

The process of assessment is a means for systematically guiding changes that over time add up to the transformation of institutions or departments in order to better achieve their goals and objectives and meet the demands of accountability. The institutionalization of assessment is transformative itself, since it implies for many institutions a new way of decision making—one based on evidence. In addition, when assessment results are used to address important questions, generally about educational purposes and specifically about teaching and learning, assessment can literally transform the culture and practices of an educational community.

Whether at the course, departmental, or institutional level, the important questions for an educational community concern the realization of its educational purposes. Therefore, the implementation of the assessment process should involve clarifying educational purposes from the course to the institutional level.

Course-Level Assessment

In developing course syllabi, instructors naturally think about what they want their students to learn relative to the purposes of their courses, that is, where each course fits into the curriculum and what its particular learning goals should be. Unfortunately, sometimes these issues are reflected only in a list of topics to be covered. However, being more specific about expected learning outcomes—not just what will be covered but also what students should learn—has many benefits for instructors and student alike (see list above).

Learning Outcomes

The generic list in textbox 9.3 provides a good starting point for defining learning outcomes. The products and performances required of students are excellent sources of information about learning outcomes. Usually, the important outcomes of a course can be deduced from the kinds of assignments, term papers and projects, written examinations, oral presentations, small group discussions, capstone course projects, senior thesis portfolios, performances, simulations, case studies, and field work internships and coop experiences that a course requires. (For a comprehensive list, see Linda Suskie's [2009b] examples of evidence of student learning.)

Many excellent resources are available on how to state learning outcomes, including *Designing and Assessing Courses and Curricula: A Practical Guide*, 3rd edition (Diamond, 2008); *Assessment Essentials* (Palomba

TEXTBOX 9.3
Generic Learning Outcomes Categories

Discipline-Specific Cognitive Goals
- Terms and facts
- Concepts and theories
- Methods and materials
- Tools and technologies
- Perspectives and values

Higher-Order Thinking Skills
- Distinguishing between facts and opinions
- Applying concepts and theories
- Engaging in analysis and problem solving
- Drawing inferences
- Synthesizing and integrating information
- Thinking creatively and divergently

College-Level Thinking Skills
- Verbal reasoning
- Argument analysis
- Use of thinking to test hypotheses
- Use of likelihood and uncertainty or estimates of probability
- Use of decision making and problem solving

General Education and Liberal Studies Goals
- Basic skills in oral and written communication
- Mathematical, scientific, and technological literacy
- Study skills
- Historical perspective
- Awareness of contemporary issues
- Appreciation of different social and cultural perspectives and experiences
- Esthetic sense
- Ethics

Professional and Career development Goals
- Teamwork
- Leadership and management
- Responsibility
- Attention to detail
- Ability to follow directions
- Effective and efficient organization and use of one's own and others' time

Personal Growth and Development Goals
- Positive self-esteem and self-confidence
- Emotional and physical health and well-being
- Ability to take responsibility for one's actions
- Disposition for acting responsibly and respectfully toward others
- Honesty and integrity in relation to one's own values

and Banta, 1999); *Assessing for Learning* (Maki, 2004); *Assessing Student Learning* (Suskie, 2009a); and, of course, the various taxonomies of educational objectives such as *Taxonomy of Educational Objectives: The Classification of Educational Goals* (Bloom, 1956); *A Taxonomy for Learning, Teaching, and Assessing: A Revision of Bloom's Taxonomy of Educational Objectives* (Anderson and Krathwohl, 2001); and *Taxonomy of Educational Objectives, Handbook II: The Affective Domain* (Krathwohl, Bloom, and Masia, 1964). In addition, the "Teaching Goals Inventory," found in *Classroom Assessment Techniques: A Handbook for College Teachers*, 2nd ed. (Angelo and Cross, 1993), provides not only an excellent set of sample goals but also a way to prioritize them relative to a given course. (This inventory can be completed and automatically scored online at http://fm.iowa.uiowa.edu/fmi/xsl/tgi/data_entry.xsl?-db=tgi_data&-lay=Layout01&-view [retrieved October 11, 2009]).

Mapping Outcomes to Experiences

Mapping outcomes to educational experiences should be familiar to professors since they intuitively consider how to best teach particular knowledge, skills, and values. However, an explicit map that provides a guide for both the instructor and students typically is not included in course materials. Such a map is not only a good pedagogical tool but also a potential foundation for the rest of the assessment process.

A simple grid or matrix, like that shown in figure 9.2, can be used by an instructor to coordinate teaching, learning, and evaluation activities of a course. Perhaps the only unfamiliar concept involved is *evaluation evidence*, which is different from learning outcomes. Learning outcomes are the specific knowledge, skills, and attitudes that are intended to result from a given learning activity. They may or may not be directly observable.

Evaluating Outcomes

In order to gather direct evidence about the extent that students have achieved the intended learning, these outcomes have to be associated with observable behaviors, sometimes called *behavioral objectives*: *what students will do to demonstrate that they have certain knowledge, skills, or attitudes*. It is important to distinguish between the learning that is expected and the evidence that it has taken place. The more general and nonbehavioral a learning outcome is, the greater the number and variety of *behavioral objectives* that are needed to provide valid and reliable evidence of its accomplishment (Gray, 1975). For example, knowledge itself and the cognitive abilities related to its application and use, as well as affective attitudes, feelings, and inclinations, are internal

Teaching	Learning	Evaluation	
ACTIVITIES	OUTCOMES	EVIDENCE	METHOD(S)

Figure 9.2.   Teaching, Learning, and Evaluation Matrix

states that are not amenable to direct observation. Therefore, operational definitions need to be developed to guide their evaluation. There are many lists of verbs that may be used to form such evidence statements; a Google search on "Bloom's taxonomy verbs" took 0.10 of a second to identify 19,300 URLs (retrieved October 8, 2009).

By implementing many different qualitative and quantitative methods for gathering evidence across time and circumstances, assessors can make valid and reliable judgments about the extent to which students have achieved a great variety of learning outcomes. It takes a *mixed methods* approach to answer all of the important evaluation questions related to educational purposes. In contrast to Einstein's statement on things measureable and not measureable (quoted earlier), while it may be *difficult if not impossible to measure* some learning, it does not follow that *useful and meaningful evaluation* is not possible. Effective evaluation in this case implies the use of quantitative and qualitative methods—often both—to document the extent to which learning has occurred (see Ewell's 1991 publication *To Capture the Ineffable: New Forms of Assessment in Higher Education*).

The last column in the figure 9.2 matrix is for describing the evaluation methods that can be used to provide evidence for decisions about improvement and accountability. The sources of student work and achievement noted above, which can be used to deduce student learning outcomes, can also be used as sources of evidence of learning if their contents are explicitly linked to outcomes. Test blueprints and rubrics, such as those described by Suskie (2009a), are excellent ways to create this linkage since they make explicit connections between learning outcomes and the evidence to be provided by quantitative items and qualitative questions.

Interpreting Information for Action

The information generated by the analysis of evaluation results provides the basis for planning improvements as well as answering questions related to accountability. However, findings must be interpreted by local stakeholders whose questions they are intended to answer. The key is to ensure that the results address the important questions that stimulated the evaluation in the first place.

It is, therefore, imperative that the ownership of relevant stakeholders be developed at each step of the assessment process, from stating educational outcomes to determining credible evaluation evidence, to selecting and implementing evaluation methods, to interpreting results, and, finally, to using the information for improvement and accountability. In other words, assessment is not something that is done *to someone* but *with someone* so that it leads to reflection and action by faculty members, staff members, and students.

Departmental- to Institutional-Level Assessment

As described by Phillips in his letter to the reader at the end of this chapter, it is dedicated leadership at all levels that determines the success of assessment efforts. "It seems so simple to me now. . . . . But it took a long time and a lot of dedicated leadership by others to create a culture where I could finally see the real point of assessment."

Creating a culture of assessment, as stated at the beginning of this chapter, is not an end in itself but rather a means for institutional transformation.

However, as Phillips also noted, "You don't have to be bad to get better, institutionalized assessment will help you get better no matter where you are starting from."

Catherine Palomba and Trudy Banta (1999) listed the following characteristics of a good assessment program:

1. Asks important questions
2. Reflects institutional mission
3. Reflects programmatic goals and objectives for learning
4. Contains a thoughtful approach to assessment planning
5. Is linked to decision making about the curriculum
6. Is linked to processes such as planning and budgeting
7. Encourages involvement of individuals from on and off campus
8. Contains techniques that provide direct evidence of learning
9. Reflects what is known about how students learn
10. Shares information with multiple audiences
11. Leads to reflection and action by faculty, staff, and students
12. Allows for continuity, flexibility, and improvement in assessment (p. 16)

Department heads, deans, and senior administrators are responsible for providing the leadership needed to build an institution-wide assessment culture. By adopting a common planning format, such as the following, which is consistent with the model in figure 9.1, administrators can harmonize assessment efforts across an institution:

- Build consensus around educational purposes.
- Map where and how purposes and goals are to be achieved.
- Implement evaluation techniques to answer important questions.
- Analyze and interpret evaluation results.
- Plan improvements and provide information for accountability.

Educational Purposes

It is important to be clear about educational purposes at all levels of an institution. There are several ways to build consensus around purposes and goals.

- Review existing internal as well as external documents.
- Analyze student work and achievement.
- Identify hopes and expectations of faculty members, students, and employers.

Many existing documents can aid in clarifying educational purposes. Departments, programs, schools and colleges, and institutions have various statements of mission and vision, descriptions of majors and courses of study, and lists of attributes of graduates. Such documents provide the starting point for clarifying educational purposes, since they express the self-image of the institution in its own words. In addition, most institutions have adopted a cohort, consortium, or group of schools, academic programs, and departments that they use as benchmarks. Looking to others that are similar and desirable to emulate can also help to clarify local purposes (both where you are now and where you want to be). The Internet Resources for Higher Education Outcomes Assessment provides a wealth of useful information, including general resources such as discussion groups and lists of links; assessment handbooks; assessments for specific skills or content; individual institutions' assessment-related pages; materials furnished by state boards and commissions, as well as accrediting bodies; and student assessment of courses and faculty members (retrieved October 12, 2009, fromwww2.acs.ncsu.edu/UPA/assmt/resource.htm#toc).

Professional organizations such as the Association of American Colleges and Universities (AAC&U) and discipline societies such as ABET, Inc., have promulgated outcomes that are intended to guide both practice and assessment. For example, the AAC&U project Liberal Education and America's Promise (LEAP) has created a set of essential learning outcomes, "all of which are best developed by a contemporary liberal education" (retrieved October 11, 2009, from www.aacu.org/leap/vision.cfm). The outcomes, listed under Knowledge of Human Cultures and the Physical and Natural World, Intellectual and Practical Skills, Personal and Social Responsibility, and Integrative Learning, along with the educational purposes behind them, described as the Principles of Excellence, may be found in *College Learning for the New Global Century* (Association of American College and Universities, 2007, pp. 12, 26).

ABET spent nearly a decade developing its Engineering Criteria 2000 (EC2000). "[These criteria were] considered at the time a revolutionary approach to accreditation criteria. The revolution of EC2000 was its focus on what is learned rather than what is taught. At its core was the call for a continuous improvement process informed by the specific mission and goals of individual institutions and programs" (retrieved October 11, 2009, from www.abet.org/history.shtml). The twelve ABET "program educational objectives are broad statements that describe the career and professional accomplishments that the program is preparing graduates to achieve" (ABET, 2008, p. 1; see also p. 2 for the twelve objectives, A–K).

Thomas Angelo and Patricia Cross's (1993) Teaching Goals Inventory described on page 20 of their book may be used with instructors who are all teaching sections of the same course, courses that are all part of a core curriculum spread across disciplines, or courses intended to provide a sequence of experiences leading to a major, minor, or track within an academic program. This inventory provides a common reference point that can be used to stimulate discussion of the perceived relative importance of various outcomes and the sequences in which they do or should appear.

The careful analysis of student work can provide insights into educational purposes and desired learning. Such performances and products, as noted above, may include major assignments, term papers, and projects; written final examinations and oral presentations; focus group discussions and exit interviews with majors; capstone course projects and performances; senior theses and portfolios; simulations and case studies; major field and licensure exams; and competitions, field work, internships, and coop experiences. By building consensus around the characteristics of exemplary, satisfactory, and unsatisfactory student work, an educational community can generate a basis for describing its educational purposes and the learning it desires of its students. The generic learning outcomes categories in textbox 9.3, along with examples of various levels of achievement drawn from student work, can be used to harmonize learning expectations across an institution.

Another means of clarifying educational purposes is to ask key stakeholders to describe their hopes and expectations for students. The leading questions in textbox 9.4 are open-ended sources of information from faculty members and students. A more quantitative approach is to have faculty members and employers rate the importance of each learning outcome area in a document such as the CDIO Syllabus (Crawley, 2001). By comparing and contrasting responses from stakeholders in various cohorts and areas of an institution, administrators can formulate some overarching purposes. Making this part of an iterative process, in which people are engaged in a consensus-building effort, can be a useful way to facilitate communication that results in a shared vision of educational purposes across a program, school or college, or institution.

Mapping

The Middle States Commission on Higher Education Standard 14 states, "The effectiveness of an institution rests upon the contribution that each of the institution's programs and services makes toward achieving the goals of the institution as a whole" (2005, p. 3). The processes just described for clarifying educational purposes can be extended to identify where and how purposes and goals are to be achieved. As people throughout an institution become engaged in consensus-building activities focused on common purposes, they also identify the extent of their own individual and their unit's collective responsibility for various outcomes.

TEXTBOX 9.4
Leading Questions about Learning

Questions for Faculty
- In general, what are the most important things a student gains from your field of study?
- What qualities and capabilities do you strive to foster in your students?
- What is the most important knowledge that your students acquire from your field of study or from working with you?
- How does your field of study or your work change the way students view themselves?
- In what ways does your field of study or what you do contribute to a student's well-being?
- How does your field or what you do change the way a student looks at the world?
- What does your field of study or what you do contribute to the well-being of society at large?
- How do people in this area of study differ from those in other areas (knowledge, skills, and values)?
- How do we know the extent to which students are getting what we hope from our field of study?
- How do we use information about student learning and development to enhance student learning?

Questions for Students
- What is the most important knowledge you have gained from taking this subject?
- What are the most valuable skills or abilities that have you developed as a result of taking courses in this subject?
- How has taking courses in this subject changed the way you look at yourself?
- How has taking courses in this subject changed the way you look at the world?
- How has taking courses in this subject changed the way you think about the future?
- How do people in this area of study differ from those in other areas (knowledge, skills, and values)?
- What changes might be made in courses or in this major to enhance student learning?

Source: Based on leading questions developed by C. Ewart, Department of Psychology, Syracuse University, 1998.

As noted above, successful leaders build a community around assessment. This occurs not only by setting expectations but also by providing incentives, recognizing accomplishments, and sharing the leadership. The process of mapping educational purposes to institutional practices provides an excellent opportunity to engage the entire community in assessment. Not only the faculty members in academic units but also the support staff in the academic units along with those in admissions, student affairs, financial aid, health services, budgeting and planning, facilities maintenance, housing and dining, computer and technology support, buildings and grounds, alumni affairs, and so on, have roles to play in the achievement of educational purposes. Engaging them, as is appropriate, in the process of identifying their own and their unit's contributions to student success can result in a strengthened sense of community and a rededication to the mission of the institution.

Evaluation Questions and Methods

Important evaluation questions naturally emerge from mapping educational purposes to institutional practices and procedures. The most fundamental ones are "as an institutional community, how well are we collectively doing what we say we are doing?" and, in particular, "how do we support student learning, a fundamental aspect of institutional effectiveness?" (Middle States Commission on Higher Education, 2006, p. 25). By tying these two questions together, an institution can break down the silos that have formed around individual units. These questions require people to consider not only how well they are performing their own functions and accomplishing their own purposes but also how extensively the functions actually support student success and institutional education purposes.

Some of the methods used to answer these questions will provide direct evidence of student learning, and others will provide indirect evidence. However, even indirect evidence can lead to more focused learning-centered questions, especially if the results are not satisfactory. For example, at the 2009 annual meeting of the Association of Community College Trustees, Camille Preus, commissioner of the Oregon Department of Community Colleges and Workforce Development, reported that the Oregon community colleges "have now agreed to collect (and discuss internally) the following 'student success indicators':

- High school students enrolling directly into college
- The percentages of those enrolling at college and non-college levels of work in math, reading and writing
- The credits earned each year toward an associate of arts degree
- The credits earned each year toward a career or technical certificate
- Semester to semester persistence rates
- Fall to fall persistence rates
- The percentage of GED students who advance to the next level of their programs
- GED fall to fall persistence
- The percentage of English as a Second Language students who advance to college level work." (Jaschik, 2009)

The extent that the information related to each metric is satisfactory can be used to demonstrate whether students are learning what is intended, since academic success underlies all of these metrics. However, numerous other aspects of a college experience involving many different units across an institution have major impacts on these metrics. Discussions intended to formulate questions about the underlying factors influencing student success can engage people in every division of an institution.

Methods described previously for gathering direct evidence of student learning may be used to deduce the important learning outcomes and then to document learning for improvement and accountability. This assumes that the contents of these evaluation methods have been mapped to the learning outcomes.

The institutional-level rubrics (and related materials) for fifteen of the AAC&U Essential Learning Outcomes in the areas of Intellectual and Practical Skills, Personal and Social Responsibility, and Integrative Learning, created under the auspices of the project VALUE: Valid Assessment of Learning in Undergraduate Education, are useful examples (retrieved October 12, 2009, from www.aacu.org/value/rubrics/index.cfm).

Many of these direct and indirect indicators of student learning are relevant to all higher education institutions and are often collected as a routine function of institutional research and academic program assessment. A modified version of the matrix in figure 9.2, in which the first column is labeled Unit Activities rather than Teaching Activities, can be used to organize the evaluation related to a campus-wide assessment effort.

Analyze and Interpret Evaluation Results

Perhaps the most important step in the assessment process is the consideration of results for the purpose of action. There are several ways to organize the discussion of evaluation findings. One is to use existing institutional governance and administrative structures. For example, at the U.S. Naval Academy (USNA), a Faculty Senate Assessment Committee was established through an amendment to the Senate bylaws. This standing committee is responsible for coordinating and providing oversight for all academic assessment. At the institutional level, a standing committee of the Senior Leadership Team, the Academy Effectiveness Board, was established to organize institutional effectiveness assessment related to the USNA mission, vision, and attributes of graduates.

Another way to organize the discussion of findings is to form ad hoc groups to focus on specific evaluation questions with the related data collection, analysis, and interpretation. These could be cross-function committees that are supported by a central unit such as institutional research. Or a more or less permanent self-study group may be formed, similar to those required in accreditation reviews, since today most accreditation bodies expect self-studies to be based on a process of continuous improvement, not just an episodic effort intended solely to prepare for an accreditation visit.

No matter what structure is used, the key feature of this step in the assessment process is communication, communication, communication! Large colloquia and institutional assemblies; small group discussions among faculty members, staff members, and students; formal reports and press releases; and informal posters and fliers of specific findings and actions are all important ways to engage the campus community in using evaluation findings to consider important issues and thus build a culture of assessment. However, it is the outcomes of campus conversations based on assessment results that are truly transformative.

Plan Improvements and Provide Information for Accountability

The *internal discussion* stimulated by the findings of direct and indirect evaluations of student success can lead to plans for improvement as well as responses to the call for accountability. As noted in Middle States Commission on Higher Education Standard 7, intuitional assessment calls for "evidence that assessment results are shared and discussed with appropriate constituents and used in institutional planning, resource allocation, and renewal to improve and gain efficiencies in programs, services and processes, including activities specific to the institution's mission (e.g., service, outreach, research)" (Middle States Commission on Higher Education, 2006, p. 29). Thus, there must be "evidence that institutional assessment findings are used to

- improve student success;
- review and improve programs and services;
- plan, conduct, and support professional development activities;
- assist in planning and budgeting for the provision of programs and services;
- support decisions about strategic goals, plans, and resource allocation; [and]
- inform appropriate constituents about the institution and its programs."

The most important requirement is for "evidence that renewal strategies made in response to assessment results have had the desired effect in improving programs, services, and initiatives" (Middle States Commission on Higher Education, 2006, pp. 29–30). In other words, calls for accountability are best answered by providing evidence that assessment findings have been used and that the impact of the resulting changes have become the focus of future assessment efforts. This is called *closing the loop*, indicating that the culture of assessment has been institutionalized.

EXAMPLES OF EFFECTIVE PRACTICES

Translating principles into action is never easy. However, reviewing examples of assessment efforts at other institutions makes it possible to get a sense of what might work and how to go about establishing a culture of assessment. A great variety of resources are available that identify different institutions that have developed effective programs, disciples, and practices related to assessment. (A search of Google using "higher education assessment" produced 36,500,000 results in 0.30 of a second.)

In addition to the references cited in this chapter, the following are notable relevant websites and publications.

- Undoubtedly the most comprehensive website is the Internet Resources for Higher Education Outcomes Assessment. Its Individual Institutions' Assessment-Related pages alone provide over 350 links (retrieved October 13, 2009, from www2.acs.ncsu.edu/UPA/assmt/resource.htm#inst).
- A site with great potential is that of the National Institute for Learning Outcomes Assessment (NILOA): Making Learning Outcomes Usable and Transparent (retrieved October 13, 2009, from www.learningoutcomeassessment .org/AboutUs.html). Established in 2008, the institute's major undertaking is the National Survey on Student Learning Outcomes Assessment. Chief academic officers from all regionally accredited two- and four-year colleges and universities in the United States were invited to participate in the survey intended to provide an informed perspective on the current state of student learning outcomes assessment at the collegiate level. The results of the first iteration of the survey were released on October 26, 2009. In addition, NILOA will conduct interviews of key respondents; analyze websites of institutions and those of organizations engaged in assessment-related efforts; produce a series of commissioned papers addressing pressing topics; and provide short, instructive case studies of promising practices in collegiate learning assessment—particularly the use of assessment data to improve student learning and approaches to public reporting of assessment data. Of particular note, on the NILOA Resources page are links to papers, articles, presentations, institute working papers, college and university associations, college and university sites, award-winning campuses, and related programs and activities (www.learningoutcomeassessment.org/resources.htm).
- Publications authored or edited by Banta, one of the founders of the contemporary assessment movement in the United States, provide a wealth of models of assessment. For example, *Assessment in Practice: Putting Principles to Work on College Campuses* (Banta et al., 1996) includes eighty-two campus case studies. *Assessment Update: Progress, Trends,*

and Practices in Higher Education, edited by Banta, has been published for over twenty years. Each issue contains articles recounting campus-based successes and raising important issues regarding assessment from the authors' firsthand experiences. Several compilations of articles have been made, including *Assessment Update: The First Ten Years* in which over thirty campus profiles are reproduced (Gray, 1999), as well as articles regarding the growing variety of assessment methods, views from the states, and community college strategies. *Assessment Update* articles have also been republished in collections on *Assessing Student Achievement in General Education* (Banta, 2007a) and *Assessing Student Learning in the Disciplines* (Banta, 2007b).

• *Outcomes-based Academic and Curricular Program Review: A Compilation of Institutional Good Practices* by Marilee Bresciani (2006) includes nineteen case studies of "institutions that are actively engaged in systematic evaluation of student learning and development, [and] gathering meaningful data about how to improve student learning" (p. 1).

These resources can be used to bring the campus community into the conversation about how best to define, develop, and implement assessment so that in the end it is meaningful, manageable, and sustainable.

APPENDIX: WHY READ THIS CHAPTER?

Dr. Andrew T. Phillips
Academic Dean and Provost
United States Naval Academy

Several years ago, I was asked what I thought of "all this assessment stuff." The question was asked of me in an interview for a provost position, and the bias was quite clear. "This assessment stuff" was code for nonsense or red tape or some other similarly pejorative term. Provosts are generally pretty used to questions of this type; there are certainly individuals who see some institutional policies as wasting their time, and they occasionally offer that observation in pretty stark terms. And I must admit that it wasn't the first time I've been asked this particular question, but usually the asking is done by a faculty colleague who genuinely wants to know why assessment is important and how it can be useful and helpful. But, this specific instance was during a formal interview where I assume the questions had been prepared by the search committee in advance. So, I figured they were either baiting me to see how I would react to a question with a clear bias in favor of an old-school attitude, or they were, as a group, truly beholden to that old-school attitude!

So, I developed my response carefully, and it went something like this. . . . As a mid-career faculty person, perhaps as recently as about ten years ago, I thought that the assessment "movement" and its focus on outcomes, measures, data collection, evaluation, action (or inaction), and feedback was making a bureaucracy out of what I was already doing pretty efficiently and effectively without all of the overhead! After all, I knew what I was teaching (I had a syllabus, you know), I created the questions for my own exams and of course I was grading those exams, and therefore I knew what the students were learning. In a nutshell, over the course of a student's undergraduate career and my participation in that career, I felt that could tell you what I had taught them and what they knew and did not know. I didn't need any elaborate assessment process to guide that.

But that was then, in the late 1990s.

It seems so clear to me now that I (perhaps among many) just didn't "get it." And I wish I could identify the key "aha" moment, but in truth I think I simply heard a steady drumbeat of sensible talk by key leaders who understood how to effectively change the culture behind assessment and keep the focus on asking the big and serious questions about student learning. They would say, "How do you *really know* if your students can think critically and solve problems? What *actual proof* do you have? And when you revise your courses and your curriculum, why do you do that and based upon *what direct evidence* do you make your decision?" As a scientist, those are questions that really rattle around in your head when someone asks them of you! So, over time, I began to see that what I really lacked was the *intentionality* aspect of assessment.

I began to see that student learning outcomes are bigger than just syllabus content, and that you should be conscious of your *real* outcomes, that measuring student learning was more complex than simply assigning a grade to an exam or paper, and that knowing whether you are truly improving student learning involves more than simple reflection about whether you THINK the students learned what you THINK you taught them. When you come face to face with that realization, it hurts a bit. So, I changed.

I realized that well-designed assessment processes enable educators to create great educational experiences. You should know what you are trying to achieve (have well-designed outcomes). You should create your teaching and learning experiences to deliver on those outcomes (design your courses and program to actually provide opportunities to achieve the outcomes). You should carefully and consciously measure the extent to which the students are achieving those outcomes (use some kind of rubric to directly assess the learning). You should then reflect on the results you get by actually evaluating the data—in an objective and dispassionate way. And you should decide upon a course of action as a result of what you find. It seems so simple to me now. . . . But it took a long time and a lot of dedicated leadership by others to create a culture where I could finally see the real point of assessment.

This chapter is about creating such a culture. To be sure, that is hard work and will take time. Lots of time. And the message can't be accusatory. It can't imply that professional educators don't know what they are doing. The message needs to be framed as a vehicle for BETTER education, for BETTER learning, for BETTER program design. In short, you don't have to be bad to get better, and institutionalized assessment will help you get better no matter where you are starting from.

NOTES

1. The idea that "good outcomes assessment involves development of meaningful, manageable, and sustainable assessment practices" was first put forward by the Program Assessment Consortium Team (PACT) at California State University, Bakersfield, in the 1990s (see Program Assessment Consortium Team, 1999).

2. Based on materials developed by the Research and Development Center for Teacher Education, University of Texas at Austin, for consulting skills workshop, described in Hall et al., 1975.

REFERENCES

ABET, Inc. (2008). *Criteria for accrediting engineering programs: Effective for evaluations during the 2009–2010 accreditation cycle.* Baltimore: ABET Engineering Accreditation Commission. Retrieved October 11, 2008, from www.abet .org/Linked%20Documents-UPDATE/Criteria%20and%20PP/E001%2009-10%20 EAC%20Criteria%2012-01-08.pdf.

American Association for Higher Education Assessment Forum. (1992). *9 principles of good practice for assessing student learning.* Washington, D.C.: Author. Retrieved October 11, 2009, from www.academicprograms.calpoly.edu/pdfs/assess/ nine_principles_good_practice.pdf.

Anderson, L. W., & Krathwohl, D. R. (2001). *A taxonomy for learning, teaching, and assessing: A revision of Bloom's taxonomy of educational objectives.* New York: Addison Wesley Longman.

Angelo, T. A., & Cross, K. P. (1993). *Classroom assessment techniques: A handbook for college teachers* (2nd ed.). San Francisco: Jossey-Bass.

Association of American College and Universities. (2007). *College learning for the new global century.* Washington, D.C.: Author. Retrieved October 11, 2009, from www.aacu.org/leap/documents/GlobalCentury_final.pdf.

Banta, T. W. (Ed.). (n.d.). *Assessment update: Progress, trends, and practices in higher education* (published bimonthly by Wiley Subscription Services). San Francisco: Jossey-Bass, Wiley Periodicals.

Banta, T. W. (2007a). *Assessing student achievement in general education.* Assessment Update Collections. San Francisco: Jossey-Bass.

Banta, T. W. (2007b). *Assessing student learning in the disciplines.* Assessment Update Collections. San Francisco: Jossey-Bass.

Banta, T. W., Lund, J. P., Black, K. E., & Oblander, F. W. (1996). *Assessment in practice: Putting principles to work on college campuses.* San Francisco: Jossey-Bass.

Bloom, B. S. (Ed.). (1956). *Taxonomy of educational objectives: The classification of educational goals*. New York: David McKay Company.

Bresciani, M. J. (2006). *Outcomes-based academic and curricular program review: A compilation of institutional good practices*. Sterling, Va.: Stylus.

Crawley, E. F. (2001). *The CDIO syllabus: A statement of goals for undergraduate engineering education*. MIT CDIO Report 1. Boston: Department of Aeronautics and Astronautics, Massachusetts Institute of Technology. Retrieved October 11, 2009, from www.cdio.org/files/CDIO_Syllabus_Report.pdf.

Curry, B. K. (1992). *Instituting enduring innovations: Achieving continuity of change in higher education*. ASHE-ERIC Higher Education Report 7. Washington, D.C.: George Washington University, School of Education and Human Development.

Diamond, R. M. (2008). *Designing and assessing courses and curricula: A practical guide* (3rd ed.). San Francisco: Jossey-Bass.

Eckel, P., Green, M., & Hill, B. (2001). *On change IV: Riding the waves of change: Insights from transforming institutions*. Washington, D.C.: American Council on Education. (ERIC Document Reproduction Service No. ED 470 841 HE 035 503). Retrieved June 1, 2009, from www.eric.ed.gov/ERICDocs/data/ericdocs2sql/content_storage_01/0000019b/80/1a/93/89.pdf.

Ewell, P. T. (1989). Hearts and minds: Some reflections on the ideologies of assessment. In *Three Presentations from the Fourth National Conference on Assessment in Higher Education*. Washington, D.C.: American Association for Higher Education.

Ewell, P. T. (1991). *To capture the ineffable: New forms of assessment in higher education*. Review of Research in Education 17. Washington, D.C.: American Educational Research Association.

Gray, P. J. (1975). A conceptual framework for statements of educational objectives. Master's thesis, Cornell University, Ithaca, N.Y.

Gray, P. J. (1997). Viewing assessment as an innovation: Leadership and the change process. *New Directions in Higher Education, 100*, 5–15.

Gray, P. J. (1999). Campus profiles. In *Assessment update: The first ten years*. San Francisco: Jossey-Bass.

Hall, G. E., Loucks, S. F., Rutherford, W. L., & Newlove, B. W. (1975). Levels of use of the innovation: A framework for analyzing innovation adoption. *Journal of Teacher Education, 26*(1).

Harris, K. (1995). Collected quotes from Albert Einstein. (May be freely distributed with this acknowledgment.). Accessed June 1, 2009, from http://rescomp.stanford.edu/~cheshire/EinsteinQuotes.html.

Jaschik, S. (2009). Whose metrics? *Inside Higher Ed* (News). Retrieved October 12, 2009, from www.insidehighered.com/news/2009/10/12/acct.

Kotter, J. P. (1990). *A force for change: How leadership differs from management*. New York: Free Press.

Krathwohl, D. R., Bloom, B. S., & Masia, B. B. (1964). *Taxonomy of educational objectives. Handbook II: The affective domain*. New York: David McKay Company.

Machiavelli, N. (1999). *The prince*. (Translated with notes by G. Bull). London: Penguin.

Maki, P. L. (2004). *Assessing for learning: Building a sustainable commitment across an institution.* Sterling, Va.: Stylus.

May, R. (1972). *Power and innocence: A search for the sources of violence.* New York: Norton.

Middle States Commission on Higher Education. (1996). *Standards of excellence.* Philadelphia: Author.

Middle States Commission on Higher Education. (2005). *Assessing student learning and institutional effectiveness: Understanding Middle States expectations.* Philadelphia: Author. Retrieved October 11, 2008, from www.msche.org/publications/Assessment_Expectations051222081842.pdf.

Middle States Commission on Higher Education. (2006). *Characteristics of excellence in higher education: Requirements of affiliation and standards for accreditation.* Philadelphia: Author. Retrieved December 03, 2009, www.msche.org/publications/CHX06_Aug08REVMarch09.pdf, xii, xiii.

Palomba, C. A., & Banta, T. W. (1999). *Assessment essentials: Planning, implementing, and improving assessment in higher education.* San Francisco: Jossey-Bass.

Program Assessment Consortium Team. (1999). *PACT outcomes assessment handbook.* Bakersfield: California State University.

Rogers, E. M. (1968). The communication of innovations in a complex institution. *Educational Record, 49,* 67–77.

Senge, P., Kleiner, A., Roberts, C., Ross, R., & Smith, B. (1999). *The dance of change: The challenges of sustaining momentum in learning organizations.* New York: Doubleday/Currency.

Suskie, L. A. (2009a). *Assessing student learning: A common sense guide* (2nd ed.). San Francisco: Jossey-Bass.

Suskie, L. A. (2009b). *Examples of evidence of student learning.* Philadelphia: Middle States Commission on Higher Education. Retrieved October 8, 2009, www.msche.org/publications/examples-of-evidence-of-student-learning.pdf.

Weiss, G. L., Cosbey, J. R., Habel, S. K., Hanson, C. M., & Larsen, C. (2002). Improving the assessment of student learning: Advancing a research agenda in sociology. *Teaching Sociology, 30,* 63–79.

WEBSITES

AAC&U project Liberal Education and America's Promise (LEAP)
www.aacu.org/leap/vision.cfm

ABET
www.abet.org/history.shtml

Internet Resources for Higher Education Outcomes Assessment
www2.acs.ncsu.edu/UPA/assmt/resource.htm#toc

National Institute for Learning Outcomes Assessment (NILOA)
www.learningoutcomeassessment.org/AboutUs.html

North Carolina State University, Internet Resources for Higher Education
    Outcomes Assessment
www2.acs.ncsu.edu/UPA/assmt/resource.htm#inst

Teaching Goals Inventory
http://fm.iowa.uiowa.edu/fmi/xsl/tgi/data_entry.xsl?-db=tgi_data&-lay=
    Layout01&-view

VALUE: Valid Assessment of Learning in Undergraduate Education
www.aacu.org/value/rubrics/index.cfm

Winthrop University, Principles of Assessment
www.winthrop.edu/accountability/default.aspx?id=6875

Chapter Ten

Putting Students First as Partners in the Learning Enterprise

Gary L. Kramer and Thomas E. Miller

When Randy Pausch, a computer science professor at Carnegie Mellon, wrote *The Last Lecture* (2008), he hoped to enable others to overcome obstacles and seize the moment to do what matters most. Essentially and in reflective ways, Pausch asked his audiences, "If we were to vanish tomorrow, what would we want as our legacy?" (front book jacket). With a similarly reflective tone, in this chapter we ask, "What would we do differently to engage students as partners in the assessment process of the learning enterprise? What is to be the narrative five years from now?" Despite uncertainties, we can affirm that senior administration has the ability to set the tone and to facilitate strategies that will enable a demonstrable data story. Or as Lee Shulman (2007) asserted, we must "summon creative energy and ambition and initiate progress in assessment needed to improve the quality of learning in higher education" (p. 25).

PURPOSE OF THIS CHAPTER

Engaging students as partners in the learning enterprise, particularly in the assessment processes, is not simple. Doing this is both challenging and essential as higher education seeks to improve student learning and development. But students need to be involved in discussing and planning assessment rather than just giving feedback about learning and program outcomes. While assessments are most effective when they intentionally involve students as partners, this ideal is difficult to achieve, especially since students often cannot see the benefits or connections of curricular and cocurricular program and unit interventions and associated learner outcome assessments. Recognizing that student success is a result of partnerships and collaboration within the campus community, this concluding chapter addresses this question: in five years, what will the campus narrative be for putting students first as partners in the learning process? If planning and assessment are good for the campus, we must seek a culture of evidence that can demonstrate the following:

- what really mattered or made a difference in engaging students in the learning enterprise and whether data have been used to drive change and improve student learning and development;
- whether the campus community has supported a campus culture of student success, including meaningful connections between curricular and cocurricular learning outcomes; and
- whether students' experiences have been aligned with the claims of the institution and have met personal and institutional expectations, including the themes, conditions, factors, or trends of student success.

Consequently, this chapter will focus on establishing a culture of evidence that leads to and supports student success in the learning enterprise—not only to engage students as partners in assessments but also to clearly identify their expectations and experiences in relation to the institution's aims and claims. An intentional culture of evidence focused on student success becomes meaningful for the institution *only* as it serves as a body of knowledge to *inform* and *benefit* stakeholders, including students.

A reading of this chapter should motivate the reader to relevant actions:

- Consider how to more effectively engage students in examining alignment of their expectations as well as experiences and feedback with assessments conducted on the campus.
- Ensure that every measurement used on the campus is intentional and of value.
- Ensure that students participate in the decisions that affect them most, especially discussions on how they benefit from learner outcomes, whether expectations are met, and especially what mattered most or made a difference to them in their educational success.

ENGAGING STUDENTS IN LEARNING OUTCOMES: AN INSTITUTIONAL EXAMPLE

Students engaged with campus assessment processes are stakeholders, as are the faculty and staff in the campus community. Like most other institutions, the following institutional example did not originally have a process or set of tools in place for managing program-level documentation. In response to the need, they launched a learning outcomes wiki site to facilitate management, publication of program documentation, and engagement of the campus community—especially students. Within the first year all programs had been documented. During both the fall and winter semesters, all students received a personalized e-mail invitation from the president of the university inviting them to review the expected learning outcomes for their majors and provide feedback.

Refinement of the content being published for each of the degree programs is attributed to the significant efforts of not only the faculty but also students. The student role in the process was extremely valuable, especially as the university considered students to be the "consumers" of education. A feedback mechanism was embedded within the wiki site enabling students to provide feedback for all degree programs concerning clarity and content. Students were enthusiastic about moving from a discussion of what classes they took to what specific outcomes they were gaining from their education, especially as they considered employment or graduate school.

In this assessment approach students were treated as partners in the assessment and learning processes; a number of students were assigned by campus senior leaders to join an institutional expected learning outcomes task force. Among other things, they were commissioned to create a video to help promote awareness and understanding of learning outcomes among students throughout the university. They created an effective product in just a few months. The video was made available to all units across campus to inform students of the benefits of understanding what their programs expected them to learn and be able to do as graduates. It also illustrated the utility for open major students in selecting a major program aligning their interests with the expected learning outcomes. The video vividly profiled actual students with the faculty in their majors, with commentary from the college deans.

Expected learning outcomes across campus were not only published electronically on the wiki site but also posted as hard copies in campus areas often visited by students, such as advisement centers and program, department, and college offices. Publishing the expected learning outcomes on campus, especially in hard copy form, resulted in additional faculty attention—facilitating faculty agreement on expected learning outcomes for each program and improving the quality of the statements. Students were involved in this process as well, with the student advisory council taking the lead in distributing the hard copies and explaining their potential utility to students across campus. Many students were excited to have a clearer, high-level understanding of the target goals for the many degrees offered across campus.

Encouraging Student Responses

In short, in this situation students were treated as partners: they were engaged in discussions about, not just "feedback" on, student learning outcomes. Student responses to questions such as the following provided valuable information to the institution on student learning expectations:

- What is the most important knowledge you have gained from taking courses, minoring, or majoring in this subject?
- What are the most valuable skills or abilities you have developed as a result of taking courses, minoring, or majoring in this subject?
- How has taking courses, minoring, or majoring in this subject changed the way you look at yourself? The way you look at the world? The way you think about the future?
- How do you know whether these changes have occurred?
- How do people in this area of study differ from those in other areas (knowledge, skills, and values)?
- What changes might be made in courses and programs of your major or minor to enhance student learning?

This example has been given to set the stage for the balance of this chapter, which will provide further points of emphasis and examples of putting students first in the learning enterprise. Certainly from the student perspective, participating in assessments on a campus that recognizes students as partners in the assessment process is not a matter of simple tasks or easy answers. But the basic premise of this chapter is that key factors or conditions applicable across institutional types can not only influence and support purposeful (intentional) assessments but also engage students before, during, and after an assessment process. This chapter seeks to assist senior campus leaders in leading assessments that involve and engage students as partners—wherever students are in the campus community: for example, the classroom, advisement centers, campus residences and learning communities, cocurricular activities, new student orientation, career advisement services, and other key performance areas of the campus.

Recognizing Students as Partners

The book *Powerful Partnerships: A Shared Responsibility for Learning* (AAHE, ACPA, and NASPA, 1998) affirmed the benefits of college engagement as opportunities for student learning and development. Adrianna Kezar (2009) commented that partnerships in academia are more espoused than enacted but went on to comment that "describing the importance of partnerships is far more productive than discussions about obstacles, especially since students and their learning experience and success are at stake." Students can be especially helpful in critiquing student development and learning outcomes and in articulating criteria that will evaluate the outcomes. Students can make the connections from their classroom learning to their cocurricular learning as well as be proactive in designing integrated learning opportunities (Bresciani, 2009, p. 541).

Gaining the student perspective in collaborative discussions about assessments (what they rave about, etc., regarding their learning and development) is important in identifying what really matters or makes a difference—asking questions that value students' engagement in the learning enterprise. Thus, a key to collaborative direct student discussions and a contribution to the narrative is to conduct occasional focus groups with students. John Schuh (2009), a distinguished scholar and researcher in student affairs assessments, provides an excellent focus group protocol in his book *Assessment Methods in Student Affairs* (see p. 249, appendix 1).

Factors That Lead to Success in the Learning Enterprise

Many things contribute to student success in higher education, including the characteristics of the students themselves as well as their precollege experiences. However, this section will focus on the success-related factors that can be influenced by institutions.

Faculty-student Contact

Research and experience have established that when students form relationships with faculty members their chances of success are enhanced (Kuh et al., 2005; Pascarella and Terenzini, 2005). Contact between students and faculty members can be encouraged, facilitated, and rewarded by institutional leaders. Small classes seem to allow students to become familiar with their instructors, while large classes may not. Classes that allow students to apply course material under faculty supervision are also opportunities for students to connect with faculty members: for example, science laboratories, art studios, and architecture workshops. Even when such structures are not available (or applicable), courses that encourage classroom student discussion can also facilitate student-faculty connections.

Some structures and programs can support the development of contact between students and faculty members outside of the classroom. For example, service-learning initiatives provide excellent opportunities for student-faculty contact, as do programs that involve faculty members as advisors for student organizations. Engaging faculty members in delivering "last lectures" can be enlightening for students and stimulate their interest in connecting with the faculty.

University leaders can establish reward systems that recognize and celebrate faculty members who form strong connections with undergraduate students. Such programs seem easier in small liberal arts institutions, but large research universities have successfully implemented them also (Kuh et al., 2005). The institution that is committed to student success, particularly at the undergraduate level, will find creative ways to promote good relationships between students and faculty members.

In a landmark article published in 1972, Burns Crookston described academic advising as a teaching function. The teacher-advisor role advanced by Crookston focused on moving students toward a positive, shared, active approach to both intellectual and interpersonal learning (Kramer, 2003). Nearly thirty years later, Richard Light (2001), after a ten-year study of more than ninety institutions of higher education, validated Crookston's work when he concluded, "Students who get the most out of college, grow the most academically, and who are happiest organize their time to include activities with faculty members" (p. 10).

Faculty advising can be strengthened in its teaching function when there is campus leadership and vision attuned to the following outcomes:

- Students participate not only in assessing programs put in place for them but also by assuming an active role and voice in discussing various aspects of advising as teaching.
- Campus leaders encourage innovation and evaluation of faculty advising, and they reward, recognize, and celebrate successful innovations.
- Faculty are supported as integral partners in advisement, especially in their important role of helping students evaluate and reevaluate the function of advising as teaching, to improve student learning and development.
- Advising as teaching is implemented to support student learner outcomes, that is, clarifying, connecting, and crystallizing life, career, and academic goals; establishing and developing a thoughtful educational plan; maximally using available resources; becoming involved in the academic community; and regularly evaluating their outcomes and progress.

Advising as teaching not only engages students as partners in the learning enterprise but also provides personal meaning to students' academic goals. And just as important, when performed effectively, it can connect the campus community resources to stimulate and promote students' intellectual and personal growth.

Cocurricular Activities

When students join organizations they have the opportunity to interact with peers who share their interest in the activity. Such interaction can become an important form of engagement and a point of affiliation with the institution, giving students a stronger sense of membership in the institutional community. That sense of membership and affiliation can generate substantial success motivation.

At large research universities, student organizations are particularly important because they are of a size and scale that enable genuine interaction with a smaller group of peers who share an area of interest. The organization itself may be only indirectly related to the success of a student, but the feeling of belonging can be very important to student success.

Quality Student Relationships

Peer relationships are very important to students, perhaps as important as any other influence in their college experience (Astin, 1993; Dewitz, Woolsey, and Walsh, 2009; Inkelas et al., 2007; Swenson, Nordstrom, and Hiester, 2008). Institutions can promote peer relationships by forming working groups for class projects or using peer tutors. Cocurriculum intramural sports, fraternities and sororities, community service activities, athletic teams, and student clubs present additional opportunities for peer interaction.

In residence halls students have regular opportunities to interact. Some interactions are required, such as those with a roommate, but many are chosen intentionally and can result in lasting relationships. Commuting students may find it more difficult to connect with their peers because they are not on campus for as much of the day as are resident students. However, commuter student organizations, places or departments that are designated for commuters, and even ride-sharing programs can give them a chance to find peers with whom they have much in common.

A common strategy for connecting students to their peers is to put students in positions to serve students. Resident assistants, orientation student staff members, peer tutors, intramural sports officials, peer mentors, and classroom-based master learners are all roles in which students support other students, engaging them in ways that can enhance their chances for success. These peer helping programs are beneficial for all, as both the helper and the recipient can grow and learn from the experience.

Institutional leaders should not assume that student relationships will automatically develop without intentional efforts made to foster them. Many students find natural and comfortable ways to interact with their peers, but some do not. The informed leader is alert to the need to facilitate and support strong peer relationships.

Experiences with Diversity

Interacting with students of different backgrounds and ethnicities promotes an appreciation and respect for diversity that is positively related to student success. Institutional programs, events, and activities that celebrate diversity convey to students the importance of diversity in the learning environment.

An institution that recognizes the powerful educational effects of diversity and is deeply committed to it will encourage students to find opportunities to interact with diverse individuals. Such opportunities are easy to find at institutions where the student enrollment is quite diverse; however, students enrolled at a relatively homogenous institution may need to become involved with other institutions, even high schools, with diverse populations to exchange information and perspective. Creative leaders will find ways to facilitate opportunities of this sort.

STEPS THAT FOSTER STUDENT SUCCESS

There are specific steps that institutions can take to enhance the prospects for student success (Kuh, 2009; Kuh et al., 2005). This section will present several that have been shown to be particularly effective.

Provide Accurate Messages during New Student Orientation

One of the challenges that institutions face is to manage unreasonable student expectations regarding the college experience. College recruiters, older siblings and parents, or popular culture and entertainment media may promote unrealistic images of success. New student orientation needs to include accurate, clear messages about the characteristics and behaviors of successful students so that new students understand the effort and time that success will require.

Preenrollment studies of student expectations can be rich sources of information about potential points of dissonance between student expectations and the reality of student experiences (Miller, Kuh, and Paine, 2006). Assessing student expectations of the college experience allows administrators to identify areas that need attention during orientation.

Promote a Learner-Centered Culture

Institutions that effectively communicate a broad focus on students and their learning set the stage for student success. Although many students focus their college expectations on friends and fun, the core purpose of higher education is student learning. The institutional commitment to student learning, as broadly applied both in and outside of the classroom, is key to enhancing student success. When students, faculty members, and staff members hear consistent messages that focus on the student learner and the learning process, all constituents have the opportunity to work toward this end.

Leaders often celebrate other aspects of institutional life, from athletic team victories to faculty research successes, and recognition of such accomplishments is important. However, the mission or central activity for most institutions is, or at least should be, to enhance student learning, which should be a regular part of communication about the institution and its efforts. Leaders should not merely assume a general appreciation of its importance.

Maintain High Academic Standards and Provide Regular Feedback

An institutional commitment to student success does not mean lower standards. Rigor and challenge in coursework are hallmarks of quality academic programs, and students respond to challenges that are balanced with appropriate levels of support. Support should include regular assessment of student learning and prompt feedback to help students remain on the paths where they are successful and make adjustments when their levels of learning need to improve.

Additional support is provided through tutoring services, study areas in student centers and residence halls, writing centers, and high-quality academic advisement. Another strategy that can help is recognizing students whose achievement has improved over time.

Leaders should also encourage and reward faculty members who give early and regular feedback to students about their performance. Faculty members should be encouraged to submit midterm grades and to give academic assignments early in the semester so that students can learn from the feedback they receive and make appropriate adjustments.

Focus on Time on Task

One of the keys to student learning is the amount of time spent on learning-related activity. Thus, institutions should help students manage threats to the time they have to engage in learning. Students with off-campus jobs, long commutes to campus, or significant family care requirements may find it difficult to prepare for their academic work and may struggle to succeed. Administrators should be aware of circumstances that threaten the time students can spend on tasks related to learning and be prepared with suggestions for students who need help.

A useful activity to assist with time management is to conduct a parent orientation program with accurate information about the time and effort required for students to succeed. Conveying this information to the parents of commuting students may be particularly important, as they need to realize that the academic demands on a college student are much greater than those on a high school student and that college students cannot be just as available for household support as they were before college.

Another important way to support students' time on task is to create opportunities for on-campus employment. Students who work on campus have better access to learning support, such as computer labs, the library, and faculty members in their offices, than do students who are employed off campus. Increased opportunity for time on task is one of many advantages of students holding on-campus jobs.

Additionally, residence hall living is efficient and can be more appealing to students when the cost is not prohibitive. Costs of on-campus living can be made more reasonable for students and their families through cooperative arrangements in which students direct their own custodial work in public areas and serve and clean up after their own meals.

SERVICES THAT FOSTER STUDENT SUCCESS

In addition to steps that institutional leaders can take to enhance the chances of student success, they can also provide particular services that can make powerful differences in student learning, persistence, and adjustment to college. Most of these are standard at typical four-year institutions; however, attention needs to be given to their quality and their focus on student success (Kramer, 2007).

New Student Orientation

Central to the highest quality programs of new student orientation are realistic introductions to the student experience and candid explanations of the approaches to learning and academic work that lead to success. Orientation programs need to be much more than academic advisement and class registration, and they also need to be more than just social opportunities for new students to get to know each other. Orientation programs that contribute to student success involve the broad institutional community and include strong partnerships between sections on academic affairs and student affairs. A properly structured and balanced orientation program will provide new students with a strong start toward success and high-quality learning. Regular assessment of the outcomes of orientation programming is essential to its quality. Measuring the effect of these programs enables them to be refined so they evolve into wonderful assets to the student success initiative.

First-Year Programs

Following the orientation program, the new student may have a perspective on what leads to success and a strategy for how to approach learning, but no orientation program can give the new student all of the information and guidance needed for the entire course of the first year of college. Actually, much of the support and perspective a student might need in the first year does not need to be completed before classes start. A strong first-year program can be constructed to help students prepare for and successfully navigate the challenges of the first academic year. First-year student programs might include a first-year experience course, an office with professional staff dedicated to supporting first-year students, a staff of peer helpers, or a series of programs and activities structured around benchmarks of the first year such as midterm exams, midterm grades, second semester registration, the Thanksgiving break, and final exams. As with orientation, assessment of the effects of first-year programs is necessary to allow for refinement and correction of the effort to provide for desired effects on student success. Many institutions have also designed a special set of programs and services for sophomore students who need continued support, but such programs are beyond the scope of this discussion.

Developmental Academic Advisement

High-quality academic advisement is central to the success of students. Whether first-year student advisement is delivered by full-time staff employed for that service, as often occurs at large or research-oriented institutions, or by faculty members as part of their assigned duties, as is more common at smaller institutions, the outcome should be the same. Students should receive individual attention, good counsel on their academic options, and personal attention tailored to their developmental needs, interests, and success. Upper-level students are often advised by the faculty in their major areas, where the objectives should remain the same. Assessment of advisement services is very important, so advisors get feedback about the most effective practices and approaches in order that supervising administrators and faculty members can have opportunities to enhance the services.

Career Services

Students' career interests often evolve over the course of their academic experience, and many students need expert advice and counsel as those interests unfold. The student whose college experience is purposeful and targeted toward some end is more likely to have success than the student who is aimlessly wandering through the academic program with no specific end in sight. Career services are central to helping students find purposes and identify targets to which they can apply their skills and their learning. The best of those operations have strong outreach programs and are not passively waiting for students to show up in their offices. A purposeful, outcome-driven career services operation benefits from regular assessment and program review, so adjustments and refinements to the program can be made.

Tutoring

When students encounter learning challenges in their coursework, they often seek expert support in the form of tutoring services associated with their discipline. Tutoring services that are accessible, private, and confidential provide students with the best sort of support for their success. Tutoring provided by peers can be particularly effective. Student organizations affiliated with disciplines can be excellent sources for tutors with talent and affinity for the discipline. Measuring the tutoring program against intended outcomes is important in informing and improving the practice, so regular assessment of available tutoring is very important to student success.

Financial Aid

Many students find themselves with financial challenges, which can lead to stress that distracts them from learning or even causes them to withdraw from the institution. A financial aid office that is accessible, friendly, and supportive can be very important in enhancing student prospects for success. Students often need expert advice regarding financial dilemmas that they face, and a helpful ally in the financial aid office can be a powerful source of support. The financial aid program should engage in some form of outreach to remind students of important deadlines and to encourage their full use of available services. As for all of the other services that have been described, the financial aid operation should be assessed against the desired outcomes, and feedback from students should be an important aspect of that assessment.

Meaningful On-Campus Work Experiences

To meet financial pressures, many students turn to part-time employment to help them fund their education. Working off campus can result in a disengagement from the learning environment and become a threat to success. When institutions can arrange meaningful on-campus employment for students, connections develop between students and the institutional community, and students are better informed about services, activities, and programs. The work should be meaningful in as many instances as possible. Washing dishes in the dining hall is not meaningful work. Work that is meaningful includes supporting a faculty member in a research task, working with an administrator on a career-related project, or designing and leading a community service project. Such work experiences do more than just generate extra revenue for students; they also enhance student success.

Residential Education and Learning Communities

Students who live in residence halls on campus are offered a collection of powerful learning opportunities associated with the living environment. Living on campus can give students a higher appreciation of diversity, opportunities to refine social skills, an appreciation for the value of community, and several other forms of learning and growing. However, the truly refined residential operation constructs purposeful learning opportunities through residential education programs, living-learning communities, faculty in residence programs, and other resourceful ways of engaging students in the learning enterprise. If on-campus housing is provided, it must be carefully and purposefully connected to student learning experiences for the purpose of enhancing student success. Routinely assessing these initiatives is important, so they can be refined and enhanced.

Individually Tailored Services

Student success is enhanced when students feel as though they are of importance—that they "matter" to institutions. They need to realize that they are considered to be more than numbers. They feel this sense of importance as they recognize that services and programs that are available to them are directed to them as individuals and are designed to address their personal needs.

A CULTURE OF ASSESSMENT AND EVIDENCE

While the above discussion frames factors, steps, and services that foster student success, substantial pressure is being applied to colleges and universities to demonstrate their effect on students and show results from their efforts. This pressure is generated by regional accrediting associations, state and federal governments, and the public. It can also be felt on college campuses from various constituencies external to a functional area. For example, faculty members may seek evidence of the effect of a student affairs program, or in challenging fiscal circumstances administrators may be called to defend the effect of intramural sports.

Establishing Outcomes That Signal Student Success

Administrators need to identify the student outcomes most closely associated with success. For example, the leadership of an institution may believe in the importance of enhancing the students' interpersonal development to promote meaningful relationships with faculty members and peers. Because establishing relationships with faculty members and peers has a positive relationship to student success, this particular intended outcome seems well considered. Other outcomes that relate to student success are easily identified, from the development of personal identity, to the enhancement of cultural competence, and to the development of behaviors that enhance wellness. The outcomes identified by an institution or a unit within the institution should be specific to the mission and values of the institution or the purpose of the unit.

Outcomes Assessment

When an outcome is identified, those responsible for achieving it need to establish a means to assess the level of its accomplishment. Considering the previous example, how would an institution measure the extent to which students' interpersonal development is enhanced as a result of the college experience? A wide array of tools can be used for such measurement. Assessors could sponsor individual interviews or focus groups of senior students, requesting their perspectives and example experiences. Alternatively, a quantitative study could easily be constructed. A number of survey instruments address interpersonal development, ranging from those available from Educational Benchmarking, Inc. (EBI), or from Noel-Levitz, Inc., to the College Student Experiences Questionnaire (CSEQ), the College Student Expectations Questionnaire (CSXQ), and the National Survey of Student Engagement (NSSE)—all available from the Center for Postsecondary Research at Indiana University.

Interdivisional Partnerships

In the best learning-focused colleges and universities, strong partnerships exist between the academic affairs section of the institution and the student affairs section. These institutional components are the principal organizations responsible for setting the learning agenda, both in and outside the classroom. Without such strong collaborative partnerships, student success is less certain. Compartmentalized and independent efforts to support success can be redundant or inconsistent in approach and effect. Coordinated support of student learning is the far better approach, so academic administrators and student affairs administrators serve students most effectively when they participate in full partnership in the student learning enterprise.

Connections between Effective Educational Practice and Research

Educational practices in support of student learning must be assessed, and research must be conducted to explore strategies for improvement. A strong institutional commitment to research about students, including the factors that contribute to or detract from their success, is necessary for students to attain success. This section will describe an effort at the University of South Florida (USF) that combines a strong research initiative with an intervention program to increase the prospects for success of students who are at risk of attrition. Comparable projects at other institutions will be mentioned as well.

The Attrition Prediction Project at the University of South Florida

The Attrition Prediction Project at USF connects research to practice in support of student success, exemplifying strong partnerships between operations of academics and student affairs. One of the principles of the project is that what students expect of the college experience may be useful in anticipating their risk of dropping out. The premise is that unmet expectations may lead to cognitive dissonance and a disconnection from the institution, so using student expectations to help predict their persistence makes sense (Miller, 2005).

The project begins by collecting data from students through administering the CSXQ prior to enrollment, during the summer orientation program. A database of the CSXQ results is constructed, supplemented by data collected by the university through the admission process, including high school grades, SAT or ACT scores, and various demographic fields.

When the cohort reaches the beginning of the sophomore year, the database is divided into two groups: persisters and dropouts. Using logistic regression, a predictive model is developed, based on a wide range of variables, to identify the risk an individual student has of dropping out. The model is then applied to the next incoming class, and students who are most at risk of attrition are targeted for individual contact by a team of academic affairs staff and student affairs staff. The contact is intended to provide support to the student and help him or her develop strategies for success at the university. The model design was created by a partnership between a faculty member and a student affairs assessment professional, and the intervention team represents both academic affairs and student affairs (Miller and Herreid, 2008, 2009).

This research project is ongoing, with the model being updated and adjusted annually. The project has also developed a model that predicts sophomore attrition, with the original database being adjusted to include real student experiences and outcomes (major choice, grade point average, number of credit hours, etc.). The academic advising system in the colleges of the university will be the source for intervention with the students who are most at risk (Miller and Herreid, 2009). The system also predicts transfer student attrition. This prediction has particular significance, since the university has one of the largest transfer student populations in the country—almost ten thousand students per year between 2006 and 2009.

The notion of developing a model to predict individual attrition and thus to enable interventions to modify attrition risk is gaining traction at other institutions. Representatives of a number of colleges and universities have contacted the researchers at USF, and several are developing models of their own using the same logistic regression approach. This method of using scientific research to identify those at risk of attrition, based upon multiple characteristics, is but one way of connecting educational practice to research.

Other Types of Initiatives

Many other types of applied research efforts exist. The aforementioned NSSE has been employed by more than one thousand institutions in the past few years in efforts by administrators to understand student engagement at their institutions. The results of the NSSE instrument can be used to evaluate student engagement and enhance the prospects of student success (Kuh et al., 2005). Similarly, the CSEQ has been used by many institutions to measure learning outcomes, the effect of first-year programs, or the efficacy of other efforts to enhance student success. In today's academe in which assessment and demonstration of effect have reached new levels of importance, using research and assessment results to inform institutional practice is the best strategy for institutional leaders.

Learner Outcomes in the Classroom and Credit-Bearing Learning Experience

In the current higher education atmosphere, learning outcomes for academic courses must be identified. Regional accrediting agencies are expecting to see evidence of learning assessment in academic programs, and such evidence has become a key aspect of institutional accreditation. In individual courses, faculty members are responsible for identifying specific learning outcomes and for designing ways to assess student attainment of those targets. The NSSE is an excellent example of a powerful tool that measures student engagement in the learning enterprise.

Learner Outcomes and Assessment in Student Affairs and Other Functional Areas

While the assessment of classroom learning is clearly the responsibility of the individual faculty member and the associated discipline, assessment of learning outside of the classroom is not as clearly aligned with the duties of an individual or a department, and the tools for assessment are less specifically intended for out-of-class activities. However, measurement of learning that results from the out-of-class experiences of students is just as important as assessment of in-class learning, and if instruments for this purpose are not readily available, then institutional officials need to develop their own.

One readily available measurement tool, the CSEQ, can be very useful for assessing out-of-class student learning outcomes. Residential living options, counseling centers, student health operations, campus recreation, and other standard services for students can readily identify learning outcomes associated with their work with students. In many cases, the results of an administration of the CSEQ can provide very useful insight into student attainment of specific targeted outcomes (Gonyea, 2003).

Learner Outcomes and Assessment in General Campus Life

In addition to its utility in measuring learning outcomes in functional areas and departments, the CSEQ instrument can provide insight about students' general attainment of learning outcomes. If intended learning outcomes relate to diversity appreciation, interpersonal growth, technology use, wellness issues, and so forth, the CSEQ can provide insight about them. The instrument includes a variety of items associated with each area, and the student respondents can reflect experiences associated with these sorts of common learning outcomes associated with their general campus life experience (Kuh and Pace, 1998).

Other Assessment Resources

The National Resource Center for the First-Year Experience and Students in Transition at the University of South Carolina exists to support initiatives that improve student learning and success. The center makes resources, including an annotated database of assessment instruments, freely available, and the reader is encouraged to review the database. The instruments described above are included in the database, as well as a number of others sponsored by the American College Testing Program, Educational Benchmarking, Noel-Levitz, and the Higher Education Research Institute at the University of California at Los Angeles. The assessment resources, including a typology of instruments, resources for the first year in college, and others for the senior year, can be accessed at www.sc.edu/fye/resources/assessment/index.html. Also, Schuh (2009) provides an excellent summary of commonly used instruments in student affairs, their purpose and information collected (appendix 3, pp. 257–260).

WHAT WORKS?

Benchmarking, a form of accountability measure, along with cost-benefit analysis, needs and satisfaction assessments, learning outcomes measures, accreditation standards, and so forth, is about how institutions compare with each other, with industry standards, or with institutional adopted standards. These assessments are applications of one approach to creating a culture of evidence—a systems or strategic approach for assessing and improving quality. As shown in this chapter, benchmarking can be used to determine whether a program or unit is on track within a predetermined framework—standards used for the benchmarking exercise. Rarely, however, would one institution measure what is of value and allow measurements to drive decisions with methodology based on or adopted fully from a similar institution. Administrators are more likely to derive principles and constructs from the successes of others and adapt good ideas or practices from other institutions.

Among several institutions that could be cited as working examples of benchmarking and assessment partnerships, especially those that involve students in connecting learning outcomes in areas of both academic and student affairs with institutional claims and mission, are North Carolina State University, California State University, Brigham Young University, and the University of South Florida. A brief description of the institution's model of student partnerships follows:

North Carolina State University, a large public land-grant university, relies on outcomes-based planning and assessment to inform decision making and provide evidence about the quality of teaching, learning, and engagement at the university. Both curricular and cocurricular departments, including those in student affairs, engage in ongoing outcomes-based assessment and evaluation—all aligned with department-specific initiatives and with the university's mission and goals (see www2.acs.ncsu.edu/UPA/index.html).

California State University Channel Islands is noteworthy for its outcomes-focused approach to its mission. Performance indicators focus on six areas: students, faculty instruction, program quality, infrastructure, finance, and funding (see www.csuci.edu/about/ir).

Brigham Young University created a university task force devoted to learning outcomes. As colleges and universities across the country are being asked to publish learning outcomes for all of their programs, and to provide evidence that the expected learning outcomes are realized by students, Brigham Young University, as part of an ongoing effort to directly involve students, created the task force, including students, to develop and launch a learning outcomes wiki to facilitate the convenient management and publication of program documentation (see http://learningoutcomes.byu.edu/).

University of South Florida is another outstanding model with an undergraduate studies website focused entirely on student success (see www.ugs.usf.edu/success.htm). In addition, USF has developed websites that focus on assessment of intended learning outcomes of the Division of Student Affairs, which is supported by faculty and student participation as members of the Division's Planning and Assessment Team (see www.sa.usf.edu/committees/SAPAC/committee.asp and www.sa.usf.edu/committees/SAPAC/content/SA%20Learning%20Outcomes%20with%20Blooms%20Taxonomy.pdf).

WHAT'S MOST IMPORTANT IN FOSTERING STUDENTS AS PARTNERS IN THE LEARNING ENTERPRISE?

Peter Ewell (2004), who wrote the foreword for this book, emphasized the importance of bipartisanship—that is, connecting curricular and cocurricular learner outcomes in academia: "It is no longer enough for institutions to measure the effectiveness of what they do, including the outcomes their students achieve. They must now be purposeful, aligning departmental goals with institutional goals. . . . Put simply, accountability in higher education and student affairs has become about "publicly acceptable performance and results" (p. 3). To achieve results in fostering students as partners in the learning enterprise, we recommend a modified version of Marilee Bresciani's (2003, 2009) questions on creating a culture of evidence—questions that institutions must ask (and answer!) to be successful:

- What are we trying to do and why? (conduct systematic reflection)
- What is my program supposed to accomplish? (conduct purposeful, intentional planning)

- What do I want students to be able to do and know as a result of my program?
- What tells us that we are getting better? (How should we improve planning and delivery processes? Do we review enough?)
- How do we know that our program is working and that students have benefited?
- How do we use the information from assessment to improve the delivery of what we are doing or to celebrate successes? (conduct systematic evaluation)
- Do the improvements we are making work? (Are student learning and development enhanced?)
- Do we celebrate successes? (Do we recognize when we have reached a worthy goal we once perceived as unattainable?)

The greatest gap between what students expect college to be like and what they experience is *the nature of the college environment.* Because institutional context and student success are inextricably connected, campus administrators need to know and connect all aspects of the environment for and in behalf of student success. When the institution's mission is aligned with its educational policies and programs, especially its institutional claims, and involves students as partners in meaningful ways, students' experiences are generally more effective in fostering their success. Moreover, when students' expectations match their experience in college, they are more likely to be satisfied and to persist to graduation (Kuh, 2009, p. 61).

Some rather significant research and related evidence (Bailey, 2006; Braxton, 2006; Bresciani, 2003, 2009; Keeling et al., 2008; Kezar, 2009; Kramer, 2007; Kuh, 2009; Light, 2001; Miller, 2005; Miller and Tyree, 2006; Schuh, 2009; Tinto and Pusser, 2006) have affirmed that student success on the campus is a direct result of students' engagement, even partnership, in the learning enterprise; the campus environment; and administrators' use of a systems approach to measure what is of value and, just as important, their use of resulting data to drive decisions.

Russell Osguthorpe and Lolly Osguthorpe (2009) represented graphically the essence of partnering with students and using curricular and cocurricular partnerships that lead to success. In figure 10.1 we share their representation, slightly modifying the title to embrace the primary concepts as they pertain to student learning and development.

Preparation for Change

What must we do to be dramatically better in five years? What will the narrative be like? Everything depends on you, the senior leader: Which areas

	Learning Outcomes	*Learning Activities*	*Learning Assessments*
Linked	Outcomes, activities, and assessments are *linked* to each other and to the life of the learner.		
Challenging	Outcomes, activities, and assessments are *challenging* yet attainable.		
Inspiring	Outcomes, activities, and assessments *inspire* students and teachers to reach for the highest in them.		

Foundation of Edifying (Caring) Relationships

Figure 10.1. Partnerships That Lead to Student Success, Development, and Learning

matter to you? What can be measured five years from now to demonstrate empirically the progress made in aligning institutional claims with student experiences, especially in partnering with students in their learning and development? Through this chapter, we hope we've been able to motivate readers to seize the moment to do what matters most and, using a culture of evidence to create the narrative, to tell the data story. At the beginning of this chapter we asked the question Pausch asked his audiences: "If we were to vanish tomorrow, what would we want as our legacy?" As authors of this chapter, we hope we could answer that readers have found ways to *put students first as partners in the learning enterprise.* Mihaly Csikszentmihalyi (1990) defined this optimal experience of student success as something *we make happen.* And we add this advice: while senior leaders can both set the tone and make things happen on the campus, they ought to proceed with productive caution. To illustrate, carved in a stone in the upper gallery of the main patio at the University of Salamanca is this carving: *Semper Festina Lente,* which translated is *always hasten slowly.* The carving also includes a dolphin, which symbolizes speed and energy; an anchor representing rooted restraint; and a circle to imply patience.

Clearly, whatever we choose to do to partner with students in the learning enterprise, given inevitable time and budget constraints, must be done methodically, be fiscally sound, and, of course, move forward with vision and will. John Rosenberg (2009) reasoned that amid our efforts to always hasten slowly is the interesting yet important mixture of "systematic" and "proportionate." *Systematic* refers to the arduous process of gathering and converting information to knowledge by organizing it according to categories we accept as useful—measuring what we value and driving decisions from what we measure. Yet, systematic invites and is balanced by *proportionate*, which suggests wisdom, balance, and pace—even a sense of urgency. Perhaps William Butler Yeats captured the essence of putting students first as partners in the learning enterprise when he urged, "Education is not the filling of a pail but the lighting of a fire of learning."

REFERENCES

American Association for Higher Education (AAHE), American College Personnel Association (ACPA), and National Association of Student Personnel Administrators (NASPA). (1998). *Powerful partnerships: A shared responsibility for learning.* Washington, D.C.: Author.

Astin, A. W. (1993). *What matters in college? Four critical years revisited.* San Francisco: Jossey-Bass.

Bailey, T. R. (2006, November). Research on institution level practice for post secondary student success. Paper presented at the National Symposium on Postsecondary Student Success, Washington, D.C.

Braxton, J. M. (2006, November). Faculty choices in teaching that foster student success. Paper presented at the National Symposium on Postsecondary Student Success, Washington, D.C.

Bresciani, M. J. (2003). Expert driven assessment: Making it meaningful to decision makers. *ECAR Research Bulletin, 21.*

Bresciani, M. J. (2009). Implementing assessment to improve student learning and development. In G. S. McClellan & J. Stringer (Eds.), *The handbook of student affairs administration* (pp. 526–546). San Francisco: Jossey-Bass.

Crookston, B. B. (1972). A developmental view of academic advising as teaching. *Journal of College Student Personnel, 13,* 12–17.

Csikszentmihalyi, M. (1990). *Flow: The psychology of optimal experience.* New York: Harper & Row.

DeWitz, J. S., Woolsey, M. L., & Walsh, W. B. (2009). College student retention: An exploration of the relationship between self-efficacy beliefs and purpose of life among college students. *Journal of College Student Development, 50*(1), 19–34.

Ewell, P. T. (2004, November). The changing nature of accountability in higher education. Paper prepared for the Western Association of Schools and Colleges (WASC) Senior Commission.

Gonyea, R. M. (2003). The college student expectations questionnaire: Assessing student expectations of their college education. Retrieved February 18, 2007, from www.indiana.edu/.

Inkelas, K. K., Daver, Z. E., Vogt, K. E., & Leonard, J. B. (2007). Living-learning programs and first-generation college students' academic and social transition to college. *Research in Higher Education, 48*(4), 403–434.

Keeling, R. P., Wall, A. F., Underhile, R., & Dungy, G. J. (2008). *Assessment reconsidered: Institutional for institutional effectiveness.* N.p.: International Center for Student Success and Institutional Accountability (ICSSIA).

Kezar, A. (2009). Supporting and enhancing student learning through partnerships with academic colleagues. In G. S. McClellan & J. Stringer (Eds.), *The handbook of student affairs administration* (pp. 405–424). San Francisco: Jossey-Bass.

Kramer, G. L. (Ed.). (2003). *Faculty advising examined: Enhancing the potential of college faculty as advisors.* Bolton, Mass: Anker.

Kramer, G. L. (Ed.). (2007). *Fostering student success in the campus community.* San Francisco: Jossey-Bass.

Kuh, G. D. (2009). Understanding campus environments. In G. S. McClellan & J. Stringer (Eds.), *The handbook of student affairs administration* (pp. 59–80). San Francisco: Jossey-Bass.

Kuh, G. D., Kinzie, J., Schuh, J. H., Schuh, E. J., Whitt, & Associates. (2005). *Student success in college.* San Francisco: Jossey-Bass.

Kuh, G. D., & Pace, C. R. (1998). *College student expectations questionnaire* (2nd ed.). Bloomington: Indiana University, Center for Postsecondary Research and Planning.

Light, R. J. (2001). *Making the most of college: Students speak their minds.* Cambridge, Mass.: MIT Press.

Miller, T. E. (2005). Student persistence and degree attainment. In T. E. Miller, B. E. Bender, J. H. Schuh, & Associates (Eds.), *Promoting reasonable expectations: Aligning student and institutional views of the college experience* (pp. 122–139). San Francisco: Jossey-Bass.

Miller, T. E., & Herreid, C. H. (2008). Analysis of variables to predict first-year persistence using logistic regression analysis at the University of South Florida. *College and University, 83*(3), 2–11.

Miller, T. E., & Herreid, C. H. (2009). Predicting sophomore persistence using logistic regression analysis at the University of South Florida. *College and University, 85*(1), 2–11.

Miller, T. E., Kuh, G. D., & Paine, D. (2006). *Taking student expectations seriously: A guide for campus application.* Washington, D.C.: National Association of Student Personnel Administrators.

Miller, T. E., & Tyree, T. M. (2006). Using a model that predicts individual student attrition to intervene with those who are most at risk. *College and University, 84*(3), 12–19.

Osguthorpe, R. T., & Osguthorpe, L. S. (2009). *Choose to learn: Teaching for success every day.* Thousand Oaks, Calif.: Sage.

Pascarella, E. T., & Terenzini, P. T. (2005). *How college affects students.* San Francisco: Jossey-Bass.

Pausch, R. (2008). *The last lecture.* New York: Hyperion.

Rosenberg, J. (2009, October). The human conversation. Paper presented at the biannual meeting of the Leadership Associates of the Center for the Improvement of Teacher Education and Schooling (CITES), Midway, Utah.

Schuh, J. H. (2009). *Assessment methods in student affairs.* San Francisco: Jossey-Bass.

Shulman, L. S. (2007). Counting and recounting: Assessment and the quest for quality improvement. *Change: The Magazine of Higher Learning, 39*(1), 20–25.

Swenson, L. M., Nordstrom, A., & Hiester, M. (2008). The role of peer relations in adjustment to college. *Journal of College Student Development, 49*(6), 551–567.

Tinto, V., & Pusser, B. (2006, November). Moving from theory to action: Building a model of institutional action for student success. Paper presented at the National Symposium for Postsecondary Student Success, Washington, D.C.

WEBSITES

Brigham Young University
http://learningoutcomes.byu.edu

California State University Channel Islands, Institutional Research
www.csuci.edu/about/ir

National Resource Center, Resources
www.sc.edu/fye/resources/assessment/index.html

North Carolina State University, University Planning and Analysis
www2.acs.ncsu.edu/UPA/index.html

University of South Florida, Division of Student Affairs Expanded Student Learning Outcomes
www.sa.usf.edu/committees/SAPAC/content/SA%20Learning%20Outcomes %20with%20Blooms%20Taxonomy.pdf

University of South Florida, Division of Student Affairs Planning and Assessment
www.sa.usf.edu/committees/SAPAC/committee.asp

University of South Florida, Undergraduate Studies Student Success
www.ugs.usf.edu/success.htm

Epilogue

Gary L. Kramer and Randy L. Swing

What can senior leaders do to rally assessments around improving student success, learning, and development? It would be easy to reply that every campus is unique and each must find its own way into and through assessment processes. We agree there is no one-size-fits-all approach to assessment. Institutions *do* have unique and varied missions that must be addressed, but a close look at the chapters in this book reveals that the authors seldom needed to qualify their advice by stipulating that it applies only to one type of institution or another. We did *not* segment the book into sections for community colleges, liberal arts colleges, research universities, and so forth. The unspoken but shared belief is that there are common leadership imperatives that impact the ultimate success of assessment efforts no matter what sector, type, or size of institution is involved.

Nobody believes that significant improvement in student learning outcomes can be wrought without the engagement of the faculty and staff or that assessment efforts can be meaningful without the goodwill of student participants. But collectively the authors—both in their advice to senior leaders and in what they did not need to write—point to the common need for senior leaders to actively *lead* assessment.

Simply put, what senior campus leaders do and say has significant impact on the success or lack of success of assessment activities. Senior leadership does, indeed, matter. In each chapter, the advice is straightforward. Senior leaders must set expectations, build and sustain an infrastructure to support assessment, provide resources, pay attention to assessment, use results, and celebrate successes. This is, of course, a tall order for busy leaders who juggle many competing priorities.

We conclude this book by acknowledging that assessments on the campus, those that contribute to supporting decision making in all key performance areas of the institution, are considerable and fraught with challenges and con-straints. This is especially challenging when consideration must be given, as this volume asserts, to the place assessments and reporting have in the larger context of aligning institutional claims with and achieving outcomes in all performance areas of the campus. Yet, perhaps, it is all the more important therefore for senior leaders to assert their political wisdom and leadership talents to guide strategic planning (including data derived from purposeful as-sessments) and existing budget constraints in meaningful and credible ways, that is, managing and supporting behavior change based on broad engage-ment of the campus community.

Clearly, these constraints and challenges and others exist on every campus. While we offer no panacea in creating and managing assessments on the cam-pus, this volume does offer essential, established, or working principles on and conditions for an assessment infrastructure that can make a difference in achieving institutional outcomes. Thus, we conclude with some insights and resources from the chapter authors of this volume in response to Peter Ewell's statement in the foreword:

> The second decade of the twenty-first century promises tough times for higher education. Money is short, infrastructure continues to crumble, and there are far too many students for an increasingly contingent and discontented faculty to teach. For a president or academic leader to put aside these urgent problems and consider assessment seems the height of indulgence. Why pay any attention to this topic at all?

In response, the authors and editors recommend the following strategies for senior leaders to "pay attention" to assessments in higher education:

- Tell the data story by augmenting written and oral communication with indicators of institutional functioning and student learning. Great stories have power, but evidence drives home the point. Celebrate successes in as-sessment. If you are not thinking about (and using) assessment, why should anyone else?
- Find your "assessment voice." Be ready to state why you invest part of your day in fostering and encouraging assessment efforts. Communicate why you are passionate about student success and how evidence can help your institution realize the highest aspirations for your students.
- Monitor and ensure that assessment results are salient for a range of stake-holders who have diverse interests and agendas and that they are disaggre-gated for underrepresented populations.
- Encourage the perception that assessment in higher education is a practice of listening, reflecting, learning, and making evidence-based decisions—

that there are no magic bullets, only engaged inquiry. At the same time, prepare to align resources to support change derived from assessment data.

- Engage the campus community in ownership of the assessment processes. Pursue faculty members and students as partners in assessments of the learning enterprise. For example, learning outcomes can be an effective foundational tool for strengthening academic programs *when* faculty members see their value and use them to improve student learning.
- Insist that assessments are transparent, that they are primarily for learning, and that they should be shared openly in the processes of planning, analysis, and reporting. Build and sustain an assessment infrastructure, one that supports decision making in all key performance areas of the institution.
- Establish that assessment processes are to be reproducible and well documented. Provide opportunities that allow campus constituents to have meaningful experiences with assessments that lead to making a positive difference.
- Assert that assessments are a means to an end—to accomplish important institutional goals and purposes. Consistently and persistently pursue what is of most value to the campus. Intentionality matters as much or more than any other factor of assessments.
- Do not worry over the small details but rather worry about building and maintaining momentum, especially in providing qualitative and meaningful feedback through timely and stakeholder-meaningful reports.
- Find and support your assessment "champions"—the faculty and staff members who are the natural leaders in assessment efforts. Grow your own assessment talent and champions by investing in professional development activities if needed.

The chapters in this volume model good assessment practice and will help senior leaders accomplish institutional outcomes. In higher education assessments, especially in assessing student learner outcomes and development, senior leadership does matter. Indeed, an institution today can no more do without assessment than it can do without a development office, especially since student learning and development is at the heart of the institutional mission. While "the second decade of the twenty-first century promises tough times for higher education" (see the foreword), this volume firmly believes that assessment is one of the key management tools available to senior leaders of colleges and universities to work their way out of the tough times.

To improve and maximize student learning and development—the central theme of this book—researchers and scholars in the field and in this volume remind us that assessment of the student educational journey ought to be purposeful, integrated, and built on and reinforced by one another. It is the way we do assessment, not just doing it, that matters. Thus, the challenge of the next decade will be not just to take stock of student learning but also to get better at generating student learning, intentionally, systematically, and continuously. Specifically, are assessments purposefully aligned with institutional claims and enable a demonstrable culture of evidence? Does senior leadership matter in higher education assessments? This volume's editors and authors affirmatively supply solid research and scholarship that, indeed, it does matter.

Subject Index

9 Principles of Good Practice for Assessing Student Learning, 182

AACSB International, 164–165
ABET, Inc., 164–165, 167–174, 176, 200
accessibility of data. *See* database
AccessUVa, 155
accountability, ix, 5, 162; external pressures for, xxii, 75–76, 174–175; research of, xvii–xviii. *See also* Spellings Commission, Voluntary Framework for Accountability, Voluntary System of Accountability
accreditation and accreditors, 9, 161–162, 174–175. *See also* disciplinary accreditation
Achieving the Dream initiative, 67–68
ACT, 8, 14, 227
administrators. *See* leadership
Albany State University, 153
Allegheny College, 144
Alverno College, 147
American Association for Higher Education (AAHE), 77, 81–82, 166
American Association of Colleges and Universities (AAC&U), 109–110, 112, 136
American Association of Community Colleges, 8

American Association of State Colleges and Universities (AASCU), 8
American College Personnel Association (ACPA), 77–78
assessment: across institutions, 7–9; authentic, xxii, 101–102; benefits of, 184–185; cost, 127–128; course level, 194; culture of, 179, 196, 225–230 (*see also* culture of evidence, transformation assessment); definitions of, 4–6; department/institutional level (*see* disciplinary assessment); examples of effective practices, 206; federal/state governments, and, 174–175; formative, 98; guiding principles of, 182–183; implementing, 185–186; leading (*see* leadership); "of learning" versus "for learning," 97–99; manageable, 187; meaningful, 21, 181–182; methodology, 83–84 (*see also* assessment measures); plan (*see* assessment plan); pressures for, 182–184; process, xxiv, 180; purpose of, 6, 10; questions addressed by, 186–189; and reflection, 104–106, 112 (*see also* common assessment measures,

self-reporting); resources, 229, 230; summative, 98. *See also* characteristics of good assessment program
assessment in student affairs, xxii, 145; contextual issues, 75–78; examples of, 87–88; a model, 82–85
assessment measures/instruments, 84–86; alignment to claims/mission, 5, 79, 114 (*see also* learner outcomes); direct (*see* direct assessment measures); grades, 7; indirect (*see* indirect assessment measures); peer review, 32, 111–112, 128; qualitative, 86–87; quantitative, 86; standardized tests, 20, 98–99; value added, 14–15, 52. *See also* common assessment instruments
assessment plan (or systems approach to assessment), xxiv, 45, 153; benefits of, 31; factors of, 29–44; developing, 54–62; institutional model. *See* culture of evidence, creating a
assessment system. *See* assessment plan
Association for Institutional Research (AIR), 64
Association of American Colleges and Universities (AAC&U), 8, 107, 200; essential learning outcomes, 204
Association of Community College Trustees, 8
Association of Public and Land-grant Universities, 8
Atlas.ti, 86
Attrition Prediction Project, 227–228

benchmarking. *See* common assessment instruments
Bloom's Taxonomy, 197
board of trustees. *See* leadership
Boston College, 148
Brigham Young University, 152, 230–231
Buena Vista University (BVU), 151
Buffalo State College, 149

calendar. *See* master calendar
California State University Channel Islands, 231
Center for Postsecondary Research at Indiana University, 226
chancellor. *See* leadership
change, 46, 232–234
characteristics of good assessment program, 166, 199
CIRP Survey, 74
Civil Rights Act, 62
closing the loop, 43, 205. *See* using results of assessment
cognitive engagement, 99–105
Cognitive Level and Quality of Writing Assessment (CLAQWA), 111
collaboration, 149–151
College Level Academic Skills Test (CLAST), 111
college of arts & sciences, 153
College Outcomes Survey, 7. *See also* Voluntary System of Accountability
College Senior Survey (CSS), 148
College Student Expectations Questionnaire (CSXQ), 226
College Student Experiences Questionnaire (CSEQ), 226
Collegiate Assessment of Academic Proficiency (CAAP), 8, 97
Collegiate Learning Assessment (CLA), x, 8, 14, 97
Colorado State University (CSU), 144
common assessment instruments, 16–20; benchmarking, 51; capstone courses, 16, 98; competency tests, 97–98, 110; course-embedded assessment, 16; course progression and success, 17; culminating project, 17; curriculum and syllabus analyses, 17; employer surveys, 18; employment and job placement rates, 18; focus groups and exit interviews, 18; institutional or departmental tests, 18–19; licensure exams, 19; portfolios

(*see* portfolios); rubrics, 19, 99, 108–109; satisfaction and self-reported learning surveys, 19, 99, 147; standardized tests, 20, 98–99; vendor or industry certification examination, 20

Community College Survey of Student Engagement (CCSSE), 137–138

consumer information and assessment. *See* transparency in assessment

Cooperative Institutional Research Program (CIRP), 74

Council for the Advancement of Standards (CAS), 77

Council for Higher Education Accreditation (CHEA), 136, 152

Council of Regional Accrediting Commissions, 9, 166

culture of evidence, xxiv–xxv, 5, 43–46, 145, 155–156, 225–230; creating a, xi, 98, 147, 206–207; for student learning, 155–156; institutional model, 47–50; sustaining, 46, 50–53; using disaggregated data, 13. *See also* assessment, culture of; assessment plan; transformation assessment; using results of assessment

database, xxi, 84; advantages of, 38–39; purpose of, 37; selecting a, 39–41

data collection, 28, 41, 47, 84. *See also* culture of evidence

data-driven decision making, xvi, 43–44, 76, 80, 129–130

DEEP (Documenting Effective Educational Practices) Project, xviii, 80, 140, 155

direct assessment measures, 15–16, 50, 52

direct evidence, 203–204. *See also* direct assessment measures

disaggregation of data, 67–68

disciplinary accreditation, xxiv, 176; accrediting bodies, 163–166;

definition, 162–166; future trends in, 174–175; model of, 167–174

disciplinary assessment, 161, 176

disciplines without accreditation, 166–167, 175

diversity, xxi; definitions, 61–64; historical influences, 61–62; and law, 62–63; types of assessment, 64–66

Diversity Scorecard project, 67–68

Eckerd College, 144

Educational Benchmarking, Inc. (EBI), 226

Education Commission of the States, 137

educational purposes: clarifying, 199–201; mapping to institutional purposes, 201–203

engagement. *See* cognitive engagement; engaging stakeholders in assessment; engaging students

engaging stakeholders in assessment, 32–37, 145–151; case study, 119–122; extrinsic motivation (motivators), 34, 192; faculty, xi, xxiii, 12, 33–36, 112–115, 153–154. *See also* resistance to assessment; intrinsic motivation, 34, 192

engaging students, xxiii, xxv, 36–37, 51–52, 80, 147–149, 213–214, 216; framework for assessment, 137–140; in learner outcomes, 214–216; involvement theory, 78–79. *See also* students, partners in learning/assessment; cognitive engagement

Engineering Criteria 2000, 200

ETS® Proficiency Profile, 8

evaluation, 5; questions, 203

faculty-student contact, 217–218

feedback, 12, 82, 127, 153, 221

First College Year Project, 151

Focus Group Kit, The, 86–87

formative assessment. *See* assessment, formative

Foundations of Excellence®, 151

grades. *See* assessment measures, grades
Grutter v. Bollinger, 62

Higher Education Research Institute
(HERI), 120, 196, 309

Indiana University Center for
Postsecondary Research, 226
Indiana University-Purdue University
Indianapolis (IUPUI), 152
indirect assessment measures, 16, 50,
52
indirect evidence, 203–204. *See also*
indirect assessment measures
institutional: culture of assessment,
xxiv; effectiveness, xx, xxii–xxiii,
151–156; improvement, 52, 80, 122,
131, 104–143; mission, 5, 79, 145,
166
Internet Resources for Higher Education
Outcomes Assessment, 200, 206
IPEDS (Integrated Postsecondary
Education Data System), 63–64

leadership, xi, 3–4, 142–144, 198–
199; board of trustees, 144–145;
challenges faced, 23–25, 53, 59–60,
114; principles of successful
assessment leadership, 189–193;
responsibilities of, xxii–xxiii,
20–23, 29; questions to ask about
assessment at the institution, 9–10;
vision, 6, 45
learning environments, 101–104
learning goals. *See* learning outcomes/
objectives
learning outcomes/objectives, xxii–xxiii,
5, 109, 152–153, 194–195, 228–229;
aligning to assessment measures,
196; aligning to institutional mission,
123–124, 197–198, 226; assessment
of, 125–128, 131, 194–196, 226;
case study of, 119–122; creating/
developing/establishing, 11–12,

80–81, 194–196, 226; definition of,
11–12; evaluation of, 12, 196–198;
feasibility of, 124–125; in student
affairs, 77–78, 80–82, 87–88, 229
(*see also* assessment in student
affairs); purpose of, 10–15; questions
for selecting, 122–125; resources,
195–196
Liberal Education and America's
Promise (LEAP), 200, 211
Lumina Foundation, 8

master calendar, 41–43
Measure of Academic Proficiency and
Progress (MAPP), 8, 97
measurement. *See* assessment measures/
instruments
Miami University of Ohio, 143
Middle States Commission on Higher
Education, 77, 166, 205
Midwestern University (MWU), 146

National Association of State
Universities and Land-Grant
Colleges (NASULGC), 8
National Association of Student
Personnel Administrators (NASPA),
77–78
National Council for Accreditation of
Teacher Education (NCATE), 107,
164
National Institute on Learning
Outcomes Assessment (NILOA), ix,
206
National Student Clearinghouse Student
Tracker, 20
National Survey of Student Engagement
(NSSE), 52, 73, 137–138, 142,
144–149, 226
National Survey on Student Learning
Outcomes Assessment, The, 206
new student orientation, 220, 222
Noel-Levitz, Inc., 226
North Carolina State University, 230

North Dakota State University, 87
Northwest Accreditation, 152

Ohio State University, 153
Oregon State University (OSU), 88

peer review. *See* assessment measures, peer review
Penn State Pulse, 88
Pennsylvania State University, 88
Plan for Researching Improvement and Supporting Mission (PRISM), 144
portfolios, 19, 97, 104–106, 147; benefits of, 106–107; electronic (e-portfolios), 107–110; assessment projects, 109–112
positive restlessness, 139, 142–143. *See also* institutional improvement
Principles of Undergraduate Learning (PULs), 152
professional accrediting bodies, 164–165
program improvement. *See* institutional improvement
program success. *See* institutional effectiveness

qualitative data, 16–20, 86
quantitative data, 16–20, 86

reflection. *See* assessment and reflection; portfolios
Regents of the University of California v. Bakke, 62
reporting data, 204–205. *See also* database, reporting capabilities
resistance to assessment, 24; faculty, xi, 34, 120, 188 *See also* engaging stakeholders in assessment, faculty

Sandia National Laboratories, xvii
SAT, 14, 227
senior leadership. *See* leadership
Southern Association of Colleges and Schools, 77

Spellings Commission, ix, 7–8, 75, 82
stakeholders, 76, 127. *See also* engaging stakeholders in assessment; engaging students
standard assessments. *See* assessment measures/instruments
St. Olaf College, 153
strategic plan for assessment. *See* assessment plan
structural diversity. *See* diversity
student: co-curricular activities, 65–66, 219; diversity, 220 (*see also* diversity); engagement (*see* engaging students); first-year programs, 223; partners in learning/assessment, xxv, 147–149, 216–217, 231–232; peer relationships, 219–220, 225; retention, 145; time management, 221–222
student involvement. *See* engaging students
Student Involvement Transcript, 87
student learning, 51, 53, 86, 95, 125–126; collaboration, 227; focus on, 220; improving, xxiii, 153–136; measuring, 86, 97–99
student services. *See* assessment in student affairs
student success, xxii–xxiii, xxv, 139, 151–152; factors, 217–220; services that foster, 222–225; steps that foster, 220–222
Student Success Project, 141
summative assessment. *See* assessment, summative
Survey of Academic Advising, 74
Survey Kit, The, 86
Swarthmore College, 145
systems approach to assessment. *See* assessment plan

Teacher Education Accreditation Council (TEAC), 164
Teaching Goals Inventory, 196, 200

Teaching, Learning and Evaluation
Matrix, 197
Teagle Foundation, 136, 150–151
technology, 85, 104. *See also* database
telling the data story. *See* reporting
timeline. *See* master calendar
transformation (transformative)
assessment, xxiii–xxiv, 182, 189,
194 (*see also* culture of evidence);
definition of, 179–180
transparency in assessment, 7–8, 75–77
TRIO programs, 87

United States Naval Academy, 204
University of Louisville, 147–148
University of Nevada, Reno, 87
University of South Carolina, 229
University of South Florida, 109,
111–112
University of Texas at El Paso (UTEP),
141

University of Virginia (UVA), 154–
155
University of Wisconsin, Green Bay
(UWGB), 142–143
using results of assessment, 12–13,
84–85, 145, 205. *See also* closing the
loop; culture of evidence; data driven
decision making

VALUE (Valid Assessment of Learning
in Undergraduate Education), 8,
109–112, 204
value added. *See* assessment measures,
value added
Voluntary Framework for
Accountability (VFA), 8
Voluntary System of Accountability
(VSA), x, 8, 76, 98

wiki, 152, 215, 231
Winthrop University, 182–183

Name Index

Akintoye, A., 33, 54
Allen, W. R., 70
Anderson, J. A., 32, 37, 41, 42, 43, 45, 54
Anderson, L. W., 196, 209
Angelo, T. A., xvii, xxvi, 33, 34, 37, 40, 44, 54, 196, 200, 209
Annis, L., 106, 115
Armacost, R. L., 36, 40, 41, 55
Astin, A. W., xvii, xxvi, 78, 79, 90, 219, 234

Bailey, T. R., 232, 234
Banks, B., 106, 115
Banta, T. W., xvii, xxvi, 14, 25, 29, 30, 32, 33, 34, 35, 36, 37, 38, 39, 40, 41, 42, 43, 44, 51, 52, 54, 55, 106, 115, 127, 131, 136, 147, 152, 157, 158, 196, 199, 206, 207, 209, 211
Barab, S., 113, 115
Barefoot, B. O., 82, 90
Barr, M. J., 79, 90
Bauman, G. L., 70
Baxter Magolda, M. B., xvii, xxvi
Bender, B. E., 235
Bender, K. K., 144, 159
Bensimon, E. M., 67, 68, 70
Bereiter, C., 103, 104, 117
Bers, T., 27

Biggs, J., 123, 126, 131
Biglan, A., 166, 167, 177
Birnbaum, R., 69, 70
Black, K. E., xvii, xxvi, 29, 30, 32, 33, 34, 36, 37, 38, 41, 42, 43, 44, 51, 54, 127, 131, 136, 157, 209
Black, P., 100, 115
Blimling, G. S., 77, 90
Bloom, B. S., 111, 196, 210
Blumenfeld, P. C., 100, 101, 102, 103, 115
Boehner, J. A., 76, 90
Bok, D., 144, 157
Borden, V. M. H., 40, 41, 54, 135, 157, 158
Boyer, E. L., xvii, xviii, xxvi
Bradley, P., 104, 116
Brainard, J., 77, 91
Braxton, J. M., 232, 234
Bresciani, M. J., 32, 37, 41, 42, 43, 44, 54, 74, 81, 91, 207, 210, 217, 231, 232, 234
Bridges, B. K., 158
Buckley, J., 150, 158
Butcher, P., 104, 117

Cabrera, A. F., 66, 70
Calderon, T., 167, 177
Cambridge, B.L., 106, 116

Carter, D. F., 66, 70
Carver, S. M., 105
Chickering, A. W., xvii, xxvi, 137, 157
Chinyio, E. A., 33, 54
Clark, E. J., 37, 55, 107, 116
Clayton-Pederson, A. R., 70
Cohen, A. M., 75, 91
Collins, A., 103, 105, 116
Collis, B., 104, 116
Connors, R., 46, 55
Cosbey, J. R., 56, 211
Cotterill, S., 104, 116
Crawley, E. F., 201, 210
Crookston, B. B., 218, 234
Cross, K. P., 196, 200, 209
Csikszentmihalyi, M., 233, 234
Currie, J., 75, 91
Curry, B. K., 189, 190, 191, 210
Cuseo, J., 77, 91
Cuthell J. P., 104, 116
Cutright, M., 90

Daft, R. L., 33, 34, 35, 55
Daver, Z. E., 235
Dean, L. A., 77, 91
Denson, N., 63, 65, 69, 70
DeWitz, J. S., 219, 234
Dey, E. L., 70
Diamond, R. M., 194, 210
Dillman, D. A., 147, 157
Dillow, S. A., 76, 92
Driscoll, A., 34, 55
Dugan, R. E., 41, 42, 55
Dungy, G, J., xvii, xxvii, 235
Dwyer, C. A., 96, 116

Eckel, P., 179, 180, 210
El-Khawas, E., 135, 136, 157
Evenbeck, S. E., 152, 158
Ewart, C., 202
Ewell, P. T., xvii, xxvi, 43, 45, 54, 55, 135, 137, 144, 157, 158, 188, 198, 210, 231, 234
Eynon, B., 37, 55, 107, 116

Fink, A., 86, 91
Fink, L. D., 106, 116, 127, 128, 131
Flateby, T. L., 111, 116
Freed, J. E., 29, 32, 33, 37, 55
Fried, J., 78, 91

Gaffney, M. A., 37, 40, 41, 55
Gamon, A., 101, 117
Gamson, Z. F., xvii, xxvi, 137, 157
Gardner, J. N., 43, 56, 90
Gardner, M. M., 43, 44, 54, 74, 91
Gawande, A., xix, xxvi
Gonyea, R. M., 229, 235
Gordon, V. N., 91, 92
Gray, P. J., 185, 192, 193, 196, 207, 210
Green, M., 179, 180, 210
Griffin, A. M., 142, 158
Grob, G. F., 85, 91
Gurin, G., 70
Gurin, P., 62, 70

Habel, S. K., 56, 211
Hall, G. E., 209, 210
Hamilton, S. J., 152, 158
Hammond, G., 104, 116
Hanson, C. M., 56, 211
Harper, S. R., 91, 146, 155, 158
Harris, K., 188, 210
Harrison, C., 115
Hayek, J. C., 158
Hernon, P., 41, 42, 55
Herreid, C. H., 228, 235
Hickmott, J., 43, 44, 54, 74, 91
Hiester, M., 219, 236
Hill, B., 179, 180, 210
Hirt, J. B., 79, 91
Hoffman, C. M., 76, 92
Huba, M. E., 29, 32, 33, 37, 55
Huisman, J., 75, 91
Hurtado, S., 64, 66, 70
Hutchings, P., 124, 131

Ikenberry, S., 136, 158
Inkelas, K. K., 219, 235

Jafari, A., 106, 116
Jaschik, S., 203, 210
Jones, C., 106, 115
Jones, E. A., xvii, xxvi, 29, 30, 32, 33, 34, 36, 37, 38, 41, 42, 43, 44, 51, 54, 127, 131, 136, 157
Jordan, S., 104, 117

Kanter, R. M., 150, 158
Kaufman, C., 106, 116
Keeling, R. P., xvii, xviii, xxvii, 232, 235
Kelderman, E., 77, 91
Kelly, W. E., 167, 177
Kempler, T. M., 100, 101, 102, 103, 115
Kezar, A., 79, 91, 150, 158, 216, 232, 235
Kimball, L., 104, 116
King, J. E., 67, 70
King, P. M., xvii, xxvi
Kinzie, J., xvii, xxvii, 91, 150, 158, 235
Kleiner, A., 211
Koschmann, T., 103, 117
Kotter, J. P., 189, 210
Krajcik, J. S., 100, 101, 102, 103, 115
Kramer, G. L., 218, 222, 232, 235
Krathwohl, D. R., 196, 209, 210
Krueger, R. A., 86, 91
Kuh, G. D., xvii, xviii, xxvii, 33, 55, 78, 79, 80, 91, 136, 137, 139, 140, 141, 145, 150, 152, 158, 217, 218, 220, 228, 229, 232, 235

Ladson-Billings, G., 62, 70
Langston, I. W., 167, 177
Larsen, C., 56, 211
Laurillard, D., 104, 116
Lave, J., 103, 116
Lee, C., 115
Leonard, J. B., 235
Lester, J., 79, 91
Light, R. J., 218, 232, 235
Lopez-Fernandez, O., 104, 116
Loucks, S. F., 210

Lubinescu, E. S., 37, 40, 41, 55
Lund, J. P., 209

Machiavelli, N., 189, 210
Madison, B. L., 167, 177
Maki, P. L., 29, 33, 34, 36, 37, 41, 42, 43, 45, 54, 55, 127, 131, 150, 158, 196, 211
Marks, H. M., 101, 117
Marshall, B., 115
Martell, K., 167, 177
Masia, B. B., 196, 210
Mason, R., 106, 108, 117
May, R., 190, 211
McKelfresh, D. A., 144, 159
McKeon, H. P., 76, 90
Milem, J. F., 70
Miller, B. A., 32, 33, 34, 36, 55
Miller, R., 108, 116
Miller, T. E., 220, 227, 228, 232, 235
Millett, C. M., 96, 116
Moonen, J., 104, 116
Morgaine, W., 108, 116
Morgan, D. L., 86, 91
Morris, L. V., 90
Mortenson, T. G., 67, 70
Muffo, J. A., 167, 177
Murphy, R., 96, 100, 101, 102, 117

Newlove, B. W., 210
Newmann, F. M., 101, 117
Nora, A., 66, 70
Nordstrom, A., 219, 236

Oblander, F. W., 209
Orfield, G., 62, 70
Osguthorpe, L. S., 232, 235
Osguthorpe, R. T., 232, 235

Pace, C. R., 78, 91, 229, 235
Paine, D., 220, 235
Palincsar, A. S., 103, 117
Palomba, C. A., 33, 34, 36, 41, 42, 55, 147, 157, 194, 199, 211

Paretti, M. C., 172, 177
Pascarella, E. T., xvii, xviii, xxvii, 79, 92, 217, 235
Pausch, R., 213, 233, 236
Payne, D. G., 96, 116
Pegler, C., 106, 108, 117
Perry, M., 106, 117
Pet-Armacost, J., 36, 40, 41, 55
Pike, G. R., 52, 54, 135, 157
Polkinghorne, D. E., 70
Ponjuan, L., 66, 70
Porter, S. R., 147, 159
Powell, K., 172, 177
Preston, D. S., 104, 117
Prior, J., 100, 117
Pusser, B., xvii, xxvii, 232, 236

Quaye, S. J., 146, 155, 158

Ratcliff, J. L., 37, 40, 41, 55
Reisser, L., xvii, xxvi
Rhodes, J., 75
Rhodes, T., 107, 109, 110, 117
Roberts, C., 211
Rodriguez-Illera, J. L., 104, 116
Rogers, E. M., 187, 211
Romm, J., 142, 158
Rosenberg, J., 234, 236
Ross, R., 211
Ross, S., 104, 117
Rutherford, W. L., 210
Ryu, M., 67, 70

Saunders, K., 84, 92
Sawyer, R. K., 105, 117
Scardamalia, M., 103, 104, 117
Schank, R. C., 104, 117
Schilling, K. J., 97, 112, 117
Schilling, K. M., 97, 112, 117
Schroeder, C. C., 90
Schuh, E. J., 235
Schuh, J. H., xvii, xxvii, 32, 37, 38, 40, 41, 45, 55, 74, 77, 81, 82, 86, 88, 91, 92, 158, 217, 230, 232, 235, 236
Schulman, L.S., xvii, xxvii

Schwartz, C., 41, 42, 55
Schwartz, S. W., 90
Senge, P., 181, 211
Shulman, L. S., 106, 107, 117, 124, 131, 213, 236
Smith, B., 211
Smith, T., 46, 55
Snyder, T. D., 76, 92
Sonnichsen, R. C., 85, 92
Soundarajan, N., 34, 55
Stahl, G., 103, 117
Stefanakis, E., 98, 117
Stefani, L., 106, 108, 117
Stoecker, J. L., 167, 177
Suskie, L. A., 5, 26, 30, 37, 41, 43, 45, 54, 55, 74, 82, 92, 128, 129, 132, 135, 136, 147, 157, 159, 166, 177, 194, 196, 198, 211
Suther, D. D., 103, 117
Sutton, R., 100, 117
Swan, R. H., 127, 132
Swenson, L. M., 219, 236
Swing, R., 21, 26, 27, 43, 56

Tang, C., 123, 126, 131
Terenzini, P. T., xvii, xviii, xxvii, 79, 92, 217, 235
Thelin, J. R., 75, 92
Tinto, V., xvii, xxvii, 145, 159, 232, 236
Torrance, H., 100, 101, 117
Torres, V., 53, 65, 68, 70, 71
Troxel, W. G., 77, 92
Tyree, T. M., 232, 235

Underhile, R., xvii, xxvii, 235
Upcraft, M. L., 74, 75, 82, 86, 88, 92

Vallejo, E., 70
Van Kollenburg, S. E., 34, 55
Vogt, K. E., 235

Wall, A. F., xvii, xxvii, 235
Walsh, W. B., 219, 234
Walters, E., 43, 56
Walvoord, B. E. F., 45, 56

Wehlburg, C. M., 30, 32, 33, 34, 42, 43, 45, 53, 54, 56
Weiss, G. L., 44, 56, 179, 211
Wenger, E., 103, 116
White, S. H., 42, 56
Whitt, E. J., xvii, xxvii, 77, 90, 91, 158, 235
Wiggins, G., 127, 132
Wiliam, D., 115

Wohlgemuth, D. R., 84, 92
Wood, S., 34, 55
Woolsey, M. L., 219, 234

Yeats, W. B., 234

Zak-Owens, J., 40, 41, 54
Zelna, C. L., 32, 37, 41, 42, 43, 44, 54
Zubizarreta, J., 37, 56, 106, 117

About the Contributors

Raymond D. Barclay is senior associate for Arroyo Research Services (ARS). Barclay brings a strong background in institutional research, assessment development, and program evaluation. Prior to joining ARS, he was associate vice president/director of Institutional Research for College of Charleston; vice chancellor for Institutional Research and Planning at Western Carolina University (one of the sixteen University of North Carolina campuses); director of Institutional Research and Assessment at the College of New Jersey; policy and planning analyst at Burlington County College, New Jersey; and director of Research and Planning at the Bonner Foundation, a Princeton-based national private foundation that supports programs engaged in service learning, civic engagement, and student development, as well as community-based programs. Barclay's assessment and research experience includes designing and implementing a decentralized portfolio assessment framework across the Bonner Foundation's network of schools, developing progressive institution-specific frameworks such as those addressing enrollment management, data stewardship and security, planning and budgeting, institutional effectiveness, transformative curriculum requirements across various pedagogies (performing arts, sciences, and education), and program-specific competency assessments (business, sciences, etc.).

Trudy Bers has over forty-five publications in professional journals and over fifty presentations at professional conferences. Her most recent publications include research on assessing general education achievements of community college students, examining parent perceptions of college choice for community college students, assessing critical thinking and program-level learning outcomes, using course syllabi for assessment, preparing the *New Directions for Community Colleges* issue on research literature about community colleges, and authoring "Effective Reporting," a monograph in the Association for Institutional Research (AIR) Resources. She is currently president of the Council for the Study of Community Colleges and has been president of AIR, the National Community College Council for Research and Planning, and the Illinois AIR. Bers works with community colleges to develop new approaches to foster student success.

Bryan D. Bradley is assessment and evaluation consultant at Brigham Young University, Provo, Utah, and a specialist in issues concerning assessment of student learning and use of assessment data to meet accreditation requirements. He has worked in the education, industry, and government services arenas as a skills training and performance measurement consultant for over twenty-five years. His work and research interests include assessing learner performance at the higher levels of cognitive behavior. He enjoys working with educators and training leaders to support them in developing assessments, course goals, and course activities that promote the highest levels and rewards of learning. Bradley is the author of over a dozen scholarly presentations and articles concerning online assessment and measurement.

Peter J. Gray holds a PhD in educational psychology from the University of Oregon and a master's degree in curriculum theory from Cornell University. He has been the director of academic assessment at the U.S. Naval Academy since 2002. Previously, he was responsible for evaluation and research as associate director for the Syracuse University Center for the Support of Teaching and Learning. During the 2008–2009 academic year, he was on sabbatical as a visiting scholar at the University of Bath and a visiting research fellow at Oxford Brookes University. Gray has over forty publications and has given over one hundred workshops and lectures worldwide on topics related to assessment and quality assurance in higher education.

Coral Hanson is currently assistant director of Assessment, Analysis, and Reporting for the School of Education at Brigham Young University, Provo, Utah. She oversees the assessment data for the School of Education and works with faculty members in reporting and understanding their data. Hanson's interests include effectively assessing student learning and understanding how to improve the education of students. She is the coauthor of "An Evaluation of the Effectiveness of the Instructional Methods Used with a Student Response System at a Large University." It was published October 2008 in *Interactive Educational Multimedia Journal*. Hanson is also coauthor of the paper "The Pursuit of Increased Learning: Coalescing Learning Strategies at a Large Research University," to be published in AIR's *Professional*

File. She enjoys working with colleagues on assessment to better inform their programs. Hanson completed her master's degree in instructional psychology and technology with a focus on assessment and instructional design at Brigham Young University. She has also presented several papers at major assessment conferences.

Trav D. Johnson is associate director at Brigham Young University's Center for Teaching and Learning. He directs center consultants in helping faculty members, departments, and colleges improve courses and programs. He also helps direct student ratings and the evaluation of teaching at Brigham Young University, including gathering feedback on teaching and using this feedback to enhance teaching and student learning. Johnson's research interests focus on the use of faculty and course evaluation in instructional improvement, including the use of online student ratings. He has published and presented over fifteen papers on topics related to educational evaluation and improvement including publications in the series New Directions for Teaching and Learning and in *The Sage Handbook of Management and Learning, Education and Development*, and has recently published "Learning-Centered Evaluation of Teaching" in *To Improve the Academy* (edited by L. B. Nilson and J. E. Miller).

Jillian Kinzie is associate director of the National Survey of Student Engagement (NSSE) Institute for Effective Educational Practices at Indiana University Center for Postsecondary Research, where she coordinates the NSSE Institute project activities. Her PhD is from Indiana University in higher education with a minor in women's studies. Kinzie joined the NSSE staff after serving as a faculty member at Indiana University coordinating the master's program in higher education and student affairs from 2000 to 2002. She has more than a decade of additional experience as a research associate and an administrator in academic and student affairs. Kinzie's research interests include college choice, first-year student development, teaching and learning in college, access and equity, and women in underrepresented fields. She is interested in understanding how institutions use student engagement data and other assessment results to inform improvement efforts in undergraduate education; how differences in student engagement are affected by gender, race and ethnicity, and first-generation status; and what forms and degrees of impact are generated by programs and practices designed to support student success (learning communities, undergraduate research, service learning, etc.).

Gary L. Kramer is professor of counseling psychology and special education and associate director in the Center for the Improvement of Teacher Education and Schooling in the David O. McKay School of Education, Brigham

Young University. He received his PhD from Oregon State University and has served in the past as dean of students, associate dean of student academic and advisement services, and director of student services on three campuses. A past president of the National Academic Advising Association, Kramer has written extensively about academic advisement, assessment, student academic services, institutional improvement, and student information systems. He has published over seventy refereed journal articles, book chapters, book reviews, monographs, grant proposals, ERIC documents, and institutional reports, including more than fifty articles and chapters in twelve different refereed journals and twelve monograph chapters and chapters in books. In addition, he has edited four monographs and four books and has delivered more than 130 professional papers, including keynote addresses for ten different professional organizations.

Thomas E. Miller has served as adjunct instructor in the College Student Affairs graduate program since 1999 at the University of South Florida (USF). He joined the faculty full time after having been employed most recently as associate vice president for student affairs and dean of students at USF. He previously held positions as vice president for student affairs at both Eckerd College and Canisius College. His latest publications have presented his research on student expectations of college and on the prediction of student attrition from college and intervention strategies. Miller recently published, with Barbara Bender and John Schuh, *Promoting Reasonable Expectations: Aligning Student and Institutional Views of the College Experience* (2005).

John Muffo is the series editor of Assessment in the Disciplines for AIR. Formerly, he was an administrator for special projects for the Ohio Board of Regents (2005–2008) and director of the academic assessment program at Virginia Polytechnic Institute and State University (1990–2005).

Danny Olsen is the director of institutional assessment and analysis at Brigham Young University in Provo, Utah. He has worked within the scope of institutional research and assessment at Brigham Young since 1986, previously having worked in various computing and analytical capacities in the manufacturing, banking, and defense industries. Olsen completed a PhD in Instructional Science from Brigham Young with emphasis in research, measurement, and evaluation. Additionally, he has earned a master's degree in information management, also from Brigham Young. Olsen is responsible for developing and implementing an institutional assessment plan that reflects a dynamic school structure, while continuing to integrate various aspects of the planning process. He is author of several publications and has presented over forty papers at national and international assessment conferences.

Russell T. Osguthorpe, professor of instructional psychology and technology, currently serves as director of the Center for Teaching and Learning at Brigham Young University. He has also served as chair of his department and associate dean of the McKay School of Education. In 1998 he was awarded the Martha Jane Knowlton Corey University Professorship. He has recently directed research studies on how assessment tools can be used on college campuses to improve student learning. He speaks several languages; has collaborated on educational projects in China, Europe, and Polynesia; and has been a visiting scholar at the University of Toronto and the University of Paris. Osguthorpe is coauthor of *Choose to Learn: Teaching for Success Every Day* (2009, with Lolly Osguthorpe) and *Balancing the Tensions of Change: Eight Keys to Collaborative Educational Renewal* (1998, with Robert Patterson).

John H. Schuh is distinguished professor of educational leadership and policy studies at Iowa State University. Prior to holding this position, he served in administrative and faculty assignments at Wichita State University, Indiana University (Bloomington), and Arizona State University, the institution at which he received his PhD degree. Schuh is author, coauthor, or editor of over 235 publications, including 25 books and monographs, 70 book chapters, and over 110 articles. Among his books are *Assessment Methods for Student Affairs*, *One Size Does Not Fit All: Traditional and Innovative Models of Student Affairs Practice* (with Kathleen Manning and Jillian Kinzie), *Student Success in College* (with George D. Kuh, Jillian Kinzie, and Elizabeth Whitt), *Involving Colleges* (with George Kuh, Elizabeth Whitt, and associates), and *Assessment Practice in Student Affairs* and *Assessment in Student Affairs* (both with M. Lee Upcraft). Currently, he is editor of the New Directions for Student Services sourcebook series and is book review editor of the *Review of Higher Education*. Schuh has made over 260 presentations and speeches to campus, regional, national, and international meetings.

Kay H. Smith is currently associate vice president for the Academic Experience at the College of Charleston in Charleston, South Carolina. Smith received her PhD in English Renaissance literature from Emory University and, in 2010, a Fulbright Fellowship to Hong Kong Polytechnic. She has published and presented extensively on Shakespeare and film. At the College of Charleston, she has primary responsibility for First-Year Experience, General Education, and academic support services like Orientation, Advising, New Student Programs, Center for Student Learning, Undergraduate Academic Services, as well as retention and early-alert programs. Prior to coming to the College of Charleston, Smith was a faculty member and administrator at Appalachian State University, where she directed the Watauga College program, Appalachian's long-standing and innovative residential college. She later went on to become chair of the Department of Interdisciplinary Studies and the Department of Foreign Languages and Literatures. At the College of Charleston, Smith is currently involved in developing the Center for Excellence in Peer Education and in various e-portfolio projects.

Randy L. Swing is executive director of AIR, a professional association of more than 4,200 institutional researchers, planners, and decision makers representing over 1,500 higher education institutions. Prior to joining AIR, Swing served as codirector and senior scholar at the Policy Center on the First Year of College and as a fellow in the National Resource Center for the First-Year Experience and Students in Transition at the University of South Carolina. He has worked with numerous research teams in Japan and has served as an advisor to the Quality Assurance Agency of Scotland. He has authored articles, chapters, monographs, and books, including *Achieving and Sustaining Excellence in the First College Year* (2006) and *Proving and Improving: Tools and Techniques for Assessing the First College Year* (2004). He is a frequent speaker at national and international conferences on institutional change, assessment, retention, and undergraduate student success. He serves on the editorial and review boards for the *Journal of General Education, Journal on Excellence in College Teaching,* and *Innovative Higher Education.*

Vasti Torres, professor at Indiana University at Bloomington, teaches courses in student affairs administration, student development theory, and research in higher education. Prior to joining the Indiana University faculty, she had fifteen years of experience in administrative positions, most recently serving as associate vice provost and dean for enrollment and student services at Portland State University in Oregon. She was the principal investigator for a multiyear grant investigating Latino students' choice to stay in college. She is active in several student affairs and higher education associations. In 2007–2008, she became the first Latina president of a national student affairs association—American College Personnel Association (ACPA). She has been honored as a Diamond Honoree and Senior Scholar by ACPA, National Association of Student Personnel Administrators Contributed to Knowledge Award, and program associate for the National Center for Policy in Higher Education.